CHALLENGING ISSUES AND ACCOUNTABILITY IN NIGERIA'S PUBLIC ADMINISTRATION

EDITED BY

B. OYENIRAN ADEDIJI, PH.D.

DEPARTMENT OF LOCAL GOVERNMENT STUDIES
FACULTY OF ADMINISTRATION
OBAFEMI AWOLOWO UNIVERSTY,
ILE-IFE, OSUN STATE, NIGEIRA.

AuthorHouse™
1663 Liberty Drive
Bloomington, IN 47403
www.authorhouse.com
Phone: 1-800-839-8640

Published by AuthorHouse 8/28/2012

ISBN: 978-1-4772-5959-7 (e)
ISBN: 978-1-4772-5960-3 (hc)
ISBN: 978-1-4772-5961-0 (sc)

Library of Congress Control Number: 2012914959

DEDICATION

This book is dedicated to:

Professor Tale Omole,

The Vice Chancellor, Obafemi Awolowo
University, Ile-Ife, Nigeria

ACKNOWLEDGEMENT

I hereby wish to register sincere appreciation to all authorities in the field of Public Administration, whose writings or speeches and/or pioneering efforts have indirectly encouraged, influenced and enriched this exercise. I particularly hereby acknowledge with respect the assistance I received from

1. Professor J.A Fabayo, Department of Economics, Faculty Social Sciences, Obafemi Awolowo University, Ile – Ife, Nigeria.

   Professor David A. Ijalaye, Faculty of Law, Obaferni Awolowo University, Ile – Ife, Nigeria.

   Professor Olu Adediran, Faculty of Law, Obaferni Awolowo University, Ile – Ife, Nigeria.

   Professor Ademola Popoola, Faculty of Law, Obaferni Awolowo University.

   Professor Oladimeji Aborisade, Former Dean, Faculty Administration, Obafemi Awolowo University, Ile – Ife, Nigeria.

   Professor Wale Adebayo, Former Dean, Faculty of Agriculture, Obaferni Awolowo University, Ile – Ife, Nigeria.

I also wish to express deep appreciation to all my colleagues and coworkers at the Department of Local Government Studies, Obaferni Awolowo University, Ile-Ife, for the support and co-operation I received from them, which made the publication possible.

PREFACE

In Nigeria. Public Administration has become the focus of attention for all and sundry: curious political scientists, jealous state government observers, apologetic practitioners of Local Government. This book Challenging Issues and Accountability in Nigeria's Public Administration is an attempt to treat in essay form a few of the aspects of Public Administration which have recently gained the trend of intensive research focus and scholarly attention of the authors. It is expected that the book would be of interest to scholars and students of Public Administration, political scientists and Nigerian policy-makers. The main aim is to stimulate and kindle more exhaustive discussions, reflections and researches on such issues. The book is made up of twelve chapters:

In Chapter 1, OYENIRAN ADED1JI [1] identifies compliance with laid down accounting and financial procedures as a way of enhancing local government autonomy, and suggests not only appointment of high calibre of persons to local government service, but also motivation of such officers to get familiar with documents relating to rules, regulations, and procedure.

In chapter 2, OYENIRAN ADEDIJI [2] identifies supremacy of national policies over those local of governments, and its disturbing effects on implementation of local government's policies as a potential source of strained inter-governmental relations sooner or later.

In chapter 3, OYENIRAN ADEDIJI [3] analyses how the abrogation of the local government service commission created ambiguous interpretation and perception, which led to what observers regard as blatant display of power, and points out the consequences of as well as the lessons from the event.

In chapter 4, Mike Adeyeye,[4] observes that the present system of

1 OYENIRN ADEDIJI (Ph.D.), Reader and former head of department of Local Government Studies, Obafemi Awolowo University, Ile-Ife, Nigeria.

2 OYENIRN ADEDIJI (Ph.D.), Reader and former head of department of Local Government Studies, Obafemi Awolowo University, Ile-Ife, Nigeria.

3 OYENIRN ADEDIJI (Ph.D. Reader and former head of department of Local Government Studies, Obafemi Awolowo University, Ile-Ife, Nigeria.

4 MIKE ADEYEYE, Reader, Department of Local Government studies, Obafemi Awolowo University, Ile-Ife, Nigeria.

Local Government does not appear to be very effective for the 21st century, he therefore suggests the need to underscore the importance of political objectives of popular participation of the citizens in service delivery/maintenance and revenue mobilization as strategy for Local Government to realize their objectives.

In Chapter 5, Isiaka 0 Aransi,[5] examines ethics at the Local Government level and states that all is not yet well, he suggests the adoption or re adoption of office ethics such as neutrality and non-partisan rather than that of having affiliations to traditional rulers and political parties in control of the council as well as punctuality at work, pursuit of general interest, respect for rules and regulations, honest handling of council resources and properties, non-misuse of official secrets as well as cordial relations with colleagues and the public.

In chapter 6, Prof Amadu Sesay & Dr Kehinde Olayode[6] study how West Africa has been in the vanguard of regionalism and regionalisation through its Economic Community of West African States; ECOWAS, founded in 1975. The paper examines efforts to combat human trafficking in the sub-region, within the context of new regionalism that emerged in the post Cold-War order. The paper uses as case study, the anti-human trafficking agencies of Nigeria, with emphasis on their successes, constraints and the nature of the war on human trafficking in West Africa.

In chapter 7, Erhun[7] studies the importance of culture of a nation in its socio-economic development and noted the fact that Nigeria is yet to recognize this fact. She suggests that Nigeria's policy makers should not this tact and take necessary measures along that path, nothing the crucial role which the judiciary could play in that matter.

In chapter 8, Prof Toriola Oyewo [8] examines some legal principles which if followed could releave Local Government councils of

5 I.O ARANSI, Reader, Department of Local Government studies, Obafemi Awolowo University, Ile-Ife, Nigeria.

6 Prof Amadu Sesay & Dr Kehinde Olayode, Department of International Relations, Obafemi Awolowo University, Ile-Ife, Nigeria.

7 Erhun, Faculty of Law, Obafemi Awolowo University, Ile-Ife, Nigeria.

8 Toriola Oyewo, Professor, Lead City, Ibadan, Oyo State, Nigeria.

litigations by disgruntled citizens which serves as draining pipe to Local Government autonomy.

In chapter 9, Prof Toriola Oyewo [9] observes that local Government is a sick institution with obvious symptom lack of fund (adequate) as officers privatize the resources, internal skirmishes which, Serves as barriers to performance. The low quality of councilors, coupled with Godfather syndromes. The acts or omissions of state governments also hampers the institution. Suggestions are made that the federal Government should effect necessary constitutional and legal changes to remove the institution from all barriers presently facing it, especially from the claws of the state Government.

In Chapter 10, Bamisaye and Ayodele Bello[10] cast a look at Nigeira's general elections of April 2011 and noted the fact that despite improvements on those of 1999 and 2003, much more improvements are necessary so as to strengthen internal democracy. He suggests that whoever would occupy the presidential position should be based on merit rather than on ethno criticism.

In Chapter 11, Bamisaye and Ayodele Bello[11] examine the implications of the agitation for resource control for Nigeria's federalism and its logic. The study concludes that the Federal Government under the current dispensation had played a crucial role in the distribution of resources in the oil producing areas in order to reduce the persistent agitation for resource control.

In Chapter 12, A.T Oyewo and M.L.A Salawu,[12] scan through the ways, the Nigerian judiciary has been handled and being manipulated within the hierarchies of government, and concludes, that the Nigeria judiciary has been terribly neglected, relegated to the background, seriously undermined, and slighted within the rank and file of the entire government.

In Chapter 13, A.T Oyewo and M.L.A Salawu,[13] examine how

---

9 Toriola Oyewo, Professor, Lead City, Ibadan, Oyo State, Nigeria.

10 Bamisaye, Senior Lecturer, Faculty of Social Science, Obafemi Awolowo University, Ile-Ife, Nigeria.

11 Bamisaye, Senior Lecturer, Faculty of Social Science, Obafemi Awolowo University, Ile-Ife, Nigeria.

12 Toriola Oyewo, Professor, Lead City, Ibadan, Oyo State, Nigeria, & M.L.A Salawu, Senior Lecturer, National Open University, Ibadan Study Centre, Ibadan, Nigeria.

13 Toriola Oyewo, Professor, Lead City, Ibadan, Oyo State, Nigeria, & M.L.A Salawu, Senior Lecturer, National Open University, Ibadan Study Centre, Ibadan, Nigeria.

corruption appears to be an endemic disease difficult to be eradicated in Nigerian scene, and how the efforts of the present administration is praiseworthy and commendable in waging a great battle against it. the paper recommends the adoption of ombudsman so as to expunge from Nigerian body politics, those parochialists, whose souls are dead, and whose motive in public life is all about primitive accumulation of wealth.

In Chapter 14, A.T Oyewo and M.L.A Salawu,[14] take the readers to a tour of legal provisions with decided cases on the chieftaincy law and suggest that chieftaincy disputes and settlement should be handled by experts on conflict resolution and management to reduces the number of cases going to the court, and that before a chief can , be deposed the principle of natural justice should be adhered to.

In Chapter 15, Oyeniran Adediji[15] reveals how the state government which constitutionally ought to nurture, sustain guide and encourage the local governments in their service delivery and performance efforts have paradoxically become an obstable, as they deny that institution of free hands to conduct their affairs through teleguidance denial of adequate fund and highjacked their lucrative functions. The paper suggests that if local government institution is considered as necessary, then it should be given free hand to operate.

In Chapter 16, Oyeniran Adediji[16] throws light on the present situation in which Nigerian leaders at all levels have not been able to respect accountability in governance and how the tolerant attitude of the governed masses has served as tact approval, or ratification for corruption and lack of accountability. He suggests that the masses need to change their attitude in order to make their leaders to regard themselves as servants of the people rather that as their masters.

---

14 Toriola Oyewo, Professor, Lead City, Ibadan, Oyo State, Nigeria, & M.L.A Salawu, Senior Lecturer, National Open University, Ibadan Study Centre, Ibadan, Nigeria.

15 OYENIRN ADEDIJI (Ph.D. Reader and former head of department of Local Government Studies, Obafemi Awolowo University, Ile-Ife, Nigeria.

16 OYENIRN ADEDIJI (Ph.D. Reader and former head of department of Local Government Studies, Obafemi Awolowo University, Ile-Ife, Nigeria.

TABLE OF CONTENTS

CHAPTER ONE

STRICT COMPLIANCE WITH ACCOUNTING AND FINANCIAL PROCEDURES AS EVIDENCE OF ACCOUNTABILITY AND STIMULUS TO AUTONOMY OF LOCAL GOVERNMENT

B.OYENIRAN ADEDIJI (PH.D)

INTRODUCTION

For some time now the issue of accountability at the grassroots level has become more and more recurrent in political, economic, academic and social discussions. The assumption of increasing financial responsibilities by Local Government with enormous amount of money flowing to them from the federal and state Government has provoked calls for more measures for ensuring that the additional funds now at the disposal of local government councils are used judiciously to provide social and other services that could improve the deplorable living conditions of the local masses.

The general impression rightly or wrongly nursed about Local Government is that of mismanagement of financial resources. The Report of the Technical committee on the Application of the civil service Reforms, 1988 could be taken to buttress this point. According to that report:

"There is relatively less commitment to the observance of rules and regulation at the local government level than at the federal and state level"

This observation was based on the fact that: "there are no adequate checks and balances at the local government level, as there are at federal and state level"

It could be argued that the said observation was not based on detailed scientific, comparative studies of relative degree of probity and accountability at all levels of government and so was a mere broad generalization. Cases of financial irregularities are observable at all levels of government, and so local government may after all not be more financially irresponsible than her big brothers (Federal and state Governments).

Yet pockets of cases of accounting and financial irregularities at the local government level could not in any way pass local government councils for angels. Given the crucial role of local government as the last hope instrument of national development- last hope of self-librations of the wretched of the nation-Local Government has now become a focal point to which all attentions are directed for salvation and survival of Nigeria. It is for this reason that the federal Government, through the implementation Guidelines on the Application of the civil service Reforms in the Local Government service (1988) and subsequent amending guidelines made it imperative for local government councils to follow certain accounting and financial procedures.

For example the local government treasurer as the chief financial Adviser and the chief Accounts officer is charged with the responsibility of budgetary control and supervising the accounts of all department with a view to: "ensuring that the Accounting system as laid down in the financial Memoranda is complied with by all the department of the Local Government".

Local Government councils themselves are becoming increasingly concerned with the question of violation of accounting and financial procedures. Thus in most local government councils exist desperate search for measures that could limit if not totally eradicate cases of financial irregularities, and eventually improve the image of the councils. The naked fact has also been brought to light in the Report of the Technical Committed that

"With the exception of a few local government in urban areas the majority of local government in Nigeria have limited financial resources and very few of them could, by virtue of their internally generated revenue, be self-sustaining"

Moreover, in a recent study, Adediji O. analysed how violation of laid down rules, regulation and procedures drain Local Government Councils of their autonomy.

This also impedes performance maximization of the councils as most of their energies and other resources are directed at answering queries from external powers at the expense of the actual functions they are supposed to carry out

For these reasons, it becomes impotent that improvements be carried out so that the enormous tasks and functions which local governments have to carry out are not impeded by internal "*draining pipes*" and by external interventions in the council's affairs.

The search for strategies which could lead t improvement in accountability and in local government autonomy would most likely not be exclusive tasks of local government functionaries alone. Stability of the local government system is crucial not only for the stability of the nation but also the survival of Nigeria as a whole. Every Nigerian of all sectors, of all cross-sections, has a stake in the stability and survival of this country proudly or jealously referred to as the "*Giant of Africa*".

The principal objective f the paper is to examine analytically how strict compliance of local government councils with laid down accounting and financial procedures could eventually lead not only to improvements in probity and accountability but also prevent erosion of the local government autonomy.

The paper is divided into 3 sections. The first is devoted to clarification of concepts. The second brings to light the relationship between autonomy, accountability and stric compliance with accounting and financial procedures. The last part is devoted to suggestions and conclusion.

A. CONCEPTUAL CLARIFICATIONS

The concepts which would be given clarifications in this paper include:

- Strict compliance with accountability and financial procedures;
- Accountability;
- Autonomy

Strict compliance with Accounting and financial procedures: implies rigid conformity with regular order of handling the accounts and finances of the local government councils as laid down by the Government.

Accountability: in this context refers to the obligation of accounts officers to handle the accounts and finances of local government according to laid down procedures and with so clean hand and mind that there is nothing to hide: since there are no skeletons in their cupboards. It also refers to acceptance of consequences of violating such procedures, etc. by those involved in culpable acts/omissions.

Local Government: in this context is defined by the authors of the famous 1976 Local Government Reforms as: "Government at local level exercised through representative councils established by law to exercise specific power within defined areas".

Autonomy: Autonomy has been defined by Adediji, O as the power and authority to determine one's actions or inaction and to bear consequences for the same. An autonomous Local Government is supposed to have power to direct its own affairs without interference from the higher tiers of Government.

With the above concepts clearly clarified, we proceed to examine the functional relations between strict compliance, accountability and local government autonomy.

B. RELATIONS BETWEEN STRICT COMPLIANCE WITH ACCOUNTING AND FINANCIAL PROCEDURES, ACCOUNTABILITY AND AUTONOMY

Functional relationship exists between compliance with accounting and financial procedures, accountability, and Local Government autonomy.

It is a feature of government based on the principle of democracy (as distinguished from government based on the principal of absolutism) that laws, rules and regulations and procedure be laid down to guide the conduct of public officers. Since public officers are not expected to base their actions and omissions on personal *whims and caprices*, rules, laws, regulation and procedures are designed and laid down. It is the existent of such rules, laws, regulations and procedures, which justifies occasional call on such officers to render account and to bear consequences for non-conformity. According to Hobbes school of thought "the performance of covenants many be reasonably expected if there is effective provision for detecting and punishing non-conformity"

Strict compliance with accounting and financial procedures becomes a *prima facie* evidence of probity and accountability.

According to Machiavelli, the world judges a person most often by appearance rather than by reality. This is because most observers draw conclusions from what they se or hear, unable or unwilling to make further efforts to go into reality.

A local government council operating on strict conformity with accounting and financial procedures would be assumed to be in order. Once this good image of a local government council is built, further attention to detail as to correctness of such a local government council, until the contrary is proved, operates thus such a local government council, , operates on probity and accountability until the contrary is proved.

Strict compliance with accounting and financial procedures is the first step towards probity and accountability. It is also a *sine qua non* of sound financial management. Conversely, violation of or non-respect for accounting and financial procedures is a forerunner of financial mismanagement and a *slap on the face* of probity and accountability. It is also a label and/or a sign of evil intention with respect to financial matters.

According Adediji, O.

"A lot extremely interventionism in the internal affairs of local government councils are brought about by constant allegation of violations of financial regulations and procedures."

When local governments given the impression of behaving like infants in the management of their financial resources they hold in trust for the people, they become militarily regimented strictly controlled, remotely teleguided, and occasionally pushed here and there by the "*settlor*": the federal and state government who have entrusted the resources to local government for the benefit of local inhabitants.

Thus local government autonomy becomes threatened and eroded. When local populations also learn of improper management of accounting and finances of the council, they become hesitant to pay levies and rates which from a major source of internally generated revenues. Consequently, Local government councils becomes the more dependent on the higher level of government for the fund they. Since whoever pays the pipe dictates he tune

"The more the degree of local governments' financial dependence on the federal and state Governments, the less would tend to be the degree of autonomy which local governments would be left to enjoy". It is now established that there are functional relations between compliance with accounting and financial procedures, accountability, and local government autonomy. The point we are driving home is that a local government council, which operates strictly on, laid down accounting and a financial procedure is presumed to operate on probity and accountability.

This good image affects the general perception of such a local government council.

- The federal and state Government who consequently would consider such a council as responsible enough and who might all things being equal decide to interfere as little as possible in the management of the resources of the council
- The local population who would be so satisfied with the image of the council and would see no justification for external *poke-nosing* into the council affairs.

As a result of non-interference from outside, a council would not only keep its autonomy intact but also have justified grounds upon which to base demand for more autonomy. Consequently, a Local Government council where the accounting and financial procedures are not respected would give itself the image of not operating on probity and accountability. The bad image would affect how the higher levels of government and the local population perceive her. Such a council would not be regarded as matured enough to be left unchecked and uncontrolled in the management of its resources.

The autonomy of such a council would eventually become constantly eroded. Thus to some extent autonomy =f (probity and accountability) = f (strict compliance with accounting and financial procedure).

C. SUGGESTIONS AND CONCLUSION

In order to enhance probity and accountability of a council on the one hand, and to keep intact or extend her autonomy on the other, local government functionaries in charge of accounts should keep strictly to laid down accounting and financial procedures.

Accounts must be kept in accordance with regulation, and laid down procedures for receipts and expenditures of the council must be followed:

1 Use of official receipts only or all money received;
2 Lodgments of revenues into the bank as soon as possible
3 Reconciliation unit of the council to check, compare and contrast monthly bank statements with entries in the cash book;
4 Internal auditor to check revenues and expenditures of the council on regular basis
5 External auditors to have free hands in the performance of their task;
6 Queries on council fund to be answered within specified period;
7 Once an alarm has been raised, processing of the expenditure should automatically be stopped.

Besides the above, the keeping of appropriate financial records at appropriate places is important. Speaking of the financial records, A.A. Marshall says "they are in fact a principal means by which progress is monitored and accountability enforced".

Local government functionaries in Nigeria could borrow a leaf from the French system of civil service whereby an average civil servant (at central or local level) operates strictly on legality of actions and of inactions, up to a point where the local administration enjoys immeasurable prestige and respect from the central government as well as from local citizens. Consequently the central government willingly grants more and more autonomy to the local administration. As a result, the French local administration ironically enjoys more measure of autonomy from the central government than its counterpart in Nigeria: the so called local government.

Such accounts officers should know that directives of superior officers would not excise them from legal implications of criminal acts. It is therefore impotent for such officers to insist as much as possible on carrying out their functions according to laid down rules and procedures.

It could happen on occasions that accounts officers find it difficult to maintain rigidity, especially when superior officers want it done the other way. Such accounts officers should take advantage of the provisions in the 1988 civil service Reform regarding the obligation of the superior to put all directives and instructions relating to expenditure of public fund in writing Although this is not an excuse for liability on the part of the "obedient accounts officers, yet it at least shows the *principal-in-crime*: the superior officer who commands illegality.

Adediji O. sees this as an effective means of preventing reoccurrence of situation in the past when political officers gave oral instructions, which were not written down and which they later denied. So carrier officers who had to carry out such instructions had no evidence to prove their innocence and so had to bear responsibility for wrongful action and omissions resulting from obeying such instruction. In short, despite the hierarchical superiority of political leaders of a council, officers in charge of accounts and financial matters should insist upon written instruction if only for record purposes.

This calls or recruitment of high calibers of persons in terms of educational, professional and moral qualities. We believe that education and professional training would not only make them to know the right thing but also to insist upon doing nothing else.This also calls for availability of documents relating to rules, regulations and procedures by which accounts and finances are to be handled. After appointment into such positions, all categories of functionaries, especially those having to do with accounts and finances should be given unlimited opportunities to acquire further educational and professional training. Such education and training packages should also aim at correcting immoralities and criminal inclinations, which stand as the root causes of financial mismanagement. Social re-orientation is also necessitous and to improve upon societal moral qualities. Of course, there is need to conduct thorough research on the adequacy or otherwise of the present remuneration given to public officers Adediji O. observes that the current remuneration are inadequate to cover social. Familiar/economic needs of the public officers.

The current endless strikes for improved salaries and allowances in Nigeria appear to prove such observations right. This calls for further research. There is need for inviting persons who are knowledgeable in salary matters to advise on how to arrive at adequate and just remuneration for public officers. In the absence of making life comfortable for public officers, particularly those who keep and/or generate funds for the Government, the Government would seem to have forgotten Bam field's observation that poverty beyond subsistence level erodes ethical and moral value of an average person. A government that wants equity must do equity.

REFERENCE

1. Report of the technical committee on the Application of the civil service reforms in the Local Government Service, Federal Government Printers, Lagos, 1988
2. Ibid.
3. Ibid.
4. Ibid.
5. Ibid.
6. Adediji, Oyeniran, Topical Essays on Nigerian Local Government Chapter Six titled "Fundamental Barriers and Limitations to Local Government Autonomy, Aberrant Publishing Company, Ibadan, 1990, p.86-1004
7. Ibid
8. Guidelines for 1976 Local Government Reforms, Federal Ministry of Information, Lagos, 1976.
9. Op. cit. P. 88.
10. Hobbes, T. leviathan, chapter XVII.
11. Quoted by J.F. Dendi, "Thinking with Machiavellian, Pen day Publication, London, 1972, and p. 106.
12. Adediji, Oyeniran, Topical Essays on Nigerian Local Government, op. cit.
13. Ibid.
14. Ibid.
15. Ibid.
16. Marshall, A.A., Financial Management in Local Government, Allen and Unwin Ltd., London, 1976, p. 43.
17. Adediji O., Topical Essays on Nigerian Local Government, Chapter Two, op. cit., p. 29.
18. Aedeiji, Oyeniran, Dilemma of Economic Rights and Moral Oblgations of Nigerian civil servants in the Nigerian Journal of Local Government Studies, Dept. of Local Government Studies, O.A.U., Ile-Ife, Vol. 3, No. 1, April 1989, pp49-57.

CHAPTER TWO

POLICY CONSIDERATIONS AS A POTENTIAL FACTOR OF STRAINED RELATIONS BETWEEN LOCAL GOVERNMENTS AND HIGHER LEVELS OF GOVERNMENT

OYENIRAN ADEDIJI (PH.D)

INTRODUCTION

For some time now, Local Government has become an accepted means which Nigeria could arrive at political, social, economic and cultural development. The birth of this new idea could be regarded as a product of necessity rather than of accident.

In the past, Nigeria did not realize the importance of development from the grassroots. Development efforts were then carried out almost exclusively by very few public officials, particularly career civil servants, who were believed to possess a monopoly of knowledge of how a nation could move from a state of underdevelopment to that of development.

As a matter of concession the state officials in question had technical knowledge from the education and/or training on or before taking up the state jobs. The state officials did all within their possibilities: many development programmes were designed and/or executed successfully. Completed sky scrappers, bridges, express roads, and magnificent installations are today living witnesses of what could be regarded as their achievements.

The problem however was that achievements made from efforts and resources sunk into those programmes have fallen short of expectations. The whole scheme of that time could be regarded as waste of time and resources. It was later realized that Nigeria was using a wrong method of development and that no nation could develop without the cooperation and mobilization of its human and other resources. Nigerian leaders finally considered it necessary to adopt "*another approach to development*".

In 1966 for example, Babangida said in a nationwide broadcast: 'our past experiences have clearly demonstrated that no self-sustaining development can take place in Nigeria without the masses of our people being effectively mobilized, genuinely motivated and properly organized for productive activity within the context of freedom, orderly progress and social justice"1. In 1987 Babangida reiterated that his government would adopt a new policy of social mobilization that would involve popular participation in the development of the country2.

Local Government has therefore become our accepted strategy for Nigeria's political, social, economic and cultural development. This is because it is now known and accepted as the Government that is nearest to the people through which mobilization of national resources would be most fruitful.

The 1976 nationwide reforms of Local Government and the subsequent reforms have been carried out with the hope and expectation that development could thereby be propelled further. It is however regrettable that the gains so far recorded from our Local Government system have been nothing to write home about.

Moreover in recent times, scholars and practitioners of Local Government have realized that apart from the disappointment over developmental achievements through our Local Government system, there is the more dangerous problem which could result from Strained *IGR* between Local Government and higher levels of government during the forthcoming republic. The major factor capable of causing strained IGR in question is the "policy considerations" and the endless unanswerable questions they engender. Local Governments have not been effectively put in a position of initiating and implementing policies necessary for regulating the affairs at the local level. Local governments are either badly consulted or not consulted at all in the formulation of national policies which eventually would affect them individually or/and collectively. Yet such national policies are made mandatory and binding on them. The state Governments also dictate the policies which Local Governments have to follow, the manner in which the policies must be carried out.

Higher levels of government have given the impression that they are not prepared to pay the price demanded by decentralization. Consequently, a lot of confusion is created over the exact status of local governments in Nigeria. The imminent IGR strained relations are feared to constitute a defect in pillars upon which the republic is being built. It is believed that unless such defects are removed or corrected before it is too late, the presents Republic runs the risk of following the footsteps of its preceding ones in terms of duration and survival. The magnitude of the present concern appears to be demonstrated by the sponsors, organizers and participants of seminars which could be regarded as contributions to the "rescue operations"

The objectives of this paper are to:

examine the logic of supremacy of national policies on Local Government policies;

analyze the problems which policy considerations pose for IGR between Local Government and higher levels of Government.

suggest strategies which could be employed to prevent such strained intergovernmental relations.

It is our belief that such analysis and suggestions would' be of some use to Nigerian policy-makers so as to ensure maximization of profits from our Loal Government system on the one band and ensuring stability of Nigeria on the other. To make this paper clearer to our readers, some clarification of concepts would now be undertaken,

CONCEPTUAL CLARIFICATIONS

Basic concepts which would receive clarifications in. this paper include: - Intergovernmental relations, Local Governments, Higher levels of governments, Strained relations, Policy considerations.

Intergovernmental Relations

There are several definitions for inter-governmental relations. The concept was defined by Nwosu as "a plethora of formal and informal relationships and transactions that develop among the levels of Government within a nation-state 3.

Prof. Anderson defined it as "an important body of activities or interactions occurring between governmental units of all types within the federal system"4

These two definitions view inter-governmental relations (IGR) as all interactions, permutations and combinations of relations among the tiers of governmental set up in a federal system 5

However, in our opinion, ICR would go beyond relations between different levels of Government. It should include human dimensions so long as governmental units are made up of persons occupying official positions. Thus according to an author, the concept of inter-governmental relations necessarily has to be formulated largely in terms of human relations and human behaviour 6.

We define IGR as the ways and manners by which persons occupying official positions within one unit of Government in a federation treat and are treated by persons occupying official positions in other units of government(s), as well as mutual reactions to such treatments.

Local Government

Local Government is simply "Government at local level exercised through representative Councils established by law to exercise specific powers within its defined areas" 7.Local Government occupies a third level in the Nigerian governmental system.

Higher levels of Government

By higher levels of Government, we mean Governments at Federal and State levels. The Federal Government occupies the first level, while the state governments occupy the second level in the Nigerian governmental system. It is because they occupy the first and second levels respectively that we refer to them as higher levels of government.

Policy Considerations

A simple dictionary defines a policy as a plan of action, a statement of aims and ideals, especially one made by a government, political party, or a business company8. James Anderson defines it as a purposive course of action, followed by an actor or a set of actors in dealing with a problem or a matter of concern 9.In this context, it is a system of laid down rules and regulations and procedures that must be followed in particular occasions or situations by a Local Government. An acceptable definition of a policy necessarily needs to stress what is actually prescribed to be done or not to be done in case of some anticipated or intended events

In this context, policy considerations are guidelines, rules, regulations and procedures prescribed by higher levels of government which local governments must take into account, must not neglect or fail to consider in the governing and administration of their areas of jurisdiction, irrespective of such guidelines, rules and regulations and procedures which individually or collectively such local governments might be following previously or might wish to follow later.

Strained relations are ill-feelings of human beings towards other human beings and consequently mutual ill-treatment. To prevent strained relations is to take desperate steps to avoid strained human relations.

With these definitions in mind, we can now enter into some theoretical analysis of factors which tend to cause unhealthy intergovernmental relations. The study of intergovernmental relations is the study of relations between human beings who make up the units of government10.. Theories which hold for human relations would therefore tend to hold for IGR. Perhaps the only tangible difference is that while human relations tend to portray relations between human beings (irrespective of their individual calibres), IGRs tend to refer to relations between people who, by virtue of their official positions, have powers and authorities which they can take advantage of in dealing with others, thus taking advantage of a combination of official and personal powers. Such public officials can also escape liabilities for their actions and inactions under the cover of Government". Ordinary persons do not normally have access to, and enjoy such, powers and privileges. It is important to examine the logic of policy considerations.

POLICY CONSIDERATIONS: JUSTIFICATIONS

As said earlier in this paper, policy considerations are rules, regulations, guidelines and procedures laid down by higher levels of Government which local governments must follow in their areas of jurisdiction, irrespective of policies which individually or collectively such local governments might previously be following or which subsequently they might wish to follow. Such policy considerations are inexhaustible and so detailed treatment would not be attempted in a paper of this nature and so our attention would focus mainly on the following:
National policy on primary education; National policy on promotion, discipline, transfer, etc. of senior staff of Local Government; National policy on the presence of Federal Government agencies at the local government level; National policy on elections; Code of Conduct for public officers; and National policy on supremacy of federal laws.

1. NATIONAL POLICY ON PRIMARY EDUCATION:

According to Constitution (suspension and modification) (Amendmnet) Decree, 1991 which transfers the running and funding of primary school education to the Local Government, The State Government would now be responsible for the provision of basic educational facilities the primary schools while the Local Government would concern itself with employing,dismissing, and paying of teachers' salaries 11.
The rationale behind this policy is not difficult to grasp. During the period when the Centre could no longer hold 12.each region had and operated its own educational policy as it liked. Uneven standards of social, economic, cultural and political development resulted, creating feelings of inferiority and superiority and consequent fears of domination, and of marginalization which jointly or severally contributed largely to the demise of the earlier Republics.
A national policy on education offers itself as attractive means of preventing re-occurrence of separatist movements, threats to unity etc brought about by the former imbalance. It could lead to balanced and even national development.

2. National Policy On Unified Local Government Service Schemes13.

Prior to the 1976 Local Government Reforms, there was no unified system of service for the then local government functionaries in Nigeria. The Local Government Service Board which was always constituted on ad-hoc basis was nothing short of an instrument of rewarding or encouraging politically useful staff and of victimizing those who were not following "correct" political routes. Through such a system of that time, many hard-working and dedicated but politically non-submissive Local Government staff had become disenchanted and had to be forced out of service, leaving mainly the submissive but inefficient ones to muddle through. As a way of alleviating this wasteful system, there was established shortly after 1976 Local Government Reforms, a Local Government Service Commission: a body responsible for recruitment, placement, promotion, transfer, short listing for training and discipline of officers on grade level 07 and above within each State of the Federation.
The Commission has also served as a symbol of unified Local Government Service and at the channel through which circulars, directives, information, etc. from higher levels of Government reach local governments. It has put a stop to the arrogant display of power and to victimization of staff, who do not belong to the party in power.

3. National Policy on the Presence of Federal Government Agencies at the Local Government Areas:

It is also a national policy to have certain Federal agencies stationed at the Local Government areas while it is also a state government policy to have some of its agencies stationed at the local government areas. Such federal agencies include: Directorate for Social Mobilization, Directorate of Foods, Roads and Rural Infrastructures, Better Life, Information Office, Immigration. office, Federal Statistics Office, Agriculture, Veterinary Office, Tax Offices, Licensing Offices, State Security Services (SSS).
The logic of the presence of these higher levels of government agencies

at the local government areas are not difficult to appreciate. They are meant to implement, or to ensure compliance of Local Government with national policies, guidelines and specifications laid down by the higher levels of Government. Take for example, MAMSER 14.It was born out of the awareness of our multiple national problems .of cultural disorientation, ignorance of peoples', rights and obligations and lack of participation of the masses in discussions and decisions affecting their general welfare, etc.

The agency could therefore be justified on the ground of its intended objectives of solving or at least alleviating these problems. The Directorate *of* Foods, Roads and Rural Infrastructures (DFFRI) could also be justified on the understanding that the problems of lack of food, amenities and rural infrastructures such as electrification, water and good roads in the majority of the rural areas had more or less got to the stage of being regarded as national problems. It would therefore be difficult to reject the presence of such offices in local government areas, especially if it is realized that a lot of formerly rural neglected areas of Nigeria thereby for the first time got development experience". The presence of the office of Better Life in all local governments of Nigeria is also a justifiable national policy. The national problem of lack of social consciousness of Nigerian women about their rights and duties as well as their lack of awareness of their social, political and economic responsibilities could not but justify' the need for a better life office in every local government area.

The presence of other higher levels of government agencies like information offices, Immigration offices, Federal Statistics offices, Adult education offices, police, Code of Conduct Bureau, National Electoral Commission, National Population Commission, State Security Services Offices, etc. could not be said to be unjustified if the need for national, policies and national standards on key areas of our national life is recognized, and if the Federal Government is accepted as endowed with some innate or acquired resources that could be used to implement or cause to be implemented, those policies, then the presence of the federal agencies In the local government areas could be justified. In addition to influencing the implementation of national policies at the grassroots level, the presence of such agencies in the local government areas attract social infrastructural and economic amenities which turn rural areas into relatively developed ones. Since there is no country in modem world where some elements of control, supervision and direction of local governments (through national policies) are not observable, the practice whereby the higher levels of governments have their agencies at every local government area to implement or ensure implementation of overall national or state government policies should therefore be understood. It is however another thing if policy considerations could turn out to bring strained IGR.

POLICY CONSIDERATIONS: POTENTIAL FACTOR OF UNHEALTHY IRG BETWEEN LOCAL GOVERNMENT AND HIGHER LEVELS OF GOVERNMENT

Policy considerations no doubt could find justification in their being capable of preventing inbalance in the Nigerian social, cultural, economic and political development, and thus preventing fear of domination and its attendant problems. However, the nature of man as revealed by some theories of human relations lends credence to fears now being expressed in certain quarters that those policy considerations may become a major source of strained relations between Local Governments and the higher levels of Government sooner or later.

Man is selfish and seeks to appropriate for himself the lion share of scarce resources, especially money, land and women 15. Higher levels of government would most likely behave greedily towards Local Government in the distribution of national resources. It could therefore not be ruled out that, for example, local government might challenge the right of Federal and State Governments to retain the lion share of the revenue from the Federation account, through the courts. If this happens, the relations between the two levels of government could become strained whether the redress is got or not. This same selfish conduct of men leads to intolerance of opposing views, values, ideas, etc. If different political parties are in power at, for example, the State and local levels, strained relations would be difficult to avoid. Where you have overlapping relationship in which the State Government bear the cost of constructing primary school buildings while the local government authorities would hire and fire primary school teachers, political differences might create situations whereby some state governments would lock up some school buildings under *cooked up pretences* and in exercise of the right of ownership and thereby paralyze the primary school system. Some State Governments, out of sheer political intolerance, might refuse to effect repairs of primary schools in local government areas belonging to opposing parties.

The same selfish intolerance could make Local Governments to intimidate primary school teachers suspected to belong to opposing political parties. Where such teachers happen to belong to the ruling party at he State level, the teachers in question may find themselves in the bad book of the State Government and be victimized in all ways possible. "On the other hand, career officers who belong to "wrong political party" at the local government level might find themselves in myriads of victimizations in all forms by the State governments who might find it unpardonable that such officers decided to "*go astray*" politically. In both cases, strained intergovernmental relations would be more likely than not.

Human beings also have territorial conduct. Robert Ardey 16. says that a human being tends to attempt to seek for territorial expansion while at the same time he tends to guard jealously, and sometimes to attack infringements upon, his own "territory". Consequently, strained relations might become inevitable between a local government and state governments if the latter attempts to usurp the functions of the former, especially functions considered by the "owner" to be lucrative. The State Governments in Nigeria often usurp some functions of Local Government, particularly markets, and so incur strained relations with the former.

Constitutional provisions appear to have removed this possibility. However evidences abound to show how State Governments cleverly violate this right of the Local Governments. An example is the new Dughe Market Ibadan, built and controlled by Oyo State Government under the guise of another name different from "market".

The Local Government Commission consisting of officials handpicked by the State Government appears to invade the jealously protected prerogative of Local Government: personnel affairs. When the Commission appoints, promotes, transfers and disciplines senior members of Local Government, she incurs strained relations with the Local Government Councils which would not understand why an organization granted autonomy should have a sensitive matter such as control over senior members/collaborators of local government political leaders, to be left, against its will, to the free disposal of "state owned" commission. In short, a local government finds it difficult to have cordial relations with the State Government on this question of Local Government Commission. The local government is also unhappy with the Federal Government for contradicting the idea of Local Government autonomy by its indirectly "mortgaging" Local Government autonomy -to the State Government' through the Local Government Service Commission. In the same way, the State Government maintains strained relations with local government for *an* attitude considered *to* be that of '*ungrateful souls*'. This is because the Sate Government see their role in "nursing' the Local Government Commissions as a help *for* which local governments should be grateful. The Federal Government is again in a state of dilemma: when it attempted to scrape the Commission so as to make for complete local government autonomy, it incurred strained relations with the State Governments. When the Federal Government became overwhelmed with public condemnation for scrapping the Commission and decided to resuscitate it, the Local Government Councils saw the Federal Government as a confused and self-contradicting big brother with whom cordial relations should not be kept. The present supremacy of the Federal and State Governments made possible by the central command nature of the Military would tend to be pegged down. The Local Government chief executives would most likely not be as docile as they are now. It is difficult to imagine that this would not have negative effects on IGR at that time. In all societies of human beings, inequality is a common characteristic. Some persons are naturally endowed with some innate and/or acquired qualities which make them to stand above others. Persons less endowed tend to consider that such special qualities would make persons having them to dominate others. Persons having such outstanding qualities tend to strive to enlarge such or at least to keep them intact.

Plato 17 and Aristotle 18 see inequalities as the natural arrangement which keep a society in its equilibrium. In fact, the society is made possible only by inequalities of all sorts. Those who then demand egalitarian arrangement of things are believed to be playing with *social dynamite* if in the present Republic, Local Governments show cold attitudes towards policies laid down by the higher levels of government, they would appear to be claiming equality19. As a result, they could be looked at and treated by the latter as out-stepping their limits. Thus all sorts of weapons within the reach of the big brothers" could be used as corrective measures for disrespect for elders consequently, the relations between Local Government big brothers could become strained.

Thus a State Government "agency" like the Local Government Commission and the Federal Government agencies such as the DFFRI, Better Life, MAMSER, etc. might be treated as "trespassers" into the jealously guarded territories of the Local Government authorities. Such agencies might there be denied cooperation and. support necessary for implementing the national policies for which they are designed. This situation could become the more resisted whenever Local Governments are called upon to meet the expenses of such agencies from the meagre annual allocation.

It is therefore evident that policy considerations constitute for now a potential seed of strained IGR. It is therefore important to offer suggestions to alleviate possible fears over the above situation.

SUGGESTIONS FOR CORDIAL RELATIONSHIP BETWEEN LOCAL GOVERNMENTS AND HIGHER LEVELS OF GOVERNMENT

To have cordial relations between Local Government and higher levels of government, the following suggestions would be made.

Firstly, local governments in Nigeria should seek for fairness rather than equality in their relations with Federal and State Governments. This becomes necessary because equality is not always possible or practicable. Adediji O. 20 once said it that the secret behind very cordial relations between the French central Government and local administration lies in the fact that the local administrative units do not claim equality with the former. This modesty and respect for the Central Government is another secret which explains why a

French local administration ironically becomes more autonomous than the so called local governments in Nigeria. Certain acquired or natural qualities, certain real or apparent magnificence of their capacities, especially in terms of resources, make it sometimes difficult, ridiculous, or at least unfair to agree on such equalities of Local Government with higher levels of government.

On the other hand, the Federal and State governments should have to moderate their paternalistic comportments and stop treating Local Governments as *infants* that have to be militarily regimented, strictly controlled, remotely tele-guided and occasionally punished here and there in order to get desired results from them. Local Government would lean and perform better under freedom and autonomy than otherwise. They should therefore be given necessary autonomy, freedom and other resources, and be treated as responsible adults to act and function with little or no control.

It is however important to note that strained relations between Local Government and higher levels of Government can hardly he totally eliminated. This is because according to Adediji O.21 there is only one place in this world where people don't disagree: it is in the in cemetery. As long as the functions, powers and actions of a Government involve control and restrictions of the activities of the citizens and other social bodies, such a government (local, state or federal) would often be in conflicts with those whose interests have been adversely affected and these may include other levels of government.

When such occasional strained IGR happen, the governments involved should not exaggerate such temporary disequilibrium". Rather, they should always be more preoccupied with how intergovernmental relations could become improved once more.

To avoid strained relations that may arise out of one level of government perceiving other level(s) as greedy. Selfish and domineering in the distribution of national resources, a constant review of what is fair in questions of financial relations between the three levels of government should be entrenched in the Constitution. This is because justice of today may become injustice of tomorrow. A National Council on IGR designed to be a permanent, neutral and technical body to monitor study and recommend solutions to problems of IGR, to evaluate the functions and powers and financial needs of the various levels of government, etc. would be a step in the right direction.

More importantly, Local Government Councils should be made up of high caliber of persons in terms of educational, professional and/ or moral qualities like those in the Federal or State Governments. We believe that education liberates a man from ignorance, which is behind most of human problems. This could make local government to gain more respect from other levels of government. *Persons perceptions* which largely influences inter-personal and inter-organizational relations would thus tend to work in favor of local government This then calls for selection of Local Government functionaries on merit in terms of moral and intellectual qualities.

After appointments or election of such local government functionaries into office, the journey should not end there. All categories of Local Government functionaries should be given opportunities for self-development: education and training should be made available for all categories of Local Government functionaries. This is because education is the *'balance wheel'* in harmonious inter-personal as well as inter-governmental relationship.

Apart from intellectual aspects of such educational and training programmes, local government functionaries should be made to enjoy in-depth studies in human relations, which could make them to cultivate tolerant political culture. Thus intolerance, which makes Local Government *'a house divided against itself'* and subject it to external aggressions of all sorts could have been removed 22 These educational and training programmes should also be extended to all other functionaries of higher levels of governments.

While it is not practicable to eliminate policy consideration, such policies should not be imposed on Local Governments. Local Government should be involved right from the conception stages of national policies to make such policies more acceptable, and to enable local governments to accommodate such national policies in their own pre- determined policies and programmes for which they have been elected into office. National policies must not be changed too often, otherwise the supremacy of such national policies would mean that local government would have to adjust their own policies to often, a situation which will make Local-Government to have no policies. Too frequent changes in national policies too, could also have another undesirable effect: Local Government may hesitate to apply new policies in anticipation of further policy changes. That is, not taking federal policies seriously any longer

Overlapping functions between Local Government and higher levels of Governments should be reduced to the inevitable minimum so as to prevent conflicting situations. Where overlapping functions are unavoidable, the mode of performing such functions should be carefully and adequately spelt out preferably in entrenched constitutional provisions

CONCLUSION

This paper examines the current trend whereby Local Government are obliged to tailor and modify their own policies in conformity with the policies of the higher levels of government. The paper concludes that unless appropriate steps are taken, such policy consideration could lead to strained relations between Local Government and higher levels of Government.

REFERENCES

1. I.B. Babangida, Presidential Speech, Federal Government Priflter, La, 1986. – p 2. 1.5.
2. I.B. Babangida, Presidential Speech, Federal Government Printer, Lagos, 1987.
3. H.N. Nwosu, 'Inter-Governmental Relations in Nigeria', a commissioned paper on the Implementaton Guideline on the Application of Civil Service Reforms in the Local Government Service. 1988.
4. Quoted from S. Deil, S. Wright, Understanding Inter-Governmental Relations, Massachusetts, Wadworth Publishing Company Inc., 1988, p.8.
5. S. Deil. Wright, op. cit.
6. Ibid
7. Guideline, on Local Government Reforms (1976), Fed. Government Printers, Lagos, 1976.
8. The Advanced Learners Dictionary of Current English, Second Edition, Oxford University Press, London, 1966.
9. See D.S. Wright, Loc. cit.
10. Adediji, 0., Enhancing Intergovernmental Relation Between Local Governments and Higher Levels of Government, Paper presented at Ondo State Seminar/Worksbop on Local Government Legislations. and Legislative Procedures, organized by Brainfield Law Chambers (Lagos), Held in Akure, August 11-12, 1992.
11. Federal Reoublic of Nigeria Constitution (Suspension and Modification (Amendment) Decree, Ministry of Information, Lagos, 1991. See again Daily Times, Lagos, September 7, 1992, p.48.
12. O. Aboyade, "The Role of the Federal Government in the Development of the States", in Report of the seminar on the Second National Development plan 1971, (|Lagos Federal Ministry of Information, 1971), p. 39
13. See Sunday Sketch "Local Government Service Commission and Autonomy of Local Governments"

14. MAMSER Handbook, published by the Directorate for Social Mobilization, Abuja, 1987
15. S. Freud, quoted by O. Pantier, Theories of Human Behaviours, Penman's Publishers, London, 1945, p. 162.
16. Robert Andrey, Territorial Imperative, Fontana Edition, 1972.
17. M.B. Foster, Masters of Political Thought, Edward McChesney Salt, pp. 46-81.
18. M.B. Foster, op. cit., pp. 124-135.
19. J.S. Mill, quoted by Brian Crozier, A Theory of Conflict, Hamish Hamilton, London, 1974, p. 50.
20. B.O. Adediji, Enhancing Intergovernmental Relations between Local Government and Higher Levels of Government, Loc. cit.
21. B.O. Adediji, Human Relations in Local Government in *The Nigerian Journal of Local Government Studies,* Dept. of Local Government Studies, Ile-Ife, Vol. 2 No. 1, Dec. 1986, p. 132.
22. O. Adediji, Topical Essays on Nigerian Local Government, Abiprint Publishing Co., Ibadan, 1990, pp. 85-104.

CHAPTER THREE

ACCOUNTABILITY OF LOCAL GOVERNMENT FOR THE DOWNFALL OF ITS OWN AUTONOMY: THE CASE OF ABUSE OF POWER DURING THE SIX-MONTH ABROGATION OF THE LOCAL GOVERNMENT SERVICE COMMISSION

OYENIRAN ADEDIJI *PH.D

On 1st Jan., 1992 during his annual budget broadcast the President of Nigeria, Ibrahim Babangida, announced the abrogation of the Local Government Service Commission (LGSC) with "immediate effect". According to that broadcast:[1]

"i|n the content of federal autonomy and democratic provision of our Constitution, the existence of Local Government Service Commission at the state level has now become untenable".

The abrogation of the Local Government Service Commission was said to have been motivated by series of complaints about, and allegations against, the Local Government Service Commission, especially by the political functionaries of the Local Government. Such allocations include the fact:

(i) that it was enough to scrape the Commission in the name of "autonomy" granted to local governments in a federal system of administration;

(ii) that they had no effective control over the senior staff of the local government they were heading. Yet they were expected to account for everything within their domain; money, men and materials.

(iii) that since the Presidential system of Government made them Chief Executives/Accounting Officers, they should take complete control of men, money and materials accruing to the Local Government;

(iv) that senior officers serving in their local governments did not owe allegiance to them but to the Local Government Service Commission which employed, promoted, transferred and disciplined them;

(v) that the Commission was an extraneous body whose relationship with Local Government was only to recruit, promote and transfer officers and for the Local Government to pay their salaries;

(vi) that the Local Government Service Commission did not respond adequately to their manpower needs and had done nothing to grant their request for staff transfer, promotion, etc.

By the implication of the abrogation of the Local Government Service Commission, Local Governments would henceforth handle the appointment, promotion, discipline and transfer of senior members (level 07 and above) of Local Government career officers. In short the abrogation of the Commission was believed to be a right step towards the enhancement of Local Government autonomy, it would ensure that local governments were in full control of their staff and that Local Government workers were loyal to their employers who would eventually be held responsible for the destiny of the Council and this would curb indiscipline and disloyalty or divided loyalty[2].

The problem was that at the time of granting the purported autonomy, the principle was not put in clear, proper and unambiguous perspectives to put its meaning, extent and limit beyond reasonable doubt for everybody, especially for those who would operate it.

Thus while the political functionaries of Local Governments interpreted, perceived and treated the issue of autonomy as *total autonomy coupled with absolute powers and authority*, the interpretation, perception and treatment have been generally held and considered by observers as misconceived and mishandled.

The objective of this paper is not to enter into controversy as to the blame-worthiness or otherwise of the Local Government Political leaders on the perception and treatment of the autonomy in question. Rather, the objectives of this paper are mainly to:

(a) Analyse how the abolition of the Commission on the one hand, and the virtually unlimited executive power and authority of Local Government ended up leading to what observers regarded as *blatant display of power, and authority arising from that autonomy*;

(b) Identify the consequences of the above on the local government autonomy itself;

(c) Identify lessons which could be learnt from the consequences.

In this exercise, interviews and research activities would be conducted in selected Local Government Councils, and extensive use would be made of known cases of perception and treatment of local government autonomy during the abrogation of that institution. The anonymity of the source of information of research findings would be maintained. In order to facilitate easy grasp of the context meanings of this paper, some clarifications of basic concepts would now the undertaken:

CONCEPTUAL CLARIFICATIONS

The concepts which would receive clarifications in this study include:

- Autonomy
- Political functionaries
- Local Government Service Commission
- Local Government

Autonomy in this context is power and authority of a Local Government Council to determine its course of action or inaction without interference from other levels of Government, to decide and execute its functions freely and without constraints and to bear consequences for the same[3].

Local Government is:

> "Government at local level exercised through representative councils established by law to exercise specific powers within defined areas"[4]

Political functionaries are "all persons elected or nominated to perform official functions in Local Government". These include Chairmen, Vice-Chairmen, Supervisors, Secretaries to Local Government, Councillors.

Local Government Service Commission hereafter referred to simply as 'The Commission' is the body charged with the responsibilities for recruitment, deployment, promotion and discipline and training of

Local Government staff and with monitoring the activities of Local Government to ensure compliance with regulations and circulars[5]

With these concepts now clarified, we can proceed to reveal some cases of "abuse of powers" during the period.

APPARENT ABUSE OF AUTONOMY DURING THE SIX-MONTH ABROGATION OF THE COMMISSION

During the six-month abrogation of the Commission the following were some of the cases *perceived* by observers as abuse of powers and authority:

Termination of Appointment:

1. By letter No. ITLG/s/22/s.4/1, Itu Local Government, Akwa Ibom State ordered all categories of employees to apply for transfer of their services from the Council on the ground that it was the interpretation and perception of the President's broadcast in respect of the new autonomy. Conclusively the letter said in paragraph two:

"Moreover, if your name is not listed through this exercise, it therefore means you have disengaged from being an employee of Itu Local Government".

2. By letter No. IRLG/20/5 dated 8th January 1992, the Irele Local Government, Ondo State, informed all officers from grade level 07 and above that their appointment had been terminated. The Local Government boss said that this action was necessitated by Mr. President's budgetary announcement, which abolished local government service commission throughout the federation.
3. By letter No. ESWLG PP.761/12 of 14 Jan. 1992, the technical officer of Ekiti South West Local Government in Ondo State, was relieved of his duties by the Secretary to the Local Government. In the same Local Government, by letter No. ESWLG PP.873/s, a Senior Health Superintendent was informed that the Local Government no longer needed his services.
4. By letters No. P.50/3, P.52/4 and P.54/4 of 8th Jan. 1992, Engineer Grade I, Higher Agric Superintendent and Technical officer (mechanical) were told that their services were no

longer required and that they should report back to the defunct Commission for reposting. The three officers were appointed by the Local Government Service Commission on 9th Dec, 1991 and posted to Ikenne Local Government before the abolition of the Commission.

5. A respectable 'big boss' of a Colanut producing local government Council in Osun State was reported to have sacked about 150 staff of both senior and junior cadre. The provisions, rules and regulations governing appointment of junior staff and unified staff were probably assumed to have been abolished along with the Commission, and so were not followed. In the same Local Government, it was reported that an engineer was appointed to replace and render redundant the substantive engineer who was not in the good book of the political functionaries.
6. The Head of Personnel Management of Mushin Local Government in Lagos State was sacked and disgracefully replaced with a subordinate from the Area office, for disobeying the big boss. The rule relating to fair hearing was probably regarded as incompatible with the type of autonomy then granted to Local Government.
7. In Oye Ekiti Local Government most of the Local Government staff were dismissed for the same reasons and illusion of autonomy.
8. In Plateau State, several heads of Director of Personnel Management of Local Government Councils were made to roll unceremoniously in order to manifest the achievement of autonomy of local governments and to show the extent of the new powers and authority of the Council.
9. In Etiosa Local Government of Lagos State, a chief engineer was rendered redundant through the appointment of an Assistant engineer to act as council engineer while an Auditor was brought overnight to replace the Council auditor. In the same Local Government, a Chief Health Superintendent was suspended for allowing his boys to serve an abatement notices at Kaiyetore Eleko area of the Local Government and the home town of the Chairman.

10. About Fourteen (14) staff of Oredo Local Government Council were said to have experienced summary dismissal from the Local Government service in the name of autonomy, especially because the 'big boss' believed that their positions in the Council was a threat to the progress of his party.
11. In Badagry Local Government of Lagos State, all non-indigene staff were ordered to resign their appointment.
12.. The 'big boss' of Aniocha North Local Government Council was said to have locked out the Head of Personnel Management and appointed an officer among the staff to be the head of personnel management.

Discipline:

13. In Mushin Local Government in Lagos State, an indefinite suspension was given to the Head of Personnel Management on 14th June, 1992 for leaking the official secret of the administration. The old order of fair hearing was ignored, probably in order to prove the existence of 'total autonomy'
14. In Ekiti West Local Government, Ondo State, a political secretary was reported to have gone to the extent of dealing physically with a Union leader for personal reasons, an incident which led to sharp reactions, protests and strikes which took some time to bring down. The political secretary must have assured that the new autonomy vested in him the authority to be a judge in his own case.
15. In Okpe Local Government of Delta State, the DPM was said to have been locked out and removed from office in such a way that the Nigerian Union of Local Government Employees, Delta State who perceived the political boss' interpretation and treatment of autonomy as wrong had to go on strike in solidarity with the embattled officers.
16. In Epe Local Government of Lagos State a level 10 Health Superintendent officer was said to have been suspended without trial and without consulting the Head of Personnel Management who was the Executive Head of Personnel Department.
17. In Surulere Local Government of Lagos State, a political appointee of a 'big boss' was reported to have manifested

physical gestures on the Union leader for personal reasons. The entire staff was said to have gone on strike in manifestation of disapproval of the treatment of the new 'autonomy'.

18. In Agege Local Government, Lagos State, a Councillor was reported to have physically assaulted a senior clerical officer who, while preparing leave advice papers of some staff, refused to go on unofficial errand for the Councillor.
19. In Ayedade Local Government of Osun State, a Town Planning Officer was reported to have been unceremoniously removed for advising that a pertrol station should not be located at a particular spot.
20. In Irepodun Local Government of Osun State a level 9 officer was reportedly sacked *on the spot* for coming late to office.

Appointment:

21. By letter No. JSLG/P ER/s/164/1, a relation of the "big boss" of Jos South Local Government was said to have been given an appointment as Higher Revenue Enforcement Superintendent, on salary grade level 08 step 4 to replace the incumbent revenue officer who was asked to go back to his Local Government of origin.
22. In Ekiti South-West Ilawe in Ondo State, four people who were appointed as level six (GL 06) officers before the Commission was abrogated immediately after the abrogation of Local Government Service Commission was pronounced had their letter of appointment changed to Higher Executive Officer Grade level 08 for personal reasons.

Training:

All over the country, training of Local Government staff was generally either suspended, staff in training recalled, or those allowed to go on training or to continue already started training were those who were found to have political substance.

23. For example, in Ado Local Government in Ondo State staff sponsored by the local government commission for two years Diploma Course at Obafemi Awolowo University were directed to return back immediately to their various offices.
24. A rate officer in Ido Osi Local Government of Ondo State who was on his post graduate course at Obafemi Awolowo

University, Ile-Ife before the abrogation of the Commission was recalled back to his job or made to choose the alternative of losing his job

25. In Ado Local Government of Ondo State also the 'big boss' was said to have directed all sponsored staff of the Commission for the two year diploma course in Obafemi Awolowo University to report back at their various offices, or otherwise to have their appointment summarily terminated.

Transfer:

26. By letter No. INLG/128 F/iv/170, Higher Agric Superintendent, Engineer II (civil), Engineer II (Electrical) and Assistant Information Officer were back loaded to the then abolished Commission by the 'big boss', Ijebu North Local Government in Ogun State.

27. In Bomadi Local Government an officer on Grade level 14 was transferred for being a non-indigene in order to pave the way for a lady who was an indigene on Grade level 13 to become the Head of Health Dept of Bomadi Local Government.

CONSEQUENCES OF THE PERCEPTION AND TREATMENT OF LOCAL GOVERNMENT AUTONOMY

As was said earlier on, the abrogation of the Commission by presidential pronouncement was not coupled with interpretation of the newly granted autonomy. The Government was also silent on the extent to which Local Government Councils could go in the enjoyment of such autonomy. This made local government bosses to treat the autonomy in their own perception. In all local governments without exception the interpretation or the perception was that the autonomy was *total, absolute* and *unlimited*. Blindfolded by this idea of total autonomy and by the accompanying absolute powers and authorities, political functionaries of Local Government decided to do away with the hitherto laid down rules, regulations and procedures relating to appointments, promotions, placement, regrading, transfer, as well as financial prudence and procedure, etc.

With the massive recruitment of officers who had little or no moral, professional and for other qualifications for the functions they were to perform came other shocking gestures:

(i) the unceremonial dismissal of old and experienced officers with a view to creating room for those whose principal qualification was their being "beloved".

(ii) the creation of parallel hierarchical posts to render redundant those officers who for one reason or another could not be dismissed or transferred.

(iii) preferential treatment and open discrimination in question of discipline: while many local government staff were able to get away with the most serious misconducts, make-up or minor 'offences' of other disfavored staff were punished to exaggerated degree.

An element of insecurity became injected into the career prospects and professional destiny of the majority of career officers. The unceremonial dismissal and the forced resignation of old experienced or/and qualified officers created artificial scarcity of human resources. The extent of the so-called autonomy, power and authority was so exaggerated, the abuse of it so carried to ridiculous degree that:

25 petitions upon petitions poured into the office of the Federal Government,

26 pressures upon pressures, especially by National Union of Local Government Employees were put upon Mr. President and his close associates,

27 myriads of appeals from traditional rulers and well-respected social critics.

At a stage Nigerian leaders decided that enough was enough and that the country could no longer afford to waste its few qualified and/or experienced Local Government staff who handled the execution of the functions. The Commission became resuscitated overnight.

The biggest and/or the most striking consequence of the perception and treatment of the Local Government autonomy was this resuscitation of the Commission, especially the fact that the Commission was given power and authority to set up general guidelines for the appointment, promotion, discipline of Local Government staff, monitor the activities of each Local Government to ensure that the guidelines were strictly and firmly adhered to and to serve as a review body for petitions and appeals from Local Government staff in respect of anything done or omitted to be done by the political functionaries. Today, Local Government does not have effective control over its Senior Staff and logically those Senior Staff do not manifest allegiance to the council. Thus Local Government is now being closely monitored and remotely controlled as a returnee 'prodigal son'.

Not only could this new development be regarded as an erosion of the elsewhile fair size of autonomy of Local Government in Nigeria, the event could equally be regarded as a sort of *paradise lost.* The question is whether Nigerian leaders have any lessons to learn from this episode.

LESSONS FROM THESE CONSEQUENCES

Nigerians have some lessons to learn from the consequences of misconception and mistreatment of Local Government autonomy.

Firstly, whenever the law makers are not the same persons that interprete it, it is usual to have occasions when the interpretation would be at variance with the real intention of the law-maker. For the simple fact that the Federal Military Government failed to clarify the meaning and the extent of the autonomy granted to local government on 1st January 1992, different perceptions have naturally cropped up. By this omission, the Federal Government appears to have given a *blank card* to the political functionaries in question of interpretation. Thus it is only a question of interpretation whether or not local government went beyond the autonomy granted it. It is a well-known fact that there exist at least 3 different ways of interpreting a law. Firstly you have the *literal rule* by which if the words are clear, then they best express the intention of law-makers and should be applied as they sound.

Secondly, you have the *golden rule* by which if words are ambiguous the interpretation may be varied to avoid possible inconvenience and ambiguity.

Thirdly, is the *mischief rule* by which a law is interpreted with special bias for the problems and wrongs against which it has been promulgated.

As long as it is admitted that the Commission was *wiped out* on the ground of its incompatibility with autonomous local government system, it is difficult to contest the fact that one of the possible interpretations of this incident is that it also meant *an end to everything about the commission,* including its rules, regulations and procedures for appointments, promotion, discipline, transfer, etc. of the local government career officers. This interpretation is the more likely to be assumed given the fact that there were problems of disloyalty, sabotage, etc. under the Commission's system which the abrogation was meant to solve.

Secondly, the so-called misconception, maltreatment and abuse of powers by the political functionaries only confirms what Montesquieu[6] predicted in 18th Century that "every man invested with power is liable to abuse it, and to carry his authority as far as it will go". The political functionaries suddenly finding themselves innundated with autonomy *windfall* became so blindfolded by it up to the extent that they perceived the autonomy as meaning that the state government had no longer any authority whatsoever in their local government areas.

And when looked at objectively, the so called abuse of powers in questions of promotion, appointment, discipline, etc. may not be so perceived by the Local Government functionaries so long as it is remembered that *political rationality* is most often at variance with *bureaucratic rationality.* And so some political functionaries did not see anything wrong with the opportunity of encouraging excellence, rewarding, dedication and loyalty, while punishing disloyalty and sabotage through discriminatory measures.

It is for this reasons that the Federal Government has to remove the issue of local government autonomy, its extent and limit from any areas of doubts, uncertainties and ambiguities in the nearest future.

No doubt, Local Government needs a measure of autonomy to enable it perform functions which the Constitution has earmarked for it. No doubt, local government has the image of notoriety, corruption, and maladministration and managerial inefficiency that an average Nigerian would not like *unlimited autonomy* granted to it. It is however important to remember the warnings of Olowu "that strict central control of Local Government is not the best way of allaying the fears and could in fact become counterproductive in negating the very reasons for investing in the institution"[7].

Finally, the Government has to learn the lesson that before embarking upon reform of an existing institution one should first be sure of what one is doing, what implications are likely, in order to avoid a repeat of a ridiculous situation whereby the Commission which was unceremoniously abrogated overnight, had to be reinstated, and made more powerful six months later and only after a lot of damages had been done to that institution and to Local Government career system!

CONCLUDING REMARKS

The Federal Government's failure to clarify the meaning, limits and extent of the autonomy granted to Local Governments following the abrogation of the Commission makes it difficult to affirm or deny that the autonomy was in fact abused. The paper however identified the cases of apparent abuses of powers and authorities on the part of political functionaries as a key factor which led to the reinstatement of the Commission and to consequent withdrawal of the autonomy, and points out some lessons which Nigerian leaders have to learn from the episode, especially that a prior study of possible consequences of abrogating an existing institution would have prevented a ridiculous situation of having to reinstate it only six months later.

REFERENCES

1. Babangida, I.B. 1992 *Annual Budget Broadcast*, Jan 1, 1992.
2. Information received from a group of Local Government Chairmen in an *Interview*, 1992.
3. Adediji, O., 'Strict Compliance with Accounting and Financial Procedures as Evidence of Accountability and Stimulus to Autonomy of Local Government in Adediji, O. (ed.) *Emerging Trends in Nigerian Local Government*, Department of Local Government Studies, O.A.U., Ile-Ife, 1994, p. 81.
4. Federal Republic of Nigeria, *Guidelines for Local Government Reforms* (Kaduna Government Printer, 1976), p. 1.
5. *Federal Republic of Nigeria Constitution*, 1979, Federal Government Printer, Lagos, 1979.
6. Montesquieu, *L'Esprit des Lois* chap. XI, 3-6
7. Olowu, D. *African Local Government as Instrument of Economic and Social Development*, International Union of Local Government Authorities, The Hague, Netherlands, 1988, p. 80.

CHAPTER FOUR

A REFLECTION ON EFFECTIVE MANAGEMENT OF LOCAL GOVERNMENT IN NIGERIA'S 21ST CENTURY

MIKE ADEYEYE, (PH.D)

Preamble

The objective of this paper is to share a thought on the strategies for effective management of local government in contemporary Nigeria. This is imperative owing to the failure of efforts made by successive governments – national, state, local and even non-governmental organizations (NGO) - in putting good practices in place. Likewise, various appraisals of local government reform efforts and decentralization strategies since 1976 indicate that but for a few exceptions, the rhetoric of decentralization to local governments has been stronger than its reality.

Indeed, it is not surprising that in the last two decades, Africa remains the most governmentally centralized amongst the world's continents, both in terms of the concentration of public sector personnel as well as the expenditure profiles of African governments. Whereas in the past the continent's poverty relative to others used to be the major explanation for adopting such highly centralized governmental structure as a major contributor to her relative poverty.

For emphasis, the aforementioned represents only one of the major reasons for the contemporary interests in the desire to strengthen local governments in Africa, nay, Nigeria's Fourth Republic. The other reasons advanced can be summarized as follows:

the realization that African local authorities may, if adequately empowered, be able to provide certain vital services that are not practical or possible for the public sector to provide efficiently due either to scarce local resources available to them, institutional limitations, scale factors or externalities. This is particularly important in rural local communities where the private sector is relatively underdeveloped;

the relatively good performance of African local governments in the short years prelude to political independence when they were allowed to operate in clearly defined areas with some discretionary authority and access to minimum resources. In contrast, the failure of centralized approaches for the provision and maintenance of basic services (schools, environment and health services, local roads, water supply, markets and public order) have led to efforts in the direction of reviving the abandoned experiments in local governance wherein non-governmental organization and private initiatives are encouraged;

the economic and fiscal crisis confronting African governments since the late 1970s have led them to adopt various forms of structural adjustment programs. One important of such a program is the reduction of deficits and government transfers to finance basic social and economic services. Strong local governments are perceived as credible alternative institutions for domestic resources to provide such services efficiently;

the growing conviction from an economic perspective (the technical characteristics of local services and the mobilization of resources) that the assignment of service provision to decentralized level of government is likely to be more efficient than the more centralized management strategies for providing these services in the recent past. Decentralization to local governments in these circumstances not only allows better adaptation to dissimilar circumstances and varying preferences for public services across local areas, it ensures that local governments will be forced to finance services from revenue sources such as taxes on income, property, revenue benefits and user charges which are presently poorly developed;

the possible role of effective local authorities in providing infrastructure and an atmosphere conducive to local economic activities, reduced population growth, and urban oriented migration. Similarly in the secondary towns/rural centres, developing local authorities may prevent some migration to large cities, and;

the possible role of effective local governments in promoting equity goals more effectively than central governments have done through the latter's promotion of decentralized development and growth-stimulating effects of redistribution policies.

While these expectations and hopes in respect of Nigerian local governments are valid, inadequate attention to the major problems confronting local government in Nigeria have undermined past efforts. This work is segmented into four separate but interrelated parts. The first part introduces the main objectives of the work. The second explains the various definitions of local government as discussed by various authors and experts on local government studies. The third part analyses the challenges confronting the local governments and suggests appropriate global good practices for achieving local good governance. The last part concludes the work.

Defining Local Government

Historically, the concept "local government" has been given different meaning by different scholars. Hickey (1966:159-168) referred to local government as "the management of services and regulatory functions by locally elected councils and officials responsible to them, under statutory and inspectorial supervision of central legislature and executive, but with enough financial and other independence to admit of a fair degree of local initiative and policy making".

Montague (1968), in the other hand, defines local government as "government by local bodies, freely elected which while subject to the supremacy of the national (or state) government are endowed in some respect with power, discretion and responsibility which they can exercise without control over their decisions by the higher authority". To Whalen (1976), however, the following characteristics are the main features of local government: a given territory and population, an institutional structure for legislative, executive and administrative purposes; a separate legal identity, a range of powers and functions authorized by delegation from the appropriate central or intermediate legislative, and within the ambit of such delegation, autonomy including fiscal autonomy.

Finally, Chief Obafemi Awolowo (W. H. A, 1952) referred to local government as "a system of government wherein local councils make, accept responsibility for, and implement their own decisions subject only to such control as may be exercised by the people through their own regional government".

From the aforementioned definitions, it is observed that there is a general trend. This is so because the authors made a distinction between local government and local administration. Those who do not make this type of distinction refer to many things that are merely the administration of local communities as local government.

Concluding on these various definitions, Oyediran (1988) posited that local administration is the administration of local communities essentially by means of local agents appointed by and responsible to only the central government be that central government, state, regional or national. While local government is referred to as a government in which popular participation both in the choice of decision makers and in the decision-making process is conducted by local bodies which while recognizing the supremacy of the central government is able and willing to accept responsibility for its decisions. In this study, Oyeleye's concluding remark will provide a useful guide for further deliberation in this work.

However, the critical question that is still confronting governments and local councils in Nigeria is the division of responsibilities for the delivery of both urban and rural services between federal, state and their agencies and the local councils. The question is a policy issue, a political issue and sometimes, the question of the division of functions is at the heart of the deteriorating state of affairs of the services in our towns and villages. Assumedly, a successful relationship between the federal, state and local councils must depend on a number of preconditions which can be summarized as follows:

1 the need and urge for a strong system of local councils in a democratic environment:
2 local councils must play a vital role as full partner in national development;
3 a fair division of functions between central, state and local bodies;
4 a fair division of financial resources between federal, state and local bodies;
5 a fair distribution of manpower resources between state and local bodies, and the need for consideration of an equitable remuneration system;
6 formal and strong checks and balances between state government and local councils;
7 full and adequate consultation and regular flow of accurate information between all levels of government;
8 full participation of the citizens of the urban and rural areas and therefore extension of democracy to all levels of government and;
9 properly defined constitutional and legal relations and the ability for local pressure on federal government to change legislation.

In summary, the criteria for a viable local authority in a democratic context are universal. The major considerations are:

1 the size of the population in the given area;
2 an informed electorate;
3 legitimate leaders to represent the local community and the feasibility of means to identify those leaders;
4 and the availability of financial resources and relative financial autonomy.

Managing challenges confronting Nigerian Local Government

Increasingly and from contemporary observations, the problems confronting Nigerian local governments can be segmented into two broad categories: the *environmental* and the *managerial*. Since our intention here is to focus on the managerial challenges, and since the latter may be so seriously impacted upon by the environmental constraints and vice versa, it is important to underscore what these environmental factors are:

Four major environmental problems can be discerned:

Historical

The relevance of inherited structures to post independence circumstances is great. These inherited structures constitute the major model that had been experimented with in Africa (the direct, indirect and conciliar local government administration models).

Particular problem areas include:

Excessive reliance on central government controls as the sole means of correcting local governments;

Primacy of central official at the local level;

The distortion and/ neglect of traditional community structures; and

The tendency to pattern new reforms along the lines of development in the former metropolitan capitals, whether appropriate or not.

Strategies adopted for Stimulating Development

As the least economically developed continent, and ravaged by extreme poverty and political instability, there is the tendency for African governments (Nigeria, a major player) to adopt political and economic programs that promise dramatic results (one party state, state capitalism or socialism, central planning, state-supported industrialization focused on major cities, etc). Local governments are perceived as not too important in these circumstances, hence, the preference for deconcentrated structures. Moreover, the structure of power is skewed very strongly in favor of the urban communities' vis-à-vis the rural areas where majority of people live.

Institutional Constraints

The central/federal government and the party are regarded as the sole development institutions, hence, the tendency to marginalize or destroy all other social institutions- the organized private sector, political parties, non-governmental organizations, trade unions, and even religious and ethnic-based organizations and, of course, local governments.

Where local governments/administration exist at all, there is tendency for the most critical resources- skilled personnel, scare capital, all major revenue sources to be allocated to the central/federal government to the detriment of sub-national government and other agencies. Hence, responsibilities that are normally performed by local governments in other continents are performed in Africa by the following institutions in this order: (1) Central Governments - 42% (2) Public Enterprises - 14% (3) Local Governments - 20% (4) Private Sector - 11% (4) Voluntary Agencies - 7%. (World Bank, 1988).

Attitudinal problems

This is the most critical of the environmental problems. A general presumption by elites within and outside government that:
local people are ignorant, poor, and lack organizational capability. They are regarded as obstacles to development rather than possible agents.
local governments are more inefficient than central/state governments;
local governments are especially prone to corruption and mis-management, much more than central/state governments; and
local governments exist solely at the behest of the central/state government and the latter can disband or restructure them at will.
Even though virtually all these assertions have been largely disproved by research conducted on best practices by various scholars within the last two decades, as nonfactual and/or immoral, the stereotypes have persisted (Olowu, 2004; Shah, 2006)

Management Problems

Though these contextual factors are quite weighty, the more serious problems are the managerial ones. Research into local organization has proven quite conclusively that problems within the environment are not so determinative of the performance of local organization. What is critical are the structures of local organizations, the operational procedures within such organizations, and the type of interventions made by external agencies. We shall examine the structural problems first:

Legal Basis of Local Governments

Local governments are agents of the central/state government, but the equally important point they exist as home-rule institutions to serve their various communities is poorly developed in Nigeria. Hence, the prerogative of the central/state government functionary (either the Commissioner for Home Affairs or Local Government) is generally very comprehensive and total. This official is expected to exercise such power on behalf of the legislature, but given the poor development of the legislative assemblies, this power has not always been used responsibly.

This is what makes the Nigerian innovation which provided for "the existence of democratic local governments" in her 1979 and 1999 Constitutions as a measure for strengthening its local government system an extremely important innovation to watch. Legal pundits disagree concerning the constitutional implications of this development, but it seems to be contributing to the long-tem development and importance of local government in the country. State governments must therefore re-examine the relevance of the large array of control powers vested in them by section 7(1) of the 1999 Constitution to allow the exercise of greater initiatives by Nigerian local governments. (FRN, 1999: Yakubu, 2003).

Moreover, the law on local governments ought to widen the range of areas in which they can be active. Currently, Nigerian local governments are not very active in the areas traditionally regarded as major responsibilities of local governments in other parts of the world. (Olowu & Wunsch, 2004)

Size of Local Government

There has been a tendency towards creating large local governments in Africa, possibly arising from the failure of smaller units of local governments in earlier years. African Local Governments including those of Nigeria have a higher average unit-size than most other nations. Two reasons are usually stressed in favor of large size: to provide a minimum population base for a wide range of basic services (Primary education, health, water, etc) and to ensure an adequate base of locally generated revenues. Research on these subjects has, however, indicated that size has no direct relationship with the efficiency or otherwise with which services are determined, neither is there a direct positive relationship between size and revenue generation for small councils which can be quite effective in mobilizing resource from their constituents. It has also been pointed out that the highly centralized tax structures and the heavy dependence of the local governments on grants from higher governments in several African countries (Nigeria inclusive) weakens the case of large size based on revenue mobilization potential. (Wunsch, J & Olowu, D 1995; Adamolekun, 2008).

Rather what has been shown to be critical for the success of local governments/ authorities is the opportunity to maintain the right type of linkages (vertically and horizontally with other local organizations and with government agencies). Yet these types of linkages (interaction for the exchange of information and other resources) are denied local governments. Organizations are not encouraged to enter into joint solutions to common problems with other local governments (nor other local organizations).

Personnel Management Problems

Three major alternatives have been developed for managing local government personnel systems in order to take advantage of either horizontal (among local governments) or vertical (state/ local) integration or both, especially important given the inherent disadvantage of local governments in competing for personnel with other public and private organizations. These alternatives are known as the integrated, separated, and unified forms. The latter (the Unified model) is expected to synchronize the merits of the other two models while at the same time mitigate their disadvantages. Local governments pool their resources to ensure the best opportunities for upward and lateral mobility for their staff and to sustain higher standards without sacrificing their semi-autonomous status. Whereas the unified model is recommended strongly for countries in similar circumstances to African nations, a sample of some 20 countries in the mid- 1980s shows that 12 of them had adopted the Integrated System (which suggests more centralized structures). Moreover, even in the five countries which utilized the Unified Model, (Botswana, Malawi, Nigeria, Tanzania, Uganda), the management of local government senior personnel was highly centralized at the central/ state government level. The secretariat and personnel of the unified service are normally owned and controlled directly by the central/ state governments. (World Bank, 1988).

High-level centralization in local government personnel management has conferred some benefits. It has enabled local government system in some countries (Nigeria) to enjoy condition of service similar to those within the state civil service. Only three of the sampled countries reported above had no pension system for local government employees, for instance. Local government employees are also protected from the worst forms of political victimization from local councilors or other elected local government functionaries. Some form of training progammes is provided for local government officers in some of the countries. All of this represents important achievements compared to the earlier situation.

On the other hand, centralized personal management has not substantially succeeded in attracting skilled professional into local government not just that these skills are scarce but for the reason that the personnel systems are not responsive enough to the needs of the local governments, because of the prevailing belief that local government can make do with less qualified staff.

Finance

Nigerian local governments are still relatively disadvantaged in terms of revenue sources, expenditure programme and the management of their budget. Pertaining to finance of local governments the following should be noted.

1 Nigerian public finance systems are too heavily dependent on indirect taxes imposed on imports /exports and have poorly

developed their direct tax systems. Local governments tend to suffer the most in these contexts: there has been too much reliance on revenue from the federation account. And also the most buoyant and productive revenue sources are regarded as "naturally" belonging to the federal government. This makes Nigerian local governments excessively dependent and irresponsible in the use of resources and careless in developing the revenue sources allocated to them.

2 More importantly, the revenue sources bequeathed to the Local Governments through the 1976 local government guidelines and the 1999 Constitution have not been well exploited by them. Only a few Local Governments raise revenue from these sources today.

3 Likewise, the State/Local Government Joint Account (JAC) as currently operated by some state governments has not enhanced the local government finances. Reports from local government best practices across the globe indicate that maximum benefits could be derived by local governments when the account is transparently and conscientiously operated.

4 Local governments in Nigeria are never going to be able to enjoy financial autonomy and provide major infrastructure services, except if they generate a substantial portion of their own revenues, have access to the capital market, are made accountable to their financiers (the private sector and the citizens for the use of these resources).

Critical Support Institutions

Certain support institutions are critical to the existence of virile local governments in Nigeria. These include:

1 Local Government Service Commission (LGSC) - a body established at the state level to coordinate personnel activities of the local councils in every state of Nigeria.

2 Revenue Mobilization Fiscal Allocation Commission. RMFAC – a statutory body established at the federal level responsible for federal revenue allocation between the three tiers of government.

3 Training Centres (with specialization for various categories of administrative/ technical officers).

4 A state government bureau (or better still, a unit located at the state level) equipped with adequate and specialized personnel both in the headquarters and the field capable of coordinating the programmes of state ministry and of local governments.
5 State Legislature & Economic Planning and Development Commission (at the local level) to integrate local government projects with those of the field administration unit of the state government. Such a commission should be chaired by a senior official either of the State or Local Government. Transparency in project performance should be stressed.

Operational problems

False dichotomy between central and Local Governments

Strong governments are required both at the centre and in the locality. Neither is naturally better than the other, but both can be mutually reinforcing. The strengthening of local governments is not a zero-sum (but positive-sum) power game between the centre/state and localities. Central/state officials must recognize the limitations of centre as well as the localities but also the strength of each. Experience shows that without the commitment of central-level politicians and administrators to improving the local government, no great result can be expected.

Too Much Control is as Bad as Non-Interest

Past disinterest in local government could easily be exchanged for too much interest which is the reason for the present array of controls on local government. A continuous stream of circulars, memoranda, rules and decrees for local governments to comply with can be counter productive. For too long, the approach to managing local governments in Nigeria has relied too much on "stick" (control) rather than on "carrot" (incentives). It should be possible for state officials to develop a whole range of incentives to local governments to ensure that they are adequately prepared to achieving their objectives.

A Framework for Local Government Performance Evaluation

In fairness to Nigerian local government, the level of performance expected of them is not commensurate with their actual level of responsibility and funding. More disturbing is the controversial status of the local government in the 1999 Constitution. A framework for performance evaluation must be people-driven and must have the input of critical stakeholders in the various communities. State government, Local governments and critical stakeholders should evolve an adequate framework for the assessment of local governments by establishing a scale of standards. Such scale would allow a better classification of local governments on the basis of performance (first, second, third classes) and would be tied to the system of incentives as earlier suggested.

Rural versus Urban

There is the tendency to treat all local governments as the same even though their problems, challenges and opportunities vary. It is important to make a distinction for management purposes between urban and rural local governments: financial powers expenditure programmes, limited use of grants in favor of commercial loans, personnel development, etc.

Rural areas for instance ought to enjoy more grants (and support) than the urban municipalities, which should be given greater access to obtain commercial loans for their capital development projects. In this way, urban areas could indirectly support the rural areas while other avenues for cooperation and assistance could also be sought. Similarly, personnel conditions ought to be skewed in favor of rural areas for both local and state government employees. On the other hand, state governments ought to take more purposive action, often in concert with donor organizations, to ensure that urban municipalities become largely self-sustaining.

Effective national policy on information and communication technologies (ICT)

Information and communication technologies (ICTs) potentially offer diverse benefits for local governments in Nigeria in relation to the production and dissemination of, and access to, knowledge and information. A major difficulty in discussing the application of computing technology in Nigeria is that local governments as a group are quite heterogeneous; they differ widely in both the extent to which they have introduced computer and networking technology and the extent to which the necessary infrastructure exist for exploring the technology. As such, the role of federal and state governments is very important in having an effective national policy on ICT. State governments could also provide assistance to local governments in strengthening their ICT potentials.

Training

Training of local government officials should proceed beyond the narrow focus of managerial/administrative staff to include the training of various local government professional and technical staff. Moreover, state/local officials need to be exposed to training in comparative local government systems, including the potential of local organizations manned by peasants, farmers, technicians, etc.

The Role of federal/State/Local Government Official and Donor Organizations

The emphasis of this paper has focused on national/state/local governments and officials. This is deliberate. It is based on the conviction that local governments have no prospects in Nigeria except with the active support and interest of federal/ state agents. State government officials (Local Government Service Commission- LGSC) must help local governments to develop adequate personnel capacity by providing them with technical assistance in critical functions (development training, finance/ accounting skills, training programme and various forms of contracting for services from other public sector agencies and private sector.) They must help to evolve a new structure of local governments that are responsive, accountable and capable of mobilizing resources for local economic development. The logic of contemporary global economic development seems to demand the adoption of a different conception of local – level institutional development that has been adopted since independence.

The implication however, is that many more responsibilities will be thrust on local government officials. A lot will be expected of them and they cannot afford to fail. In particular, they must carry out internal decentralization, improve their strategies for mobilizing revenue even from the present sources, stimulate the participation of various social groups in their activities, and provide relevant services in the right quality and quantity which will enable their increasingly sophisticated citizens to regard them as credible institution.

Nigerian government should persist in this important experiment in spite of possible initial disappointments. Institutions, like the human beings who create and run them, require time to grow and learn from their experiences both good and bad. International Development agencies might assist Nigerian government in these efforts through some form of specialized technical aid schemes which focus specifically on the development of local governments.

Finally, Nigerian government with the assistance of international organizations should promote training in specialized fields related to local governments (e.g. property valuation and development, local government personnel systems, portfolio management for local governments, the development of standards for regulating state-local governments.

Conclusion

Perhaps the most important points made in the above presentation may be summed as follows. Tremendous opportunities exist for the development of local governments in Nigeria. It is however, critical that both state and local government officials adopt the appropriate mental dispositions in tackling the major environmental problems confronting the development of local government in Nigeria. This places great emphasis on the need to develop effective management strategies for tackling these environmental challenges.

Of the two strategies for managing local governments in Nigeria, those associated with state control have been overused, while those which rely on motivation through appropriate incentives have been poorly developed. Since management deals with the effective utilization of resources to achieve predetermined goals, some issues will seem to be important for the future of effective local governance in Nigeria.

First, there is a need to underscore the importance of the political objectives of popular citizen participation if local governments are going to be effective in realizing their objectives, such as service delivery/maintenance and revenue mobilization. Second, certain resources are crucial for the existence of virile local governments in Nigeria. These include: adequate constitutional/legal power; revenue resources (to finance recurrent capital programmes); appropriate training on personnel arrangement; support institutions which can provide technical assistance to local governments in the key areas of data management; and accountability and management innovations. A most important resource which Nigerian local governments will require is time within which they can learn and make mistakes.

The emerging consensus from the major studies carried out thus far on the strategic management of local government in Nigeria emphasizes the following points:

1 The concept and practice of local government in Nigeria has not emerged beyond those introduced in the late colonial era, namely local governments as producers of basic social services including law and order. Even in this limited sense, local governments have been severely circumscribed. Their fortunes have tended to ebb and flow with the times.

2 Local governments in Nigeria with a few exceptions, have not really penetrated into playing critical roles in economic development activities. Certain conditions would seem essential for this to happen but it is a moot point whether or not this is feasible, given the prevailing political and economic context in which local government operates in Nigeria.

3 The effectiveness, efficiency and accountability in Local Government operational management depend greatly not on the presence or absence of central government intervention in their operations, but on the nature of such intervention whether destructive or catalytic. The present situation can only be effectively tackled if some of the major issues raised above are urgently addressed. (Olowu & Wunsch, 2004; Meredith, 2006).

REFERENCE

1. Adamolekun, Ladipo (2008) The Governors and the Governed – Towards Improved
2. Accountability for Achieving Good Development Performance (Ibadan, Spectrum Books Limited).
3. Federal Republic of Nigeria, 1976, 1984 and 1988 National Guidelines on Local Government Reforms in Nigeria.
4. Federal Republic of Nigeria, (1976) Guidelines for Local Government Reform
5. (Kaduna: Government Printers.) & The 1988 Civil Service Reform at the local government level in Nigeria.
6. Federal Republic of Nigeria, The 1999 Constitution.
7. Hickey, T. J. D. (1966) "Enemies Within and Enemies Without the Gates", The Political Quarterly, Vol. 37, No. 2, April – June 1966, pp. 159 – 168.
8. Meredith, Martin (2006) The State of Africa. A history of fifty years of Independence (UK, The Free Press).
9. Olowu, D & Wunsch, J(1995) The Failure of the Centralised State (California, ICS Press).
10. Olowu, Dele (2004) Local Governance in Africa. (London, Lynne Rienner Publishers, Inc.
11. Oyediran, Oyeleye (1988) Essays on Local Government and Administration in Nigeria (Lagos, Project Publications Ltd).
12. Shah Anwar, ed (2006) Local Government in Developing Countries (Washington: The International Bank for Reconstruction and Development/World Bank).
13. Whalen Hugh, "Ideology, Democracy and Foundations of Local self-government" in L. D. Feldmann & M. D. Goldrick (eds.) Politics and Government in Urban Canada: Mathuen, 1976, pp. 28-48.
14. Western House of Assembly Debates, July 1952.
15. World Bank (1988) World Development Report, 1988 (New Oxford University Press).
16. Yakubu, John (2003) Socio-Legal Essays in Local Government Administration in Nigeria (Ibadan, Demyaxs Law Books).

CHAPTER FIVE

OFFICE ETHICS AND CONDUCT IN NIGERIA LOCAL GOVERNMENT SYSTEM

ISIAKA O. ARANSI, (PH.D)

INTRODUCTION

Within the Nigerian political/constitutional arrangement, Local Government can be considered as the third tier or the third level of governmental activity. In other words, Local Government constitutes a group of relative local communities within an identified geographical expression, involved in the management of their affairs in an organized fashion of self government, with some roles, functions and powers devolved to them through statutory provisions and relative degree of autonomy. Local Government is the closest level of government at which the art of participation in the affairs of the state can take place. It is the tier of government whose activities directly impinge on most Nigerians.

Local Governments exist not only as representative organs of the people but also as a veritable channel through which goods and services can be delivered to the people within the ambit of the laws establishing them. To be able to discharge their duties allocated to them and deliver goods and services efficiently and effectively, Local Government functionaries are expected to behave in a very responsible manner, realizing that they are holding fiduciary responsibility to the public to whom they are accountable. It becomes absolutely necessary for Local Government functionaries to be conversant with office ethics and conduct in Nigeria Local Government system.

Our concern in this paper therefore is going to be restricted to the discussion of Office Ethics and Conduct in Nigeria Local Government system. Consequently, the paper has been divided into five sections.

Section one of the works is the introduction. The second segment is an attempt at conceptual elucidation and clarification. The third section focuses attention on what constitutes ethics and conduct. Section Four discusses the various problems responsible for poor ethical conduct within the Nigerian Local Government system. The last section, section five is the conclusion to the paper.

CONCEPTUAL ELUCIDATION AND CLARIFICATION

To avoid conceptual confusion and facilitate a comprehension of their usage in this paper, four concepts contained in the topic of this paper are worthy of elucidation and clarification. These are: "Office", "Ethics", "Conduct" and "Local Government".

An Office can be simply defined as a place where business is done. It can also refer to a place where written work is done in connection with a business. Similarly, an office is seen as a government department. We would not want to belabor ourselves with the meaning of an office since we are all familiar with this concept.

The second concept that comes readily to mind, and much more relevant to our discussion, is ethics. "Ethics" can simply be defined as "moral rules or principles of behavior for deciding what is right and wrong". In other words, ethics means a general idea or belief that influences people's behavior and attitudes. A code of ethics therefore refers to a set of moral rules.

The third concept worthy of elucidation and clarification is "conduct". "Conduct" can be considered as "the way someone behaves, especially in public, in their job" etc. or the way a business activity is organized.

The last concept employed in the topic of this paper is "Local Government". Local Government has been defined in various ways by different authors and scholars. The Federal Republic of Nigeria Guidelines for Local Government Reform, 1976 conceptualizes Local Government as:

> ***Government at local level exercised through representative councils established by law to exercise specific powers within defined areas. These powers should give the council substantial control over local affairs as well as the staff and institutional and***

> ***financial powers to initiate and direct the provision of services and to determine and implement projects so as to complement the activities of the state and Federal Government in their areas and to ensure, through devolution of functions to these councils and through active participation of the people and their traditional institutions, that local initiative and response to local needs and conditions are maximized.***

To Olowu (1988), there are two approaches to the definition of Local Government in the literature. One approach, which is usually adopted in comparative studies, is to regard all sub-national structures, below the central government as local government. A second approach is more circumspect in that local governments are identified by certain defining characteristics. These characteristics usually focus on the following five attributes: Legal personality, specified powers to perform a range of functions, substantial budgetary and staffing autonomy subject to limited central control, effective citizen participation and localness.

In summary therefore, local government can be said to refer to that tier of government closest to the grassroots people.

Local government as a third tier of government exists upon the basis of two fundamental justifications; namely: the democratic principle; and developmental principles. The democratic principle enshrines the idea of participatory democracy and of political responsibility to every citizen; and on the other hand, the developmental principle implies the mobilization of human and material resources for local development.

The under-listed roles are performed by local government, which make them the pivot of national development.

(a) There are many amenities and services which can best be produced on local basis rather than on central basis especially where the need of the people are many and the resources of the central government are insufficient to cover all the requirements' demand. In such cases, local initiatives and efforts must be intensified to provide the money, material and manpower for services, which are beyond the capacity of the central government.

(b) The central government, in most cases, is remote from the local community and cannot be expected to know the individual wishes of the many communities all over the country. Having local government better solves these problems.

(c) Different towns and districts have tradition and customs, perhaps different languages and the people are proud of their hometown and their fellow citizens who live there. These traditions and customs are better preserved under local government.

(d) Local government provides a healthy spirit of competition between units of population making them jealous of each other's standard and of course eager to develop their own standard.

(e) Local government provides services, which members of the community want and prepare to pay for, but as individuals they could not buy and provide for themselves e.g. road, water supply, Motor Park, Markets etc.

Local government can therefore be considered to be very important for an effective community development. Since local government exists purposely to enhance development through rural mobilization and encouragement of democratic practices, it stands to reason that it is the most appropriate agency of community development where clear understanding of institutions, customs, religions, social structure, kingship system and nature of co-operation among the citizens of communities can be got.

Having clarified the key concepts employed in the topic of this paper, the next section discusses the issue of office ethics and conduct particularly as obtain in Nigeria Local Government system.

OFFICE ETHICS AND CONDUCT IN LOCAL GOVERNMENT

Olojede (1992) observed that from time immemorial, philosophers have often argued about the relative merits of methods of looking at and measuring moral behavior. Diverse kinds of virtues and human goals have often been identified as the best or ultimate ways to understand and implement what is "good". In modern times, ethical pluralists have argued that unillinear laws of ethics cannot define the means to good ends. They further argued that a battery of tests must be employed to ascertain or determine when choices and decisions serve morally justifiable purposes/ends. Elaboration of no one virtue such as **honesty, justice, selflessness or courage** will provide the satisfactory measure. **Moral/good behavior** emerged from applying them all. There is no doubt that the pluralist approach has the appeal of commonsense and would seem most applicable to performance in the public service.

To many people, **unethical performance** in public positions is synonymous with **blatant, overt corruption, involving fiscal gains such as the acceptance of bribes in return for dispensing some favor or exemption from governmental imposition or actions designed to advance one's financial interests.**

The problem of ethical performance in the Nigerian public service is not a recent phenomenon. Historical records sustain this view. As early as the colonial period, corruption was a glaring feature. Many junior public officials were involved in corrupt practices. These were messengers, court interpreters, court clerks, tax collectors, and judges of native courts. **Malpractices took the form of bribery, nepotism, extortion and embezzlement.**

Corruption is another word, which is synonymous with unethical conduct. Corruption is a common word and it has become part of everyday usage. Adebayo (1986) has listed some acts of corruption, which fall under the realm of unethical conduct and/or behavior. These include:

1 Using official stationery – envelopes, papers, etc. for private purposes
2 Using government drugs, dressings and hospital equipment for private purposes.
3 Using government labor for private work.
4 Using government time for private work.
5 Misuse of government motor vehicles for private purposes
6 Demanding sex from female applicants for jobs.
7 Demanding money from applicants for jobs and contracts.
8 Tampering with applications, contract documents and payment vouchers.

9 Misuse of overseas tours
10 Election malpractices – contriving to get one person to vote more than once in one particular election.
11 Obtaining import licenses under false pretences.
12 Inflation of contracts in order to receive kick-backs
13 Misuse of Security funds by Chief Executives.

Throughout most of the post-independence period, corruption became an outstanding feature of public life. Corruption took another dimension. Old malpractices in the colonial period were inherited. New malpractices were also added. Corruption became a household word. Policemen, Customs Officials, Electoral Officers, Cabinet Ministers, Parliamentarians, Military Personnel were effectively involved in violation of legal practices. Nigerian police became synonymous with corruption. Tolls were collected from drivers on a wide range of offences, which include traffic licenses, permits and criminal activities. Civil Servants, Politicians colluded and received kickbacks from government contractors. Moreover, contractors that gave ten percent kickbacks to government officials perform their duties poorly. Gross mismanagement of public funds was a recurring feature of the first and second republics. One of the most glaring case of corruption was in 1983 when the National Youth Service Corps Directorate (N.Y.S.C.) which in 1983 alone overspent its vote of N64 million by N30i9 million in a free-for-all-rip-off of public treasury.

The problems of unethical behavior of top public officials were aptly highlighted and summed up in the various declarations of Buhari and other military officers when Shagari's regime was overthrown. The following extract illustrates:

You are all living witnesses to the grave economic predicament and uncertainty which an inept and corrupt leadership has imposed on our beloved nation for the past four years...Our economy has been hopelessly mismanaged. We have become a debtor and beggar nation...Unemployment figures, including the graduates have reached embarrassing and unacceptable proportions. In some states, workers are being owed salary arrears of eight to twelve months, and in others there are threats of salary cuts, yet our leaders revel in squander mania, corruption and indiscipline continue to profile public appointments in complete disregard of our economic realities...

Military administration which crept into the Nigerian political scene on account of corrupt charges against civilians were not immune from corruption, On the contrary, it was tainted with numerous acts of bribery and corruption. For instance, during Gowon's regime, corruption came to a climax. The military governors, commissioners, and those closely associated with the regime were not only believed to have amassed huge fortunes, they in fact flaunted their wealth in a manner, which most people found extremely distasteful. The findings of numerous probes revealed the extent of abuse of office or official negligence, which was rampant in high places.

The problem of unethical conduct is not restricted to the military regimes. The civilian regimes are not excluded from this cankerworm that has eaten deep into the Nigerian body politic. The current corruptive tendency noticeable among public officials during the current civilian regime led by President Olusegun Obasanjo is a testimony to this fact.

It is pertinent to note that many public officials abdicate oaths of office to form powerful cliques to optimize their personal goals, thereby displacing corporate or public goals. As public projects are abandoned or shoddily performed, the publicity given to such instances leaves the impression to the public that the public service is rotten to the core and that the public officials are not committed to public interest.

The Local Government service is not immune to corruption and unethical conduct. For example, the Neswatch report of December 20, 1993 describes local government as "**Fortresses of Corruption, audit report indicts local government of fraud and corruption:** In a seventy-four page audit report, the following were the major issues:

1. that all the Chairmen of the twenty one local governments in a particular State were pronounced guilty of financial irresponsibility;
2. that the local government councils had become fortresses of financial malpractices;
3. that these financial malpractices include; inability to produce payment vouchers for monies paid out, non availability of revenue receipts, loss of public funds, irregularity in stores accounts, irregular payments and inflated contracts, non-

retirement of imprest advances as well as non-refund of personal advances collected by some local governments on behalf of other agencies. To be precise, the following amount could not be accounted for, seven million naira for payment vouchers, one million naira was paid out and the contractors never touched the work. In fact, the auditor's report revealed that a total sum of nine million naira was outstanding as personal advances against local government officials. It was found that five million naira was deducted under various headings such as PAYE trade unions, but never paid to the respective agencies.

Local governments have proved to be a big disappointment. The allegations of impropriety, scandalous mismanagement, illegal payment, fraud, abuse of office, diversion of council's funds i.e. internally generated revenue, usurpation of functions, embezzlement, misuse of funds, reckless management (spending/disposal), siphoning of funds, impeachment, withdrawal of money from frozen accounts etc., all constitute unethical conduct at the local government level.

ETHICAL BACKGROUND OF LOCAL GOVERNMENT STAFF

Like every society, Local Government service contains various categories of individuals. It will be recalled that there was really no scheme of service for the Local Government service since 1916 until 1976 Local Government Reforms, which gave recognition of third tier of governance to the Local Government in the Federal system instead of Administrative Department of the States. This was followed up by the 1988 Approved Scheme of Service, which spelt out entry requirements of Council staff into various cadres of the Local Government Departments. All these really brought recognition to the Local Government as a viable service with necessary ethics entrenched in the service.

The Ethical codes in Local Government service are as highlighted below:

(i) Neutrality and non-partisanship in the council service as opposed to the past affiliations of staff to traditional rulers, chiefs and political parties. In the past, it is expected that a

Local Government staff should not be neutral. At least, staff must show open support to the party in control of the council such as the Action Group (A.G.), N.C.N.C., and N.P.C. Should the party loose the Council governance in the next election, staff members already know they would be sacked. In the present day Local Government system, the ethical codes of neutrality and non-partisanship have obliterated the above position. Local Government staff members are expected to be neutral and non-partisan.

(ii) With the reforms, eras of absenteeism without permission and non-punctuality are gone. All staff are expected to come to office as early as 8.00 a.m. without necessarily first paying homage to a Kabiyesi or political godfather.

(iii) Each Council staff is now deemed to represent the general interest of the service as against a township, special or parochial interest of individuals.

(iv) All Council Staff are expected to work towards clearly set rules guiding their duties, conduct and promotion. It may be disastrous for any staff to toy with rules and staff regulations as set up in 1978, since Section 39 of the Staff Regulation has clearly set disciplinary measures for various misconducts. For instance, a staff who absconds from duty for seven official days is deemed to regard himself as summarily dismissed from service. Promotions are now on the basis of qualifications, seniority and APPER score as well as non-serving of disciplinary sanctions.

(v) A Council Staff is expected not to constitute a financial embarrassment to the Council either in terms of fraud, embezzlement or being in debt to the public members.

(vi) A staff is expected to be well behaved. Appointments of some Council staff have been terminated on the platform of stealing and intoxication with alcohol. This is most common amongst the junior staff.

(vii) Disclosure of privileged information, otherwise called official secrets are also forbidden in the council service. Staff members are not expected to photocopy files and payment vouchers for the use of petition writers and oppositions to the government of the day.

(viii) A staff should keep good relationship with his fellow staff member. He should demonstrate pleasant relationship with staff of the Local Government. He should cooperate with other members of staff in order to ensure efficiency and effectiveness in local government service.

(ix) Every Local Government staff should relate positively with the public. Staff should have a friendly personality and should not cause unnecessary delay in the discharge of their services. Staff should be patient especially when a member of the public seems to be arrogant and unreasonable. Staff should be courteous, sincere and specific to public members.

(x) A Council Staff shall not be a member of, or belong to, or take part in any society, the membership of which is incompatible with the functions or dignity of his/her office.

(xi) All staff shall resign their appointments in accordance with the existing laws and regulations on appointment.

(xii) All staff shall give adequate notice (as stipulated in the Regulations) to the appropriate officer of the Council and obtain prior approval before traveling out of the Council or before extending their approved stay.

(xiii) It shall be the duty of every member of staff to keep and preserve any Council property entrusted to him with due care and diligence. If the Council sustains a loss by reason of neglect or default of a member of staff, he shall, as far as practicable be liable to make good, the loss or damage.

FACTORS RESPONSIBLE FOR UNETHICAL CONDUCT IN NIGERIA LOCAL GOVERNMENT SYSTEM

In the Nigeria Local Government system, several factors are responsible for unethical conduct. Amongst these include the following:

(i) **Personal Interests:** - The personal interests of most local government staff often override the interests of the public they are meant to serve. Most local government staff neglect their official duty in order to pursue their personal interests.

They are hard to find in their offices because they are always away on private business. As a result, a citizen who wants to see a public official may have to go to his office numerous times before meeting him. Even those who manage to stay in their offices tend to work mostly on things that favor their interests. A little inducement from client will always expedite work.

(ii) **Tradition of Aloofness:** - The Nigerians who first got into the public service were not representative of the general populace. They were educated ones and so felt superior to other Nigerians. Since they were in daily contact with the British officials some of the goodness of the British demy-gods rubbed off on them. The Nigerian officials followed the British in looking low on the rest of the citizenry. Therefore, they became more British than the British. This tradition of aloofness from the people became accentuated after independence in 1960. The Nigerians belief themselves to be the "best and the brightest". Till today aspects of this attitudes stay on.

(iii) **Role Ambiguity:** - Role ambiguity exists when an occupant of a position does not know exactly what his job entails. This may result from unclear directive from superiors. It may also be cause by the occupant misunderstanding his job specifications. Role ambiguity creates confusion in the minds of employees. Some officials arrogate more power to themselves than their position gives them.

(iv) **Disillusionment:** - Any one who talks with civil servants will find out that most of them are disillusioned with their jobs. They always complain of low salaries, delayed promotions, or restricted job opportunities. Experience has shown that the Nigerian public service generally often frustrates its employees.

(v) **The oath of Secrecy:** - Every staff is expected to take an Oath of Secrecy as laid down by the Official Secrets Act, 1962. The act prohibits civil servants from divulging any confidential information they come across in the course of their duties. If they must disclose any information, they must obtain the necessary permission from superiors. On the surface, the Oath of Secrecy should make any civil servant unresponsive but it does. Many Officers hide behind the Oath when they are not willing to reveal information, no matter how unimportant.

(vi) **Corruption:** - Worst amongst the factors is corruption. Corruption has eaten deep into the fabric of the nation. All the tiers of government in the Federal Republic of Nigeria are affected by this cankerworm. Naturally, some local government staff members are corrupt. It is noted that Nigerians worship material success, no matter by what means the success is achieved. This is a big problem bedeviling ethics and conduct especially in Nigeria Local Government.

CONCLUSION

This paper examines office ethics and conduct in Nigeria Local Government system. It has been established that corruption and/ or unethical conduct, like a hydra-headed cankerworm, has eaten deep into the fabric of the Nigeria nation. This vice has affected and infected all the tiers of government in Nigeria, Local Government inclusive. It becomes important for Local Government staff to jettison unethical conduct and imbibe the noble culture of ethics and good conduct in the discharge of their duties and official responsibilities. To achieve the above objectives, the following suggestions become germane.

In Nigeria today, what is urgently needed is to grow and develop a culture that will inculcate the right sense of values. This will in turn, produce an ethical and moral climate in which unethical conduct and/or corruption will find it difficult to survive. These cannot be achieved through statutory legislation. The culture has to grow and develop among the people. The surest and perhaps the only way to develop this culture and the moral climate that will accompany it, is through education.

Secondly, citizen participation constitutes another panacea. This entails the involvement of citizens in making decisions about things that affect them. It is believed that if this is done, the needs of the citizens would be better serviced and proper ethical conduct will be assured.

Thirdly, accountability is another way to ensure proper ethics and conduct in local government service. This involves making local government staff answerable for their actions to the Legislature, the Executive and even the public. Accountability will make them to be more responsive because if they fail to carry out legitimate directives, they will be subject to penalties. This ensures ethics and good conduct.

Fourthly, the law court is another place where citizens can seek redress if the Council staffs are found to be unresponsive and violate ethical conduct. The staff can then be compelled to satisfy the citizens' needs.

Finally, public opinion is another thing that could be employed where it has been established that Council staff have violated ethical conduct. What the people think about the local government should affect its behavior toward them. If people feel that the local council is unresponsive and the staff there are unethical in their conduct, the public opinion should serve as a signal to the local government to change. A Local Government that wants to survive must respect public opinion. Public opinion may not always be wise, but in a democracy it is always right.

REFERENCES

1. Aborisade Oladimeji (1994): "Allocation of Financial Memoranda for Local Government", in *Commissioned Background Papers for National Orientation Workshop on the Use of The Revised Financial Memoranda for Senior Local Government Functionaries,* Ministry of State and Local Government, Abuja, pp. 15 – 16.
2. Adebayo Augustus (1986): *Power in Politics,* Spectrum Books Limited, Ibadan, pp. 20 – 27.
3. Adewumi, J.B. (1994): *Commissioned Background Papers for National Orientation Workshop on the Use of Revised Financial Memoranda for Senior Local Government Functionaries,* Ministry of State and Local Government, Abuja, p. 1.
4. Ali, D. Yahaya & Caleb I. Akinyele (1992): *Human Resources Development and Utilization, Policies and Issues,* Administrative Staff College of Nigeria, Spectrum Books Ltd., Ibadan., p. 160.
5. Federal Republic of Nigeria (1976): *Guidelines for Local Government Reform,*The Government Printer, Kaduna, p. 1.
6. Fowler Alan (1980): *Personnel Management in local Government,* Institute of Personnel Management, Martin's of Berwick, England, p. 64.
7. General Muhammadu Buhari's Speech/Declaration on "The State of the Nation" regarding why President Shehu Shagari was overthrown in 1983.
8. *Newswatch Magazine,* December 20, 1993.
9. Ola, Robert F. (1990): *Introduction to Nigerian Public Administration,* Department of Political Science, University of Benin, Benin City, pp. 20, 144-147.
10. Olojede, Iyabo (1992): "Public Sector Ethic and Democracy in Nigeria", in *The Quarterly Journal of Administration, Volume XXVI,* Numbers Three & Four, April/July, 1992, pp. 1 – 9.
11. Olowu, Dele (1988): "Development, Decentralization and Local Government", in *African Local Government as Instruments of Economic and Social Development,* IULA Publications 1415, The Hague, Netherlands, p. 2.

12. Procter Paul et. al. (Eds.) (1980): *Longman Dictionary of Contemporary English,* International Student Edition, Longman Group Limited, England, p. 2.
13. Summers Della et. al (2001): *Longman Dictionary of Contemporary English,* Pearson Education Limited, England.

CHAPTER SIX

REGIONALIZATION AND EFFORTS TO COMBAT HUMAN TRAFFICKING IN WEST AFRICA: THE NIGERIAN EXPERIENCE

PROF. AMADU SESSAY AND
KEHINDE OLAYODE (PH.D.)

Introduction

Human trafficking has had a long history in West Africa and cuts across all the fifteen member countries of the Economic Community of West African States, (ECOWAS). Thousands of women, children, youths and men are trafficked within and outside the sub-region into conditions that constitute a blatant abuse of their fundamental human rights (Sesay, 2004:12-13). Many of them are sold into virtual slavery and work in extremely inhuman conditions that can best be described as 'modern day slavery' (Ibid.) In spite of efforts by national governments, donor agencies and the Non-governmental Organizations (NGOs), human trafficking continues to flourish in West Africa. It is estimated that between 200,000 and 800,000 people are trafficked each year in the sub-region (NAPTIP, 2006:15).

Several factors have been identified as responsible for trafficking in persons in West Africa. The first and perhaps also the most important, is poverty; occasioned by the declining economic fortunes of most families who are unable to meet their daily needs. Economic inequality, so pervasive in the sub-region and its accompanying deprivation and marginalization of most citizens is the single most important cause of trafficking. It is also significant to note that traffickers usually target women and children, the most vulnerable groups in local communities (Sesay,op.cit., p.13). Another important factor has to do with age-old long cultural practices which place a very low value on the girl-child, and generally allocate low status to women in society. Thus, women are in most African communities, subordinated to the men, making them vulnerable to exploitation.

At the sub-regional and institutional level, ECOWAS, becoming increasingly concerned about the menace of human trafficking and its implications for socio-economic development in the sub-region, has organized a number of fora and conferences to create public awareness and raised the issue of trafficking with governments in the sub-region. As a result, a number of ECOWAS countries have participated in bilateral and multilateral initiatives, including the creation of a Common Platform for Action (adopted in Libreville, February, 2000) to address the problem of child trafficking , and the establishment of inter-ministerial committees to find solutions (Togo, Benin, Gabon and Nigeria); (ECOWAS-ODCCP, 2001). There have been other initiatives adopted by ECOWAS to tackle the menace of trafficking in the sub-region, though limited success has been recorded so far. All this is aimed at promoting and enhancing human security broadly defined, in the sub-region.

In spite of the various challenges facing the war against human trafficking in West-Africa, which have limited its success, the Nigerian experience in that regard stands out boldly as the best practice in the sub-region. Apart from being the first country in Africa to properly domesticate the United Nations Convention Against Transnational Organized Crimes and the Protocol to prevent, suppress and punish Trafficking in Persons, especially women and children; Nigeria, through the enactment of the Trafficking in Persons (Prohibition) Law Enforcement and Administration Act, 2003, has demonstrated its total commitment to the crusade against trafficking in West Africa.

As further evidence of the country's leadership role in the war against human trafficking, the National Agency for the Prohibition of Traffic in Persons and other Related Matters (NAPTIP) was established in

2003, and is charged with the responsibility of investigating and prosecuting offenders, as well as rehabilitating victims of trafficking in persons. Against this background, the paper uses the Nigerian anti trafficking campaign to highlight dissonant regionalization with particular reference to the war on human trafficking which the Economic Commission of West African States has taken up in an attempt to enhance human security in the sub-region. Given its relative resources and lead nation status not just in West Africa and the continent, it is reasonable to suppose that the success of the Nigerian example will provide a template for the rest of the Commission's member, and a pointer to the future of the war on human trafficking in West Africa.

Conceptual Issues

Regionalism and Regionalization

The concept of region is used differently in different disciplines: in the field of geography, regions are usually seen as sub-national entities, either historical provinces (which could have become nation-states) or more recently created units. In International Relations, regions are often treated as sub-systems of the international system. The minimum definition of a region is typically a limited number of states linked together by a geographical relationship and with a degree of mutual interdependence (Nye, 1971). More precisely, a region consists of 'states which have some common ethnic, linguistic, cultural, social, and historical bonds' (Cantori and Spiegel, 1970: 12). Thus they can be differentiated in terms of their social cohesiveness (ethnicity, race, language, religion, culture, history, consciousness of a common heritage), economic cohesiveness (trade patterns, economic complementarily), political cohesiveness (regime type, ideology) and organizational cohesiveness (existence of formal regional institutions) (Hurrell, 1995).

Regionalism on the other hand, refers to a tendency and a political commitment to organize the world in terms of regions; more narrowly, the concept refers to a specific regional project, for examples; the

ECOWAS or the European Union (EU). According to Anthony Payne and Andrew Gamble, regionalism is a state-led or states-led project designed to reorganize a particular regional space along defined economic and political lines (Gamble and Payne, 1996:2). In that regard, regionalization denotes a process or processes of weaving members of a region together either economically or politically, or both. Regionalization also refers to the more complex processes of forming regions, which implies that a geographical area is being transformed from a passive object (an arena) to an active subject (an actor) that is increasingly capable of articulating the transnational interests of the emerging region (Hettne,1993).

The West African region as presently constituted, is a clear consequence of the colonial era and experience. For instance, 4 of the 15 states in ECOWAS were British colonies; 8 were Francophone while 2 were Portuguese colonies. These historical accidents continue to influence the West African states separately and also their relations with each other. West Africa remained largely divided into Francophone and Anglophone zones long after independence. Former French colonies developed different forms of cooperation between each other and 'their political, economic and military relations to France remained important' (Adedeji, 2004:34).

Despite the ideological division among West African countries, efforts were made immediately after independence in the 1960s to start the processes of integration. The need to create sub-regional and regional economic cooperation and integration organizations in Africa was reinforced by the experiences in other parts of the world: the Latin America Free Trade (LAFTA); Caribbean Community (CAICOM); Association of South East Asian Nations (ASEAN); the Central American Common Market (CACM) in Latin America and the Caribbean Region; European Economic Community, now European Union; among others. Thus, the Treaty signed in Lagos on 28 May 1975 creating the Economic Community of West African States (ECOWAS) covered wide areas of economic activities. Article 27 of the Treaty affirms as long-term objective the establishment of a community citizenship that could be acquired automatically by all

nationals of Member States. This reinforced the preamble to the treaty that outlined the key objective of removing all obstacles to the free movement of goods, capital and people in the sub-region.
In line with the current of the new regionalism that emerged in the post Cold-War order, ECOWAS has incorporated monetary union, security concerns, democracy and good governance and developmental issues into its framework. It was in line with this paradigm that various protocols that cover broad political, social, economic and security issues were ratified by member countries of ECOWAS, thus leading to the regionalization of economic, security, political and humanitarian issues in West Africa. Some of the new concerns that emerged in the new regionalism in the sub-region are gender equality, youth empowerment, natural resource governance, money laundering, community welfare, the fight against drug and human trafficking and the proliferation of small arms and light weapons in the sub-region.

Human Trafficking

Despite divergent interpretations, there is a growing agreement that trafficking in persons 'involves movement of people for the purpose of placing them in forced labour or other forms of involuntary servitude' (OSCE, 1999:2). Trafficking has been defined in many different ways, and in recent years, it has been variously defined, among others, in term of human rights; criminal activity; irregular migration; labour exploitation; and modern slavery (NAPTIP, 2007:14). However, it should be noted that how trafficking is defined and perceived by a people is one possible but neglected dimension in the search for factors that sustain human trafficking. When trafficking is wrongly perceived or defined in the context of one's interests or to the advantage of a group, then the components and processes of human trafficking may be compromised deliberately or subverted.

The Protocol to Prevent, Suppress and Punish Trafficking in Persons, especially Women and Children, supplementing the United Nations Convention Against Transnational Organized Crime (the UN Trafficking Protocol), which was opened for signature in December, 2000, defines trafficking as:

The recruitment, transportation, transfer, harboring or receipt of persons, by means of threat or use of force or other forms of coercion, of abduction, of fraud, of deception, of abuse of power, or of position of vulnerability or of giving, or receiving of payments or benefits to achieve the consent of a person having control over another person for the purpose of exploitation (Article 3 (a))

Sex trafficking is defined in the Act as the recruitment, harboring, transportation, provision, or obtaining of a person for the purpose of commercial sexual activities.

The International Labour Organization (ILO) in its synthesis report titled '*Combating Trafficking in Children for Labour Exploitation in West and Central Africa*' provided an operational definition of trafficking within the African context as 'a form of child abuse and neglect involving the migration of children from one place to another for the purpose of exploitative labour' (ILO, 2001:23). Global Rights (2004:7) in its publication titled '*Nigerian Anti-Trafficking Laws: A Guide for Public and Policy Makers*' defines trafficking simply as 'the movement of person from one place to another by any means for forced labour or services, slavery or practices similar to slavery, servitude or the removal of organs'. This paper adopts the OSCE framework for the operational definition of trafficking. Trafficking in human beings is thus defined as:

All acts involved in the recruitment, abduction, transport (within or across borders), sale, transfer, harboring, or receipt of persons by threat or the use of force, deception, coercion (including abuse of authority), or debt bondage for the purpose of placing or holding such person; whether for pay or not, in involuntary servitude, forced or bonded labour, or in slavery-like conditions. (OSCE, 1999:5).
Trafficking in person would also include trafficking for sexual as well as non-sexual purposes and all actions along the chain from the initial recruitment of the trafficked person to the end purpose or result- the exploitation of the victim

ECOWAS and the War on Human Trafficking in West Africa.

West African countries are agglomerations of peoples arbitrarily merged by colonial maps that traversed ethnic lines, such as the Yoruba in Nigeria and Benin; Ewes in Togo and Ghana; Vai and Kroo in Liberia and Sierra Leone; Hausa-Fulani in Niger and Nigeria, and so on. The existence of ethnic kith and kin across many of the porous inherited colonial borders makes it hard to fight trafficking in the sub-region, as people belonging to the same ethnic group move freely in and out of national borders, with little or no restriction. The elaborate visa and passport regulations, customs and controls that existed in the flush of independence and the need for "foreign" workers to obtain work permits ushered in a period of restrictions on intra- regional free movement of person across West Africa. These regulations, aimed at preserving available employment opportunities for nationals in fulfillment of election promises, also introduced a subtle distinction between internal and international migration both of which once involved free movement across wide space of the sub-region.

It is in that context that the Protocol on Free Movement of Persons and the Right of Residence and Establishment, of May 1979 capitalized on free mobility of labour. Phase 1 of the Treaty, the Protocol on the Free Movement of Persons - the first to be ratified and put into effect – was ratified by Member States in 1980 and came into effect forthwith. It guaranteed free entry without visa for ninety days, ushering in an era of free movements of ECOWAS citizens within member countries. The Revised Treaty of ECOWAS of 1992 among other concerns affirmed the right of citizens of the Community to entry, residence and settlement and enjoined member states to recognize these rights in their respective territories. It also called on member states to take all necessary steps at the national level to ensure that the provisions are duly implemented.

The magnitude of trafficking in the West African sub-region is so alarming that it caught imagination of ECOWAS policy makers. The result is that the organization has put in place a concrete Plan of Action to tackle the menace. Human trafficking is the subject of attention at the highest political levels, which has led to a number of countries participating in bilateral and multilateral initiatives to address the problem. Some ECOWAS states have also signed and ratified a number of relevant international instruments. These include the Universal Declaration of Human Rights; the United Nations Convention on the Rights of the Child; the UN Convention on the Elimination of All Forms of Discrimination against Women, and; International Labour Organization (ILO) Conventions on the minimum age at work and forced labour and the African Charter on Human and Peoples' Rights.

In recognition of the seriousness of the challenge of the human trafficking network especially between Cameroon and Gabon, which serve as the hub of child labour in plantations and West Africa; the Libreville 2000 Common Platform for Action builds on a growing cooperation and efforts of countries in the West and Central Africa to address child trafficking. The participation of eight countries at ministerial level, gave the Common Platform high political exposure and endorsement. The Platform marked the beginning of regional processes that have grave political and strategic implications for the elimination of child trafficking in Central and West Africa. As a follow up to the Libreville Platform, and increasingly concerned about the protection of children, ECOWAS organized a meeting of experts from Member States on trafficking in persons in Accra, Ghana in October, 2001. This was followed by the adoption of a Declaration and a Plan of Action against Trafficking in Persons (2002-2003) during the annual ECOWAS Summit held in Dakar, Senegal, in December, 2001.

In continuation of ECOWAS' regional efforts to address the problem of trafficking, a meeting of sub-regional experts on trafficking in persons was held in Lome, Togo, from 2nd to 3rd December, 2002 and jointly organized with the United Nations Office on Drugs and Crime (ODC). The meeting assessed the status of implementation of the ECOWAS sub-regional Plan of Action against trafficking in persons adopted in Dakar in December, 2001. The meeting also recommended the following measures:

1. Member States should increase efforts to ratify all international and regional instruments referred to in the ECOWAS initial Plan of Action on Trafficking in Persons, particularly the Convention on Organized Trans-border Crime and the Supplementary Protocol on the fight against trafficking by 2003;
2. Member states should harmonize their national legislation with the Conventions, after ratifying them. ECOWAS, in collaboration with the United Nations Centre for International Crime Prevention should provide technical assistance to Member States for the ratification process;
3. Member States should ensure social rehabilitation of victims through education, vocational training, provision of micro-credit, and their involvement in income-generating activities. (ECOWAS/ODC, 2002:4-10)

The ECOWAS Convention on Extradition (A/PI/94) and the Convention on Mutual Assistance in Criminal Matters (A/PI/92) are also important tools in combating trafficking and the activities of criminal groups. The Convention on Extradition empowers national courts of law with an effective instrument to arrest, try and enforce penalties against offenders who flee one member Country to seek shelter in another. The Convention also enables ECOWAS Member States to request from one another the return of persons wanted for the prosecution of an offence or the carrying out of a sentence in the requesting country. .

The ECOWAS Conflict Prevention Framework (ECPF) was adopted at Ouagadougou on 16th January, 2008 to serve as a comprehensive reference source for ECOWAS and Member States in their efforts to strengthen human security in the sub-region. Article (68), of the Framework deals exclusively with Cross-Border Initiatives and the overall objectives is that '...to reduce tensions, fight cross-border crime and enhance communal welfare and harmony, as well as community citizenship as espoused by relevant ECOWAS Protocols (ECPF, 2008:4). These objectives are intrinsically intertwined with initiatives regarding natural resource governance, gender equality, humanitarian crisis prevention and preparedness, youth empowerment, money laundering, the fight against drug and human trafficking and weapons proliferation (Ibid). The following initiatives are to be taken by ECOWAS and partners under the cross-border initiatives component of the ECPF:

1 ECOWAS shall set up an inter-departmental committees within the Commission to map out the challenges at sensitive borders and identify specific threats to peace, security and human well-being at different cross-border zones in the sub-region
2 Members shall enforce compliance with the Protocol on Free Movement of Persons, the Right of Residence and Establishment among security and custom agencies, and shall sanction extortion and erection of illegal check points along regional routes and at crossing points.
3 Member States shall promote cross-border cooperation, facility and intelligence sharing, as well as joint operations, between security forces along borders within the framework of the West African Police Chiefs' Committee. (ECPF, 2008:3-6)

Impediments to the Regionalization of the War on Human Trafficking in West Africa

The implementation of the Plan of Action on trafficking in persons and other protocols in the sub-region has been hampered by the low level of commitment of some countries, sporadic and uncoordinated actions, lack of adequate data and technical incapacity for surveillance and tracking down of traffickers. There is also little inter-state dialogue partly as a result of failure to grasp the trans-border nature of trafficking and the origin/transit and destination chain of the phenomenon. While some bilateral and sub-regional arrangements and conventions exist on issues relating to trafficking such as the ECOWAS Convention on Extradition and the Convention on Mutual Assistance in Criminal Matters, which are very important tools for combating trafficking, however, the existing conventions have not been fully signed and ratified by all member countries of ECOWAS.

In addition, there is limited intelligence sharing among law enforcement agencies, and little cooperation on investigation, prosecution, identification of offenders, and on the methods used by criminal organizations in human trafficking. There is no effective and practical framework for exchanging of information between law enforcement and criminal justice agencies of member countries in the fight against trafficking. This situation is partly due to the non-ratification of the ECOWAS Convention on Mutual Assistance in Criminal Matters by all member states.

The ECOWAS Protocol on the Free Movement of Peoples was designed to facilitate the free movement of goods and persons within the sub-region. The Protocol is supposed to simulate efforts towards a return to the homogenous society that once existed in the sub region. However, the protocol, which allows free movement of West Africans across the borders without visas, has been abused by fraudsters. Besides that, it has also led from time to time to an influx of refugees, some of whom are involved in armed crime a situation that also created resentment among some citizens in the sub-region that have affected by these negative impact of the free movement Protocol. The abolition of visa requirements among ECOWAS states also tend to favor the activities of traffickers since they do not have to procure visas for victims taken out of national frontiers within and outside the sub-region. This problem is further compounded by the porous national borders and the dual 'citizenship' in border regions, which makes it hard to distinguish who is a 'citizen' and who is not. All these tend to encourage trafficking in the sub-region, while also making it difficult to curb.

Finally, corruption especially within some strategic national security agencies, constitute a serious impediment in the fight against trafficking. In many countries in the sub-region, some of the security agencies, especially the police and immigration officers, are linked to trafficking rings and as such, they would not decisively move against them. Some security agents even facilitated travel documents for victims while others procured the necessary visas for those repatriated to leave almost as soon as they were returned to their country.

The Nigerian Initiatives in Combating Human Trafficking

With the economic downturn of the 1980s and 1990s in Nigeria, human trafficking assumed new dimensions as increasing numbers of young girls and women were being transported to Europe, North Africa and other neighboring countries for prostitution and commercial sex. This new trend soon gave rise to the emergence of middlemen and organized crime syndicates, specializing in the illicit transfer of young girls and women who are often deceived by and or carried away promises of better employment opportunities and the 'good life' abroad. On many occasions too, such victims are either bonded or asked to swear to oaths of secrecy before they are taken out of the country.

The negative exploits of Nigerian girls who work as prostitute in Europe, notably in Italy, attracted global condemnation and caught national attention in the 1990s. Despite the widespread condemnation of the booming business in women trafficking, the Nigerian government did not take any concrete step to address the issue until the return of Nigeria to a democratically elected government in 1999. Since 1999, the following steps have been taken by the Nigerian Government to address the issue of trafficking in the country:

1 Ratification of the Convention on the Elimination of All Forms of Discrimination Against Women (CEDAW);
2 Ratification of the ILO Convention 182 on the Elimination of the Worst Forms of Child Labour;
3 Ratification of the African Charter on the Rights and Welfare of the Child;
4 Ratification of the ECOWAS Plan of Action, the Libreville Platform of Action, and the Gulf of Guinea Committee Agreement;
5 The setting up of the Inter-Ministerial Committee on Human Trafficking (September,2001), now Office of the Special Assistant to the President on Human Trafficking and Child Labour ;

6 Domestication of the Convention on the Rights of the Child through the enactment of the Child's Rights Act 2003;
7 The enactment of the Trafficking in Persons (Prohibition) Law Enforcement and Administration Act, 2003;
8 The establishment of the National Agency for the Prohibition of Traffic in Persons and Other Related Matters (NAPTIP) in August, 2003, and ;
9 Bilateral agreements on human trafficking with various countries.

- (NAPTIP, 2007)

Prior to the establishment of NAPTIP, NGOs were in the vanguard of the campaign against human trafficking. Among these NGOs, the efforts of Women Trafficking and Child Labour Eradication Foundation (WOTCLEF) then run by the wife of former Vice President Atiku Abubakar and the IDIA Renaissance in Edo State stood out. While WOTCLEF was remarkable in its campaign against trafficking in women, the IDIA Renaissance focused attention on campaigning against the illicit involvement of Edo State girls in prostitution in Italy. Apart from putting considerable pressure on government to act, it was WOTCLEF that in an unprecedented move, submitted a Private Bill to the National Assembly for approval, which led to the enactment of the Anti-trafficking Law and the setting up of NAPTIP. The signing of the Bill into law in July 2003 by former President Olusegun Obasanjo was to mark a watershed in the fight against human trafficking as it provided the necessary legal framework for combating the crime. By this gesture, Nigeria became the first country in West Africa, Africa and one of the very few in the world, to have domesticated the United Nations Convention on Trans-national Organized Crime and its Supplementary Protocol.

The National Agency for the Prohibition of Traffic in Persons and Other Related Matters (NAPTIP) was established pursuant to the Trafficking in Persons (Prohibition) Law Enforcement and Administration Act of 2003. The Agency came into being on the 8th August, 2003. Among its responsibilities are the following:

1. Enforcement and the due administration of the Act;
2. Coordination of all Laws on Traffic in persons and related offences and the enforcement of the laws;
3. Adoption of measures to increase the effectiveness of the eradication of Traffic in persons;
4. Enhancing the effectiveness of Law Enforcement Agents to suppress Traffic in persons;
5. Taking charge, supervising, controlling and coordinating the rehabilitation of trafficked persons; and participating in proceedings relating to traffic in persons;
6. Reinforcing and supplementing measures in such bilateral and multi-lateral treaties and conventions on trafficking as may be adopted by Nigeria to counter the magnitude and extent of traffic in persons and its grave consequences.
7. Strengthening and enhancing effective legal means for international cooperation in criminal matters for suppressing the international activities of human trafficking;
8. Taking such measures and or in collaboration with other agencies or bodies that may ensure the elimination and prevention of the root causes of the problem of trafficking. (NAPTIP, 2007)

The Act also prohibits and prescribes severe penalties for trafficking in persons, particularly women and children, and mandates the Agency to be the focal point for combating human trafficking in Nigeria. For the effective conduct of its functions, the Agency has the following departments and units:

1. Investigation and Monitoring Department
2. Counseling and Rehabilitation Department
3. Legal and Prosecution Department
4. Public Enlightenment Department
5. Planning, Research and Statistics Department
6. Administration and Finance Department
7. Press and Public Relations Unit

Under the Act, the Investigation and Monitoring Department of the Agency has the responsibility of liaising with the police for the prevention and detection of offences in violation of the provision of the Act, and to work in collaboration with the Immigration Service, the Police, the Custom Service and other security agencies in the fight against human traffickers. Public enlightenment and awareness creation is one of the core mandates of the Agency. NAPTIP has carried out extensive and regular sensitization and advocacy campaigns among various groups in Nigeria, which is aimed at educating the public on the problem of trafficking in persons, thereby stimulating interest in and awareness about the problem. NAPTIP also works with many other government agencies and NGOs such as, immigration and the police, faith and community based organizations, educational institutions, especially primary and secondary schools.

The Legal and Prosecution Department has the responsibility of prosecuting suspects of human trafficking and employers of child labour in courts of competent jurisdiction. The Department offers legal advice/opinion to the Executive Secretary as well as other Heads of Departments in the anti-trafficking Agency. In addition to offering legal advice and prosecuting offenders, the Department prepares Memoranda of Understanding between the agency and foreign embassies, international organizations and NGOs as well as other technical and legal issues on behalf of the agency. Between 2003 and 2007, and through its Legal and Prosecution Department, NAPTIP filed 58 cases in various high courts across the country, out of which, 12 cases were successfully prosecuted resulting in 10 convictions and 2 acquittals (NAPTIP, 2007).

To enhance its operations, the anti trafficking agency has also established six operational zonal offices in Lagos, Uyo, Kano, Enugu, Benin and Sokoto, which are among the worst offenders, in a bid to effectively policing those zones. In addition, the Agency also established seven operational shelters across the country where the victims of human trafficking are provided with temporary accommodation, welfare packages, medical and counseling services. The victims are also trained in life and economic skills and thereafter they are provided with micro finance to start business or to go back to school as appropriate.

The big gains and pioneering efforts the organization has made in the crusade against human trafficking since its inception have not gone unnoticed in the sub-region, Africa and the rest of the world. For example, Nigeria which used to be on the Watch List of the US State Department's rating on human trafficking countries has now been moved to the Second Tier List of Compliant Countries, a clear recognition of what NAPTIP has achieved since its inception. Also, Nigeria is today regarded as a model for other countries to emulate due to its anti trafficking legislation and the establishment of NAPTIP which was set up specifically to combat human trafficking. It is worthy noting that only Nigeria and Mauritania have such model in the whole of Africa.

Constraints and Challenges to the War on Human Trafficking in Nigeria

In spite of the remarkable achievements recorded by NAPTIP within a short period of its establishment, the agency faces lingering challenges which tend to slow down the pace of its work. First is the delicate nature of its assignment which also requires mobility, state of the art communication gadgets and other sophisticated equipment for surveillance, tracking, recording and documentation. The agency is also handicapped in this critical area and has had to rely on donations from development partners. As a government agency that gets its funding directly from the government's budgetary allocations has also constrained the activities of the Agency due in part, to the fact that the funds released are never enough to cover all its activities. Funds are also sometimes not released as and when they are needed. All this limitations have affected NAPTIPs' war on human trafficking in Nigeria in particular and the West African sub-region in general. There are also some institutional weaknesses and inadequate capacity especially with regard to proactive investigation, surveillance and monitoring, rehabilitation and research. There is therefore urgent need to build these capacities through regular and adequate funding, training and re-training of appropriate staff of the Agency.

CONCLUSION

This paper has examined the regionalization of the war against human trafficking in West Africa focusing on the ECOWAS and using the activities of the anti-human trafficking Agency, NAPTIP, as the Nigerian case study. The achievements of ECOWAS and NAPTIP as well as their challenges were also highlighted, focusing in particular on *modus operandi of the latter.* The study identified poverty, ignorance, corruption, cultural practices and beliefs, institutional inadequacies, lack of strong political will and commitment on the part of some governments in West Africa, as well as poor coordination among anti-trafficking agencies in member countries of ECOWAS, have been identified and discussed, as some of the major factors responsible for sustaining human trafficking in West Africa. Arising from this broad conclusion, the following recommendations are offered to aid the effective prosecution of the war against human trafficking in Nigeria and West Africa:

1 ECOWAS Member States should be encouraged by the Commission to ratify and implement without delay, the various agreements and protocols that have been put in place to combat human trafficking as a matter of collective strategy, priority and responsibility in the sub-region. The Commission should also to explore ways and means of providing technical assistance, institutional support especially to those members that lack such capacities.

2 Possession of basic education would go a long way in empowering rural folks through enlightenment and value-added orientation to appreciate the hollowness of the promises and antics of human traffickers in their midst. Emphasis must also be placed on the education of the girl-child, who is perhaps the most vulnerable among the groups that are most at risk. The campaign to entrench respect for everyone's basic human rights must also not be relented at the sub-regional and national levels in West Africa.

Finally, while there are still many formidable obstacles and challenges to the successful regionalization of the war on human trafficking in

West Africa, there is no doubt that the sub-region is moving in the right direction and the gains made so far should be consolidated. The success of NAPTIP in Nigeria is particularly commendable. The Agency had given the war on trafficking high visibility and credibility like never before in the history of the country and sub-region. It is hoped that successive governments would only build on the achievements made thus far by the organization. It is obvious that once development partners are convinced of the sincerity of governments and agencies responsible for anti-trafficking in the sub-region, they would be ready to give them the assistance that they need to 'get on with their business.'

REFERENCES

1. Adedeji, Adebayo (2004) 'A Retrospective Journey' In Adebayo Adekanye and Rashidi Ismail (eds.) *West Africa's Security Challenges. Building Peace in a Troubled Region* (London: Lynne Rienner Publishing Incorporation)
2. Amadu Sesay (2004) 'Human Trafficking in West Africa', A Report Submitted to ECOWAS (Abuja, ECOWAS Secretariat)
3. Cantori, L.J. and Spiegel, S.L. (1970) The International Politics of Regions: A Comparative Approach (Prentice-Hall, Eanglewoods Cliffs)
4. ECOWAS Secretariat (2001) *Trafficking in Persons in the West African Region* (Background Paper for ECOWAS-ODCCP Expert Group Meeting, Accra, Ghana)
5. ECOWAS Secretariat (2002) *Report of Joint ECOWAS/ODCCP Regional Meeting of ExperT on Trafficking in Human Beings* (Lome, Togo)
6. ECOWAS Secretariat (2008) *The ECOWAS Conflict Prevention Framework (ECPF)*
7. Gamble, P and Payne, A. (1996) 'Introduction: the Political Economy of Regionalism and World Order' In Gamble and Payne (eds.) *Regionalism and World Order* (Macmillan)
8. Global Rights (2004) *Nigerian Anti-Trafficking Laws: A Guide for the Public and Policy Makers* (Abuja: Global Rights)
9. Hettne Bjorn (1993) 'Neo-Mercantilism: The Pursuit of Regioness' *Co-operation and Conflict* 28(3)
10. Hurrel Andrew (1995) 'Regionalism in Theoretical Perspective' In Fawcett, L. and Hurrel, A. (eds) Regionalism in World Politics (Oxford: Oxford University Press)
11. ILO-IPEC (2001) *Trafficking of Children. The Problem and Responses Worldwide* (Geneva: ILO)
12. NAPTIP (2006) *Annual Report 2005-2006* (Abuja: NAPTIP Secretariat)
13. NAPTIP (2007) *Report on NAPTIP Activities: From Inception to Date (2003-2007)* Abuja: NAPTIP Secretariat)
14. Nye, Joseph (1971) *Peace in Parts: Integration and Conflict in*

Regional Organization (Little Brown and Co)OSCE (1999) *Trafficking in Human Beings: Implications for the OSCE* (Background Paper, Review Conference, September, 1999).

15. UNODC (2000) *The Protocol to Prevent, Suppress and Punish Trafficking in Persons, especially Women and Children* (Palermo, Italy)
16. USAID (2003) *Trafficking in Persons: The USAID Strategy for Response* (Washington: USAID)

CHAPTER SEVEN

THE RELEVANCE OF CULTURE TO THE SOCIO-ECONOMIC GROWTH AND DEVELOPMENT OF NIGERIA – A LEGAL PERSPECTIVE

MRS. MERCY O. ERHUN

ABSTRACT

Nigeria is an example of a nation born out of a cultural womb foreign to it. As a result, participation of Nigerians in cultural life is poor. Nigeria's lofty overall development aspirations remain largely unachieved as a result of the fact that we are yet to recognize the pride of place culture occupies in development. Development in Nigeria fails to reconcile with the present and the demands of the challenges of the future. We are yet to fully acknowledge the cultural dimension of development. Because of this there has not been adequate sensitization of our policy makers and the public as a whole to the cultural component of development. This is what this paper aims at achieving. In this paper, the issues of population, culture and development, impact of colonialism on the socio-economic development shall be looked into.

*Mrs. Mercy O. Erhun is currently a Lecturer in the Faculty of Law, Obafemi Awolowo University, Ile-Ife.

INTRODUCTION

Nigeria is blessed with enormous potentials of both human and natural resources. Inspite of this, the country is confronted with one of the greatest challenges facing most nations of the world which is underdevelopment. The quest for development is one of the most critical issues in the Nigerian state. Development involves two basic processes – improving and refining that which is already in existence and adapting same to contemporary requirements and finding solutions to new problems or new forms of solutions to old problems. It is a creative response to social, economic and political affairs. One can only develop what is already in existence but where what is in existence is destroyed there is nothing to develop for you cannot put something on nothing. In Nigeria, cultural values have been thrown to the air and consequently fading away. Culture is seen as falling in the realm of preservation of the heritage of the people rather then been seen as a process of enrichment and renewal of our values. Consequently, development fails to reconcile with the present and the demands of the challenges of the future. Rather than making use of Nigeria's culture for national building, Nigerian has discarded her rich and enviable cultural heritage for an alien one.

Right from 1960 when Nigeria attained independence, there has been an endless search for development in this country. Nigeria is faced with an appalled state of poverty in the midst of plenty. Economic growth is impeded despite all attempts to achieve socio-economic growth and development. Nigeria's lofty overall development aspirations remain largely unachieved. None of its elegant economic policies have succeeded in resulting in improved welfare for the citizens of this country. Nigeria remains a sick society. This is reflected in collapse of family institutions, increase in crime, religious crisis, breakdown in social order, decay in social infrastructure, breakdown in law and order etc. In this paper there will be an investigation into the root cause of lack of development in

Nigeria and solutions will be proffered in order to attain accelerated development in Nigeria. The hope of the generality of the people was that the country would develop or grow in leaps and bounds considering the fact that the country is now under the control of indigenous ruling elites. Instead, the economic problems have continued to manifest in form of increase in unemployment, poverty soaring in prices of goods and services etc. Despite various measures taken by successive administrations to steam the tide of economic problems, the Nigerian economy continues to manifest signs of stress and strains as a result of underdevelopment.

CULTURE AND DEVELOPMENT

Development involves two basic processes – improving and refining that which is already in existence and adapting same to contemporary requirements and finding solutions to new problems or new forms of solutions to old problems. It is a creative response to social, economic and political affairs. One can only develop what is already in existence but where what is in existence is destroyed there is nothing to develop for you cannot put something on nothing. As a result of the fact that Nigeria has failed to recognize the place of culture in the attainment of socio-economic development, we have not been able to harness same for our national development.

The word culture came from a Latin word *cerele* meaning to cultivate or to tend. It means to take active care of something. It is defined[17] as the sum total of the material and intellectual equipment wherewith a people satisfy or meet their biological or social needs and adapt themselves to their environment. It is a society's total way or pattern of life.[18] It is the totality of the way of life evolved by a people in their attempt to meet the challenges of living in their environment, which gives order and meaning to their social, political, economic, aesthetic and religious norms and modes of organization thus distinguishing a people from their neighbours.[19] It is that complex whole which include the knowledge, belief, art, law, morals, customs and any other capabilities acquired by man as a member of society.[20] Culture is what man interposes between himself and his environment in order to ensure his security and survival.[21] The word culture was described[22] as the embodiments of the attitudes of a people to their traditional values which are essential for factors of development

---

17 Piddington, R. (1950): Introduction to Social Anthropology, Oliver and Boyd, London, 1950 p. 3

18 Thompson L. A (1991) Culture and Civilization, in Culture and Civilization, Ed. By Thompson, Lloyd et al, 1991, Afrikalink Books, Ibadan, 1991 at p. 10

19 Cultural Policy of Nigeria, Published by Ministry of Information and Culture, 1988 p. 1

20 Taylor, B.B. (1971) "Primitive Culture", cited by Ayisi, E.B. (1972 in An Introduction to the Study of African Culture, London, 1972

21 Ayandele, E. A. (1981). "Using Nigerian Culture for National Building" In. Perspectives in Nigerian Cultural Diplomacy Abuja National Institute for Cultural Orientation, Abuja 1981 p. 81

22 Duro Oni, (2001) Cullture and Development, Journal of Black and African Arts and civilization (JBAAC) Vol. 1 No. 1, p. 6

and progress. According to Udu Yakubu,[23] for human beings to build houses, cultivate farms construct bridges, dams, electricity generating plants, provide qualitative education, manage successful businesses or organizations, control population growth, prevent or cure sicknesses and diseases, ensure social trust, good governance , law and order etc., they need an established critically receptive body of ideas and beliefs, designs, techniques and methodologies rules and regulations. In other words, they need culture. Culture entails all that people have learned and preserved from past collective experience and transmitted into the future by learning.[24] Culture is the primary means of survival and adaptation of man, offering a summation and distillation of the past that provides sound basis for living in the present and marching into the future. Bates et al posited that in the absence of culture man is prone to loosing all knowledge of even the basic means of survival and that it will be catastrophic for the prevailing culture of mankind to be wiped out.[25]

That which gave order and meaning to our fore-fathers have since been lost. What we have in Nigeria presently is super-imposed on us by our colonial masters. There can be no true socio-economic development in the absence of culture. The Nigerian culture has not been harnessed for the socio-economic growth of this country. As a result, our primary means of survival is not guaranteed. This accounts for the downward trend of socio-economic development inspite of laudable measures put in place to attain socio-economic development in Nigeria.

THE IMPACT OF COLONIALISM ON THE SOCIO-ECONOMIC DEVELOPMENT OF NIGERIA

Colonialism and its dimensional impacts remains one major factor of socio-cultural economic significance which partly accounts for the twist of fate in Nigeria. Colonial economy was said to be marked by the introduction of socio-economic formulations for social

23 Udu Yakubu, (2002) "Cultural Erosion and the Crises of Development in Nigeria," Journal of Cultural Studies, vol. 4 No. 1 p. 4

24 Tunde Babawale, (2007) Culture, Politics and Sustainable Development: Lessons for Nigeria, CBAAC Occasional Monograph Series No. 4, Concept Publications Ltd., Lagos, p.9

25 Bates, Alan P. and Joseph, Julian (1975) Understanding Social Behaviour, Houghton Mifflings Publishing Company, Boston pp 23 - 41

production[26]. Colonialism ensures that Nigeria lost the sense of pride and confidence in her own traditions and culture. Every society is organized and directed on the basis of some fundamental principles commonly referred to as ideology. The economic foundations of any society shape the ideological outlook of that society. The ideology of any society ought to be an expression of that society. The ideology of a given society is supposed to mirror the internal dynamics of that society. Ideally, the ideology of a given society ought to originate from such society rather than being imposed from an external source. Rather than emanating from the process of internal socio-economic and political dynamics, the Nigerian ideology is a product of colonial imposition and domination. The process of Nigerian autonomous socio-economic development was truncated by the colonial exploiters in a bid to impose the capitalist ideology on the people. There was thus the confrontation of indigenous system with alien economic formation which has generated immense contradictions that virtually destabilized the Nigerian society bringing about an ailing economy that has refuse to bow down to any remedy so far. As a result of imperialist ideology, dominant Europeans are held in high esteem and technically superior. Hence the strive to copy anything and every European to the neglect and destruction of anything and everything traditional, thus resulting in hybridization of the Nigerian elite.[27] The main cause of the current underdevelopment of the African Personality was attributed[28] to the phenomenon of colonialism which was defined[29] as a form of political, economic, intellectual and even physical control by a small but alien country over another country or a state of inferiority or servitude experienced by a country which is dominated politically, economically and culturally by another and more so called developed country. We have no sense of Nigerian

26 Bode Onimode, (1985) The Violent Creation of the Colonial Economy in Imperialism and Underdevelopment in Nigeria The Dialectics of Mass Poverty, The Macmillan Press, Nigeria, p 31 - 41

27 Otonti Nduka (1964) Western Education and Nigerian cultural Background, Oxford University Press, Ibadan 1964 p. 5

28 Okpo Ojah, "The Revivial of African Personality: A Challenge to African Youths in the 21st Century in Okpo Ojah (ed) AFRICA: Basic Issues in Cultural Orientation for Sustainable Development, Centre for Black and African Arts and civilization, Lagos,

29 Julius Gould and Willaim Kolb (eds), (1964) A Dictionary of the Social Sciences, Tavistock Publications, London.

personality. What I mean is that the sum total of the basic ways a Nigerian feel, think, talk and behave have been thrown away for an unwholesome romance with the lifestyle of the Western world. As a result of harsh restraint deliberately imposed by the European colonial system, the Nigerian personality is bounded. The total cultural expression of what is common to all Nigerians has been eroded. The colonial system made every thing possible to reduce and in some cases to exterminate the Nigerian personality.[30]

It was asserted[31] that the principal reason why education and related growth-promoted activities were neglected in the developing world is the indoctrination promoted by Western Leaders who promoted different ideas in the developing world in the West. According to Ogbimi, these Western leaders only pretend when they talk of a global economy. In the real sense, they are only interested in promoting the ideas which will sustain economic and political confusion in Africa. This accounts for lack of growth in Nigeria. Nigeria's strategy of development is derived from theories of economic, political and philosophical development which have been developed during the colonial and new-colonial periods to rationalize the colonial patterns of production and organization in general. These alien theories link the rate and direction of internal socio-cultural, economic changes with imports of skills and technology, capital and consumer goods but negative lifestyles.[32]

Cultural imperialism is the most dangerous tool of diplomacy. Nigeria's inability to attain socio-economic development is connected with her non recognition of the primacy of culture which is a function of total development. The very strategies of development which Nigerian government has been pursing since independence have been externally masterminded. The Nigerian personality whose ideals were manifested in a distinct and collective Nigerian identity characterized by unfettered freedom, auto-centric growth and

30 Gideon-Cyrus Mutiso & S.W. Rohio (eds) (1973) Readings in African Political Thought, Heinemann, London, p. 75

31 F. E. Ogbimi, (2006) Understanding Why Education and Training Are Indispensable to Rapid Industrialization, Society for Linking Education and Problems Publication, at p. 11

32 Adebayo Adediji, (1975) Perspective of Development and Economic Growth up to the Year 2000" in Michael Doo Kingue (ed), Building Africa in the Year 2000, African Press, Adiss Ababa p. 59

development, global impact and the preservation of African culture, customs and traditions has been lost.

The underdevelopment of Nigeria is an outcome of the subordination and distortion of Nigeria by the requirements of metropolitan capitalism. According to the orthodox school of thought underdeveloped countries can attain development only if they abandon their traditional features in preference for those of the western developed world. One of a very glaring example is the issue of population. There is this general idea sold to us by the Western world that unless population is reduced, it will be impossible to attain development. This idea is foreign to us. In Nigeria, children are regarded as assets to many poor families because they provide labor usually for farming. Cultural norms in traditional rural societies of which Nigeria is one commonly sanction the value of large families. Unlike what happens in developed countries where considerable political and financial support is provided for, lack of, or little or no family planning is not helping matters in Nigeria. Given the above, high rate of population growth is inevitable in Nigeria. Population growth and high economic growth are mutually supportive. Population is regarded[33] as a multiplier, an active factor in determining the material wealth of a society. In the words of Ogbimi, we can only talk of overpopulation in relation to numbers, resources, technology and the differences between the poor and the rich. According to him, population growth is limited by inability to provide enough food and good health care to support a higher population growth. He considers high population growth as essential for the growth of productivity.

THE ROLE OF THE JUDICIARY IN ATTAINING SOCIO-ECONOMIC GROWTH AND DEVELOPMENT

Law serves as an impartial mediator reconciling competing interests in society. According to Ehrlicks,[34] law is a living reality (living law) which reflects the true value of society. Fagbohun[35] traced

---

33 F. E. Ogbimi, (2003) Understanding Why Capital Investment Cannot Promote Sustainable Economic Growth and Industrialization, Society for Linking Education and Problems Publication, at p. 73

34 Ehrlick *Fundamental Principles of the Sociology of Law* (1862 – 1922)

35 Fagbohun, F. O. (1998) "Public Environmental Litigation in Nigeria – An Agenda for

the problems of the courts to outdated guiding rules of the common law some of which have found themselves into the constitution and other statutes and that law makers themselves have totally ignored innovation and initiative which represent the strength of the legislative process. In Nigeria today, our outdated laws are not a reflection of the true values of the Nigerian society. In most cases, they reflect the values of the western world. The judiciary, which is the arm of government responsible for the role of law, is the bastion of hope for the common man and the hope of the survival of the nation as a corporate entity. Oyebode[36] viewed judges as selected group of persons invested by their fellow men and women with the power responsibility to do right to all manner of people which they have sworn to perform a responsibility they should strive to perform as priests in the temple of justice. Judges in Nigeria are yet to rise up to the responsibility of upholding the Nigerian culture as sacred and one to be upheld in the performance of their duties as priests in the temple of justice.

The judiciary is the hope for achieving socio-economic development in Nigeria. If the judiciary refuses to play its role, the law will stand still while the rest of the world goes on. According to Cardozo[37], the role of the judge is to solidify the multifarious strands that hold society together. He is the interpreter of its sense of law and order. He supplies omissions, corrects uncertainties, and harmonize results with justice through a method of free decision.

The judiciary, which is the arm of government responsible for the rule of law, is the bastion of hope for the common man and the hope of the survival of the nation as a corporate entity. It is also the hope for achieving socio-economic development in Nigeria. If the judiciary refuses to play its role, the law will stand still while the rest of the world goes on. The response of the judiciary to the threatening and debilitating socio-economic state of affair in Nigeria should be tapped.

Reform" in: *Environmental Law and Policy*, Struan Simpson & Olarewaju Fagbohun (eds), (1998), Law Centre, Faculty of Law, Lagos State University, p 115 -158

36 Oyebode, Akin (2005) Law and Nation Building in Nigeria, Centre for Political and Administrative Research (CEDAR), Lagos

37 Cardozo, B.N. (1921) The Nature of the Judicial Process p. 16

RECOMMENDATION

Nigeria is a country that is densely populated. High rate of population growth is inevitable in Nigeria. All that is needed is an active population that can make input into the production process. Inspite of Nigeria's high population we can still attain high standard of living by making use of what we have as a means of getting what we do not have. Manual subsistence farming which results in low productivity should give way to mechanized farming. We can go into mechanized farming which can lead to the production of large quantity of food to support the high density of population. This can be achieved by making use of commercial fertilizers, large scale irrigation and agricultural machinery in order to tackle the problem of infertile land. We can get ourselves involved in high-tech industries. By employing our economic and human resources etc, agricultural productivity can be boosted.

Without a Nigerian identity, we cannot make our proper impact in international affairs. We should begin to act at both Nigeria's individual and collective interest at any particular time, and be determined to chart our destiny using our own ideology. We should cultivate, revive and defend the Nigerian personality if Nigeria is to have a rightful place in the harmony of all nations. Nigeria lacks a viable culture compass and an ideology rooted in culture. There is a need to recreate a polity based on the culture and traditions of our people and tailored to her peculiarities and based on the dynamics of globalization and the underlying principles of globalization tailored to suit our peculiar situation. We must affirm and enrich our cultural identity. There is a need to broaden the participation of Nigerians in cultural life.

There should be a deliberate effort to sensitize the public and policy makers in Nigeria to the adoption of a legal framework that will reflect the cultural components of development. For us to experience meaningful growth, there must be a synergy between our traditional values and modernity. We must be proud of our culture, taste, and values. This is what obtains in China where, even though the country is opened up to capitalist influences, the rudiments of its industrial base were built on Chinese culture and its traditional practices. The diversity of our culture not withstanding, we can still make good success story in development through respect for our culture and making our economy to be rooted in our culture by responding guidedly to the dynamics of globalization, information and telecommunication technology like what obtains in Singapore.

Hereditary qualities are fundamental to the survival of any society. Rather than replacing them by any human agent, they are to be improved upon and assisted. We should strive to develop and maintain Nigerian personality if Nigeria is to be reckoned with in all fields of human endeavour. We should recover the lost legacy of Nigerians while discarding with passionate enthusiasm towards unprofitable western ideology in the match from the part of dependence to the path of self reliance and self-sufficiency in all facets of life. The Nigerian personality is to be construed, not as a simple reaction to a colonial past, but as a complex reaction to a re-creation of the distant past. We should recapture and re-assert the dignity of Nigerians. This can be done by sticking tenaciously to the Nigerian culture, traditions and customs handed over to us by our ancestors before the incursion of the Europeans.

Nigerian laws should be revised to reflect the present day aspiration of bring cultural dimensions into our socio-economic development process. Nigerian law makers should be innovative enough to bring issues of culture to bear in our law making process. Judges in Nigeria should rise up to this responsibility in doing what is right by upholding the Nigerian culture as sacred and one to be upheld in the performance of their duties as priests in the temple of justice.

CONCLUSION

Culture and development have strong potentials for modulating and accelerating socio-economic development. Nigeria has an enviable culture, full of aspiration and vitality. Despite this we discard our traditional life-style for foreign ones. Our dispositions, organizations, orientations and values are tailored to suit those of Western societies without any form of adaptation to suit our peculiar situation. We substitute our rich cultural heritage for alien socio-economic structures. The general crisis in the Nigerian economy is a logical outcome of the continued subjugation and control of the

Nigerian economy by external powers. The trivialization or outright bastardization of Nigeria's rich cultural heritage has done great damage to Nigeria. The Nigeria's cultural diversity remains a treasure largely unexplored in her quest for socio-economic development. For Nigeria to truly and actually attain the status of a developed nation, we should identify the critical elements of the culture of Nigerians and harness them for national development

Culture is relevant to Nigeria's socio-economic growth and development. For Nigeria to truly and actually attain the status of a developed nation, we should identify the critical elements of the culture of Nigerians and harness them for national development. There can be no socio-economic development without a strong indigenous foundation. If Nigeria is to be reckoned with we should discontinue from being an appendage to foreign ideas and practices. In order to overcome the next phase of neo-colonialism and neo-imperialism which are being euphemistically dubbed "globalization", there is a need for a dynamic cultural orientation.

The Judiciary is the bastion hope of the common man and the continued existence of democracy in Nigeria. The judiciary is the arm of government responsible for the rule of law. It is the bastion of hope for achieving socio-economic development in Nigeria. If the law is not to be allowed to stand still while the rest of the world goes on, the Judiciary should be steered to respond to promote socio-economic development in Nigeria.

REFERENCE

1. Ayandele, E. A. (1981). "Using Nigerian Culture for National Building" In. Perspectives in Nigerian Cultural Diplomacy Abuja National Institute for Cultural Orientation, Abuja 1981
2. Bates, Alan P. and Joseph, Julian (1975) Understanding Social Behaviour, Houghton Mifflings Publishing Company, Boston
3. Bode Onimode, (1985) The Violent Creation of the Colonial Economy in Imperialism and Underdevelopment in Nigeria The Dialectics of Mass Poverty, The Macmillan Press, Nigeria
4. Cardozo, B.N. (1921) The Nature of the Judicial Process
5. Cultural Policy of Nigeria, Published by Ministry of Information and Culture, 1988
6. Duro Oni, (2001) "Cullture and Development", Journal of Black and African Arts and civilization (JBAAC) Vol. 1 No. 1
7. Gideon-Cyrus Mutiso & S.W. Rohio (eds) (1973) Readings in African Political Thought, Heinemann, London.
8. Ehrlick *Fundamental Principles of the Sociology of Law* (1862 – 1922)
9. Fagbohun, F. O. (1998) "Public Environmental Litigation in Nigeria – An Agenda for Reform" in: *Environmental Law and Policy*, Struan Simpson & Olarewaju Fagbohun (eds), (1998), Law Centre, Faculty of Law, Lagos State University.
10. F. E. Ogbimi, (2003) Understanding Why Capital Investment Cannot Promote Sustainable Economic Growth and Industrialization, Society for Linking Education and Problems Publication.
11. F. E. Ogbimi, (2006) Understanding Why Education and Training Are Indispensable to Rapid Industrialization, Society for Linking Education and Problems Publication.
12. Julius Gould and Willaim Kolb (eds), (1964) A Dictionary of the Social Sciences, Tavistock Publications, London.

13. Otonti Nduka (1964) Western Education and Nigerian cultural Background, Oxford University Press, Ibadan.
14. Okpo Ojah, "The Revivial of African Personality: A Challenge to African Youths in the 21st Century" in Okpo Ojah (ed) AFRICA: Basic Issues in Cultural Orientation for Sustainable Development, Centre for Black and African Arts and civilization, Lagos
15. Oyebode, Akin (2005) Law and Nation Building in Nigeria, Centre for Political and Administrative Research (CEDAR), Lagos
16. Piddington, R. (1950): Introduction to social Anthropology, Oliver and Boyd, London.
17. Thompson L. A (1991) Culture and Civilization, in Culture and Civilization, Ed. By Thompson, Lloyd et al, 1991, Afrikalink Books, Ibadan.
18. Taylor, B.B. (1972) "Primitive Culture", London cited by Ayisi, E.B. (1972 in An Introduction to the Study of African Culture, London.
19. Tunde Babawale, (2007) Culture, Politics and Sustainable Development: Lessons for Nigeria, CBAAC Occasional Monograph Series No. 4, Concept Publications Ltd., Lagos.
20. Udu Yakubu, (2002) "Cultural Erosion and the Crises of Development in Nigeria," Journal of Cultural Studies, vol. 4 No. 1

CHAPTER EIGHT

AN EXAMINATION OF SOME LEGAL ASPECTS OF LOCAL GOVERNMENT IN NIGERIA

PROF. A. TORIOLA OYEWO

INTRODUCTION

Many articles have been written on the history administration, theories. Finances and strategies of local government in Nigeria but with a negligible few on the law, statutory? rules and regulations which have prompted many litigations that have adversely affected both the administrative efficiency and management effectiveness of such local governments. Thus, this article is written to examine and unearth some principles contained in some legal aspects of the law which are promotive of litigations in local governments in order to evolve a saving value against litigation on the one hand, and provide on the other hand a panacea for the settlement of disputes when they do arise.

Corporate Personality Principle

Local Governments in Nigeria are creatures of statutes, hence ti-icy must act within the laws that establish them. They are body corporate with perpetual succession hence all their actions will continue to bind them cvcr when the composition of the membership has been completely changed. Sec ***Frcncis UBA vs The Onitsha Urban County Council*** (1966:67) ENLR. 18. Here the effects of Edict No. 14 of 1966 dissolving the Councillors and appointing a Sole Administrator was considered. The defence raised the point that since the council was dissolved *no* action could be brought against it for one cannot sue a dead person or ride a dead horse. It was held that although the Council was dissolved, the instrument creating it was not revoked, that means that the council still exists, but the Councilors only have gone. Dissolution of members does not revoke the instrument creating Local Government and ii does *riot* ffccl. the corn mon seal of the Local Governments. Thus, it was held that local government continues even if the membership has changed since it has a perpetual succession. In another case, it was held that once a council tias been dissolved and the affairs and functions of it have been given to a Caretaker Committee, Caretaker Committee must be sued because they step into the shores of the former Council. See the case of ***L,CC. (Trading*** *rn-zder* the *name of Lagos City Transport* **Service vs R. Ago *Ogunnu3i*** CITCI 5/3/018.

Vicarious Liability

A Local Government is usually liable as an employer for the acts or omissions of his employee committed in the course of his employment. In other *words*, a local government will be liable for the tort of his servants so long as they are committed in the course of the servant's employment. Thus, the liability of the local government is predicated on the liability of the servant because the servant is the principal tort feasor while the master is the accessory. See the case of ***Obi vs Water Shellabear Nig Ltd*** (1997) INWLR (pt 484) at page 722, ***Oshinbosi vs Foge Builders Ltd*** CCHCJ/8/74 (atp 128).

Pease note that all authorities have agreed that a tort comes within the course of the servants employment if:

(a) It is expressly or impliedly authorized by his master, or

(b) It is an unauthorized manner of doing something authorized by his master.

(c) It is necessarily incidental to something which the servant is employed to do.

However, it must be noted that the interpretation and application of these principles to the realities of life are fraught with difficulties which could not be resolved in an article of this nature. For example, where the acts done fall within the scope of employment but are done in an unauthorized manner, in such a situation the master/ local government will be liable. See ***Ibadan City Council vs Odukale*** CAW/ 102/68 ***Brown vs Citizen's Life Assurance Co*** (1902) 2 NSWR 212 (1904) AC. 128, Mutual ***Aide Society Ltd vs Akerele*** (1965) 1 ALLNLR 336 at p. 340.

But if the servant does something which he is not employed to do and thus acts outside the scope of his employment, the master or local government will not be liable. See the case of ***Jarmakani Transport Ltd vs Abele*** (1969) 1 ALLNLR 180. Similarly, a local government will not be liable for injury sustained by an unauthorized passenger carried in a vehicle owned by it and driven by its servants. Finally should be borne in mind that a servant has the implied authority to delegate his authority and if he does that and an injury is sustained through such an act a local government will be liable.

In conclusion three basic distinctions have been made for determining liability as follows:

i. Negligence of the servant in the course of his employment.

ii. Excess or mistake of the servant in the execution of his duty- the master will be liable, and

iii. A master/local government will be liable for willful wrong committed by the servant in the course of employment although forbidden expressly by the master even though constituting a crime and committed solely for the benefit of the servant himself. ***See such case like: J.O. Davies vs. LCC and anor,*** suit No. LD/70/73 CCHCJ/10/73/115. Where a meter was transferred from a taxi car to another by a local government worker; ***Benjamin 0. Unachukwu vs Godwin Umeoibi*** LC.C. CCHCJ5/73. 113, where a local government car damaged the Plaintiff's vehicle hence, the council was held liable. In ***George Anyaghorne vs Akughe District Council*** (1962) WNLR 116, the contract for bided -wire was paid by the Council despite the fact that it was alleged that no original vote was made by the council to meet the contract. In **A.C. *Obianwnu vs. Ukwani Council*** (1960) WNLR 62, the Council was held liable to pay for damages when the Secretary of the Council unlawfully terminated the contract in respect of building a classroom.

The facts of some of these cases and reasons adduced for decisions are as follows:

For example, in ***George Anyagborne vs Akugbe District Council,*** the Plaintiff was originally awarded a contract for the tarring of a motor park and for the fencing of the market with barbed wire. One of the terms of the contract was that the Plaintiff would be paid on the stages of the work done by installments. The Plaintiff reached an appreciable stage in the work and demanded for payment in accordance with the term of the contract, but the Secretary refused to pay him and terminated the contract stating that there was rio vote originally to meet the contract and his predecessor ought to have pointed that out in the first instance and before the contract was awarded. Thus, when all efforts to make the Secretary see reasons became abortive, the Plaintiff came to the Court for the determination of his rights. It was held in this case that the Council is bound to pay the Plaintiff since the law stipulates that a person entering into a contract with a local government shall not be bound to inquire whether the standing orders of such local government was complied with before the award of such a conlraei or in the case of a contract exceeding the prescribed limit whether the prior approval of Ihe Council has been obtained, and that all contracts entered into by a local government if otherwise valid, shall have full force and effect notwithstanding that the standing orders applicable thereto have not been complied with or that the approval of the council has not been obtained.

Also in the case of ***A.C. Obiawu vs Ukwuani*** *Council,* the Council was held liable to pay damages because the Secretary of the Council terminated an existing contract with the Plaintiff because as it was alleged, the Plaintiff failed to give three councilors' a kick back before the Plaintiff started the work. In. ***J.C. Davies vs Lagos City Council Caretaker and Active,*** suit No. 10/70/73 the Defendant Council was held liable for the tortuous acts of his servants by causing the Plaintiffs car to be seized and detained in order to remove the meter which the Plaintiff transfered from one taxi cab to the **other.** They were also found liable in trespass to the goods for exercising their lawful duties by committing serious contravention of the law through overzealousness. This decision was reached because the regulation under which they acted did not provide for the seizure or detention of the vehicle, for what ihc, ought to have done was to revoke in writing the authority or permit granted to the Plaintiff to ply the road as required by the interpretation and application of the law under which they purported to have acted.

In ***Benjamin vs Unachukwu Godwin Ume Ob*** trading under *DE* ***Games Social Brothers vs L.L.C. Caretaker,*** the Council was found liable because his servant, the second Defendant in the course of his employment drove the Council's bus so negligently that it entered the Plaintiff's shop at Tinuhu in

Lagos and broke the front walls of the shop.

Cases of vicarious liability are numerous and of various dimensions which should be shelved in the meantime so as not to get us out of the grip and focus of this work.

Ultra Vires Action

Since local authorities are statutory corporations, it is contended by many writers that they are therefore subject to all implications of the ultra vires doctrine. This means that the ambit and extent of the powers and duties conferred on them by statutes or instruments must be strictly complied with and not exceeded otherwise their action may be termed ultra vires and void.

However, many actions instituted against a local government may be lost on the following grounds:
In the first instance, the plaintiff may not have *locus standi*; secondly, wrong action may be brought on Certiorari when as a matter of fact the local government is performing an administrative duty. In other words, many applicants failed to realize the fact that certiorari actions are never appropriate for administrative actions when such administrators are not acting in a quasi- judicial manner.

All these points can be well understood through judicial decisions as follows:

1. In the case of ***Ekundare vs. Governor-in-Council and anor.*** It was held that the passing by the Ilesha Urban District Council of a resolution to the effect that the Owa of Ijesha should abdicate was ultra vires the instrument creating the council which gave the council no such power for such a resolution. The Court held that the passing of such a resolution was not merely ultra-vires the council's powers, but that the council was in passing the resolution not functioning in accordance with the provisions of the law which brought it (the council) into being.

The governor-in council was therefore praised for dissolving the council accordingly since Section 87 of the Western Regional Local Government Law (1957) which enjoins ihe Governor--in-Council to dissolve any Council when it is satisfied that the council has made default in the performance of its legal duties Quashi-Idun C.J. in the course of his judgment said:

"The Ilesha Urban District Council was created by law and vested with special powers and functions. I have not been shown any power or function vested in the council and entitling the council as such *to be* ***concerned with the appointment or deposition*** *of* ***a*** *Chief or* *an It **is my** view **that an invitation (to Oba to** abdicate expressed in a **resolution of this kind infringes not only the** provision **of the** local **government law but also the chieftaincy law..) This action is neither in accordance with Native Customary** Law nor **can it be calculated as haven been performed in accordance with the provisions of the local government law.. the Ilesha** Urban District **Council has therefore not acted intra vires.. and I hold** therefore that **the Council acted ultra vires in passing the** resolution **calling upon** the **Oba to abdicate".***

2. The Court will not intervene where the Plaintiff has no locus and where the individual suffers no greater damage than that suffered by other members of the public, nor will a local government be held liable where was done was not a judicial or quasi judicial function.

For instance in ***Nyako vs. Ministry of Local Government,*** it was held that the plaintiff failed because the appointment of traditional authorities was by the terms of local government Ordinance Cap. 64 of 1951 section 2(3) not a judicial or quasi judicial act, but was merely an administrative act in which discretion was vested in the governor which was properly applied.

Also in ***Chief J.LG. Onyia vs. The Governor-in-Council and 10 Others,*** it was held that the Plaintiff cannot sue in his private capacity to enforce a public right or restrain interference with a public right in which he has no particular or special interest, or where he has suffered damages without joining the Attorney- General. The action therefore failed as in the words of ***Maughan J. in London passenger Transport vs. Moser-op*** where he said: ***"I think it is plain that there has been no interference with any private right of the Plaintiff, nor has he suffered special damage peculiar to himself .he therefore should not sue without joining** the **Attorney-General. The persons really interested were not before the Court. All persons interested should be made parties whether by representation orders or otherwise, before a declaration** by its terms **affecting their rights is made"***

3. It must be noted that all executive acts are not subject to judicial control; hence in ***Mallam M. Arzika vs Governor Northern Region*** it was held that orders of certiorari or prohibition would not lie to the Governor because, in making the removal order, he was not under any duty to act judicially. Bate J. held that in exercising his power under section 2(1) of the Ordinance the Governor was not under a duty expressed or implied to act judicially. Other Nigerian cases abound which establish the fact Ihat one cannot bring actions of Certiorari against local authorities when such authorities are acting in their administrative capacities and for a passing mention are the cases of ***Q vs Ondo Divisional Council Ex-Parte Joseph Akinbote, and*** *MacZakin* ***Akente vs A.G. Benue, Plateau State and Wukari Local*** *Administration.* The facts of Ihe case in ***Queen vs Ondo Divisional Council Ex-Parte*** *Joseph* ***Akinbote,*** are as follows: The applicant was engaged along with seven others as a forest guard on probation for three years; and this appointment was later terminated as a result of resolution passed by the council to reinstate eight forest guards who had been previously laid off and or dismissed, and whose pots he and seven others were engaged to fill.

Because of the aforementioned reasons he applied for a writs of Certiorari so that the resolution of the Council to re-absorb those people should be declared illegal and thereby quashed. The application was accordingly refused because the resolution of a council was an administrative arid not a judicial act. Furthermore, it was held that the applicant was not an aggrieved person, because he accepted an appointment which could be terminated at any time; and as such he was terminated after the receipt of a month's salary in lieu of notice; hence order of Certiorari was refused accordingly.

Power To Sue and Be Sued

Human beings like to live in groups or societies, and as a result of this interactions, conflicts of interest and disputes usually ensue for settlement. Since local authorities do make bye-laws and are given statutory functions to perform, they usually come into conflicts with people on so many occasions. For instance, many problems and cases usually emanate as a result of structural changes in local governments. Also vehement boundary disputes between one local government and another usually ensue. And on many occasions two or more Communities have added manifold problems to the management effectiveness of local government which in the end also engendered law suits.

Disputes usually arise as a result of chieftaincy declarations in many local governments which need to be settled in law courts. Many other disputes and actions usually arise as a result of the administration of the Council's bye laws, while some disputes are always associated with the intricate provisions of the Customary Court-Laws. Hence actions are usually taken in Courts by and against the councils since such councils are Corporate bodies. However, certain statutory provisions must be complied with before any action can be sustained against a local government as follows:

For instance, there is in law limitation of suit against a local government since all actions against it should be brought within six months next after the commission of the offence alleged; and no suit shall be commenced against it until one month (at leas after) written notice of intention to commence the same has been served upon the local government by the intending plaintiff or his agent.

The law further provides that such notice shall state the causes of actions, the name and places of abode of the intending Plaintiffs, and the relief's claimed. And subject to the directive of the court the notice and all appertaining documents or summons must be served by delivering same to the secretary of the council or by getting same to be registered to the secretaries at the principal offices of the local arguments, Section 171 to 173 of the 0yo State Local Government Edict 1976 (now 2000 Law of Oyo State) and sections 160-168 of the Bendel State Local Government Law 1980 for example deal with the limitation of suits against local governments as follows:

Section 171:

"When any suit is commenced against any local government for *any act done in pursuance or execution or intended execution of any law of any public duty or authority, or in respect of any such law, duty or authority such suit shall not lie or be instituted unless it is commenced within six months complained of, or in the case of a continuance of damage or inquiry within six months after the ceasing thereof'.*

Section 172:

"No suit shall be commenced against a local government until one month at least after written notice of intention to commence the same has been several upon the local government by the intending Plaintiff or his agent"

"Such notice shall state the cause of action, the place of abode of the intending Plaintiff and the relief which he claims" **Section 173:**

"The notice referred to in section 172 and any summons, notice or other document required or authorized to be served on a local government in connection with any suit by or against such local government shall be served by delivering the same to, or by sending it by registered post addressed to, the sectary to the Local government at the principal office of the local government.

Provided that the court may, with regard to any particular suit or document, order service on the local government to be effected, otherwise, and in that case services shall be affected in accordance with the terms of such order. Please, note that the courts have been very strict with any non-adherence to the provisions of this law which apply not only in Nigeria but also in many other countries". For example, in ***Alexander D. Yaskey vs. The President Councillors and Citizens of Freetown.*** The provisions of the Freetown Municipality were considered which were on the same footing with that of Nigeria. Thus section 180, sub-section (1) of the Freetown Ordinance are identical with those provisions mentioned above in the Nigerian Local Government Law.

Also in ***Aiyembuwa vs. Ondo Western District and another*** where the applicants sought for an order of Certiorari, it was held that before a Council can be brought to court, the provisions of sections 246 and 247 of the Local Government Law of the Western Region, 1959 must be complied with. That the matter before the Court is a suit within the provision of section 245 of the Local Government Law, and since the statutory notice has not been given to the council, the council was not properly before the court and the proceedings against it was accordingly dismissed.

Equally in ***Alexander D. Yaskey Case, the Freetown Municipality Ordinance*** .1927 Section 180(1) which protests the officers from being sued under it was considered.

Here, it is provided that writs shall not issue against local government officers until the expiration of one month after notice in writing, (setting out certain details) has been served on them.

The Court also held that an allegation of failure to serve the required notice is a defence by statute and as such, must be specifically pleaded as a defence under the above Country's rule.

However, in the case of ***Animotu A. Yesufu vs (1) Ibadan City Council*** and (2) ***Ibadan Divisional Council,*** the court amplified on what constitutes sufficient notes.

In this Animotu case, the Plaintiff's claim against the defendants was for a declaration that the construction of a drain and pavement in front of his house constitutes a nuisance, a declaration that the Plaintiff's land on which the defendants had constructed the drain or pavement had not been acquired by the defendants or anybody, and an injunction to restrain the defendants or their servants or agents for carrying on the construction. The Plaintiff's solicitors had earlier in a letter drawn the attention of the defendants to the nuisance and indicated that unless it was removed and the trespass on the plaintiff's land stopped within a month they had instructions to commence legal proceedings against the defendants without further notice.

The defendants pleaded that the plaintiff had not served them with the statutory notice of her intention to institute the action.

It was further contended by way of a preliminary objection, that the letter from the Plaintiff's solicitors did not state clearly the relief sought. The court however over-ruled this preliminary objection and held as follows:

(i) That the provisions of section 247 of the local government law arc mandatory and therefore any failure to comply with them will debar a court from entertaining any action brought against any local government council established under the provisions of that law;

(ii) That the letter in question constituted sufficient notice under Section 248 of the Local Government Law; and

(iii) That it is not necessary for a Plaintiff to state the relief sought in clear legal terms, for it will suffice if sufficient indication is given of the relief sought.

The court cited the case of ***Dramai Ngelega vs Mongowa Tribal Authority*** in supporting the first contention that the provisions of Section 247 of the local government law are mandatory and accordingly sub-section (2) of it stipulaicd that the notice must contain.

(a) the cause of action;

(b) the name of the intending plaintiff; and

(c) the relief which he claims

But in considering the letter in this case which reads; ***"You have without any legal sanction by way of acquisition or otherwise taken part of her piece of land to construct the road*** *and* ***even gone further as to erect a monstrosity of a wall in front of her door step" This is***

to say the least a nuisance of the first order for not only her right of going in and out of her house has been impeded, *but* ***also people coming to see her do so at some*** **risks of** *themselves* ***especially in an arena where there is no streets lighting"*** The court gave further directives: -

(i) that the warning in the last paragraph of the letter to the effect that proceedings would be commenced against the defendants unless the nuisance was removed and the trespass stopped was a relief claimed by the plaintiff and that:

(ii) ***this amount to an abatement of the nuisance and*** *the stoppage* of ***the acts thereof.***

Hence it is seen that it may not be all that necessary to state the relief claimed at any time in clear legal terms provided that the relief is known and ascertainable from the languages used in such a notice. That is, it will suffice if sufficient indication is given of the relief sought. To hold otherwise is to put a heavy burden on an intending plaintiff who could not afford the services of a Solicitor.

Also in the case of ***Julius Eweniran and Aihaji Jimoh Afolabi vs Ogo Southern District Council*** decided on the *7th* October, 1958, the court had the occasion to determine, whether the receipt of the required notice as stipulated in section 243(2) of the Local Government Law, 1957 should be reckoned from the day an applicant/plaintiff posts his letter or from the date the letter was received by the Council.

The facts of the case are as follows to throw more lights on the position of the law reached.
The Plaintiffs who were members of a society claimed a declaration that a resolution for the payment and the levy of a 1O/=d higher education rate at Awe were ultra vires and an injunction to restrain the collection of the said rate. They had been fined for refusing to pay this rate along with normal rate on the ground that they had voluntarily agreed to pay the former for a period of 4 years only which had expired.

In a letter registered by post at Ibadan on the 21st January, 1958, where their solicitor had informed the defendant council that if the latter persisted in demanding the higher education rate, they would be sued in the High Court. Evidence was tendered to show that this letter was in fact received on the 1st of February, 1958.
On the 24th February, 1958, the Plaintiff brought the action which was dismissed on the following ground:
Held:
"That assuming the letter written by the Plaintiffs solicitor to have given proper notice of an intention to sue in conformity wit section 243(2) of the Local Government law, 1957. it has not given a month's statutory notice required by section 243(1) before the action was commenced, and that it would be against reason and common sense to calculate the one month notice from the date of the registration of the letter at the Post Office, and not from the date it was received and the defendant had notice of its contents."

Statutory Powers and Duties of Local Government

This is an important area of the law in Local Government affairs and care must be taken to differentiate between a mandatory duty and a permissive power in deed. Mandatory duties are obligatory functions and they all imply clement of compulsion; with the result that a local government must of necessity perform those functions or duties that are mandatorily imposed on them by statues, On the other hand, local governments many or may not perform those permissive functions conferred on them by powers. In such cases of permissive powers therefore, local governments have elements of discretions to exercise in the circumstances.

Liability

It is not always easy to know the liability of local governments on actions for damages brought against them for a breach of statutory duty or a failure to exercise a statutory power, but Cross told us that an action generally for damages will not lie against a local government for nonfeasance; that is, for failure to do an act which ought to have been done by it. And that an action will lie for misfeasance if a local government exercises its statutory duties negligently so that injury results. This liability is based on negligence which is the failure to exercise reasonable care in discharging such duties as demanded by the occasions. See ***Dutton vs Bognor Regis English Urban District Council***

If a local government is compelled or directed to perform a positive duty by statute, that duty must of necessity be performed irrespective of any mishaps or injury that it may cause to an individual. Such a power is mandatory and it deals with an element of compulsion. It is unlike a permissive or discretionary power which a local government may or may not do at its own discretion.

The Law therefore presumes that if an individual is injured by the exercise of mandatory duties, the excuse for such interference is based upon the fact that the statute by imposing the duty must be taken as abolishing those previously conceded rights of such individuals, hence the local government will not be liable.

On the other hand, where a local authority has a dissection to perform a duty, the discretion must be exercise reasonably and in conformity with the law. The local government must therefore exercise a reasonable duty of care not to be negligent towards people in the exercise of such a power.

The point is, nobody compels a local government to do a discretionary duty and as such no liability will accrue for nonfeasance, but if it does it, the local government must do it well and in such a way as not to negligently interfere with the people's vested or contingent rights. If a local government therefore does negligently interfere with the people's rights during the performance of such a duty and caused injury to them in the process, the local government will be liable for an action based on Tort. For instance, it was decided in ***Metropolitan Asylum vs Hill*** that a Statute which simply gave permission to a local government to build a small pox hospital gave no defence to the local government in building it in such a way and position which amounted to a nuisance to private individuals, because that hospital could have been built in another convenient place without such injury. The fact of the case is that in exercising its powers under the Mefropolitan Poor Act 1867, the Board (herein called the Local Government) built a Small Pox Hospital in a residential area of Harnpstead.

This was alleged by residents to be a nuisance; and as such it was held, that the statute by which the Board acted was no defence; which would have been diffetent had the statute directed the construction of the hospital in a given spot. A similar decision to this was reached also in the case of ***Manchester Corporation vs Farmworth.*** However, it must be noted that in the case of ***Hammaersmith Tailwag Company vs Brand and Marriage East Norfolk Rivers Catchrnen Board*** novel doctrines have been evolved by the English writers.

END NOTE

1. Francis UBA vs The Onitsha Urban Country Council (1966 - 67) ENLR18
2. LCC (Trading un'4er the name of Lagos City Transport Services) vs R. Ayo Ogunnusi CHCJ 5/73/108.
3. J. O. Davies vs L.C.C. nd anor — Suit No. TD/70/73 CCHCJ/1 0/73/115
4. Benjamin 0. Unachukwu vs GodwIn Umeobi L.C.C. - CCHCJJ/73/113
5. George Anyagborne vs Akugbe L)istrict Council (1962) WNLR ii.
6. A.C. Obianwu vs Ukwani Council (1960) WNLR 62.
7. Exundare vs Governor —In-Council & anor WNLR 149
8. Nyako vs Ministry of Local Governmci;t 2 WNLR 147
9. Chief J.1.G. Onyia vs The Governor-in-Council and 10 others (1962) WNLR 89.
10. Mallam M. Arzika vs Governor Northern Region (1961) NLR 37$.
11. Q. vs Ondo Divisional Council Ex-Parte Joseph Akinbote (196J) WRNLR 24.
12. Madakin Akentc vs A. G. Benue, Plateau State and Wukari Locri Administration (1976) Vol. 1 NMLR 18
13. Animotu A.. Yesufu vs Ibadan City Council
14. Drama, Nyelega vs Mongawa Tribal Authority
15. Lagos Town Council vs Night Soil Movers Union
16. SIaitery vs NayIo (1988) A. (446
17. Razak A. Ajayl vs E. C. of Nigeria. (1961) pt 11, WNLR 107
18. Arkinson vs Newcastle Water Works Co (1877) 2 Ex.D 441
19. Cutler vs Wands Worth Stadium Ltd. (1949) A. C. 398
20. Chairman of the Board of Inland Revenue vs Joseph Recalla and Sons Ltd.
21. The Kings vs Dunsheath, Ex-Parte Meredott.
22. The King vs Housing Tribunal
23. Regina vs Cotham (1878) 1 KB 802
24. I4RE Barnes Corporation Ex-Parte Hutter (1933) 1 KB 668
25. Banjo & anor vs Abeokuta District Council (1965) NMLR 295

26. Odukate vs Ibadan City Council — Suit No. CAW 102/68
27. R.V. Fluthshire Country Council (1951) QB 350
28. Merchandise Transport Case (1962) 2QB. 173
29. The Queen Ex-Parte Sunday Odje vs Western Urhobo Ratios Authority (1878) 1 KB 02.
30. W Fredmans—Statutory powers and legal Duties Modern law Review (1945) 31 at page 35.
31. Cross E. A. — Principles of Local Government, Sweet and Maxwell, England

CHAPTER NINE

A SEARCH FOR VIRILE AND EFFECTIVE LOCAL GOVERNMENT OPERATIONAL SYSTEM IN NIGERIA

PROF. A. TORIOLA OYEWO

INTRODUCTION

Local government in Nigeria is sick. The list of its symptoms is long and depressing it. suffers from an acute shortage of funds orchestrated and manipulated by the state government. The State governments have not ceased from encroaching into Local Government functions — thus making local government ineffective and ineffectual. Bickering and internal conflicts excessively prevail among the officials and politicians thus making cooperation and consoli4ation of efforts a sycyphean task, while the traditional rulers have been terribly unutilized to make local government veritable and advantageous in all respects. Local government attract few substantial, energetic and public — spirited people because of the application of God fatherism, thus producing inefficient and unproductive persons to work there in, as councilors without adequate skills. It is infested by party of an unyielding kind. It excites little electoral Interest and takes a low place in a ranking of public institution in order of popular esteem. Local government is in fact creaking and wasteful in Nigeria, hence the need for radical development in order to make the institution viable and self sustaining.

MANAGEMENT OF LOCAL GOVERNMENT

Although some ills have been identified in local government as stated above, yet one feels that 'management' bears the greatest and repeated salvos of attack.
The Word management has been described as getting things done through the people hence the success of any local government is a function of its administrative efficiency and management effectiveness.

Really and as suggested by a renowned author thus:

"Managing local government is where the action lies. It requires the skills of a corporate executive, the sensitivity of a statesman, and the endurance of a long distance runner; the demands are great, the expectations are high and the pressures are intense. Yet if we are to have local governments that are responsive to the needs of the citizens, they must be managed by individuals who have the ability to operate in a fish-bowl environment while creatively carrying out local government policies and programmes".

On this score, a critical appraisal of local government administration tends to show that internal skirmishes and unenhanced ability to perform coupled with inept knowledge of the appropriate translation and application of the law on local government do constitute a deterrence to make local government in Nigeria virile, viable and effective.

Oyewo writing on the councilors is of the opinion that one of the factors - determinants of a council's administrative and management performance is the quality of its Councillors, and where the Councillors are found to be young, foolish and corrupt, but handpicked on the alter of God fatherism without merits, the councils administration and management will be hampered. A similar bad effect will ensue where the councilors are illiterates, indolent and arrogant; and or where they arc found to be doing their work for selfish interest and personal aggrandizement.

Literature on these assumptions is replete and will need no further elaborations here.
Improving the performance of local government therefore requires improving the capabilities of the people who work for it, hence there must be a spirit of co-operation between the councilors and the members of the staff unlike what has been noticed in some local governments up till now.

It is equally noticed that where co-operation exists between the political leaders and the administrative executives, lots of attention would be devoted to the realization of the local government's objectives; but where the relationship is not cordial and or degenerates to that of the wolf and the lamp, the administration and management of the local government will be adversely affected.

Therefore, if we would desire an emergence of a viable and self — sustaining local government in Nigeria, we should do away with hand picking councilors on the alter of God fatherism and improve our management orientation.

We must remember that political God fathers lack every moral rectitude, integrity and decorum for they sometimes thrive in bestiality. Thus, they do anything and they get away with it as evidenced in the anomaly that took place in Anambra State and some parts of Nigeria like Ibadan, Oyo State sometimes ago. The God fathers do not expect the dividends of democracy to go round even to the grass roof, but to themselves alone. They see the nomination of Councilors as errand boys to deliver goods and services to them alone. Thus they are always pre-occupied in getting returns in terms of money from the councilors.

Hence, any Councilor or Chairman who fails to make a monetary return monthly to them has reached his waterloo or has incurred a great disfavor and thus risks termination of his further services in local government. The whole scenario looks offensive, and terrible to relate, while honesty of a councilor to his God father must be shown like a mirror; since the more money brought to the God father dictates the pace and the extent of a Councillor's retention in office. This has produced frightening situations like macheth before the ghost of Banquo to all lovers of democracy; and it is as dreadful as a gathering storm. Therefore to enhance the qualitative representation in local governments, the qualification of membership with regards to the State House of Assembly as contained in section 106 of the 1999 constitution should be used, while God fatherism should be discouraged in its entirety.

Also, we should stop the appointment of people who are not elected to be made supervisory councilors since the Constitution guarantees only; democratically elected local government. Thirdly the appointment of the political secretaries must now stop.
They are unnecessary wastes and particularly when they serve no useful purpose to the effective growth of local government. They are aberrations of the government but imposed from above to serve what one may call personal urge and aggrandizement and it looks like finding jobs for the boys at the expense of the down trodden masses. Finally one would suggest that the present unjustifiable salaries being paid to these Couneilors should be reviewed. This will plug to a vanishing extent the present drains that arc existing in our local governments.

Also must be advised that we should not allow anybody to throw dusts into our eyes as far as a virile system of local government operational system is concerned and we should resist the urge to be on the horns of a dilemma in Nigeria any more over this system.
Hence, it is high time to set Thames on fire, take the bull by the horns and cut the Gordian's knot by reverting to the parliamentary system of running our local government as opposed to the obtaining presidential system which is incongruous, baseless and wasteful in Nigeria.

Afterwards the Americans, who are the protagonists of the Presidential system of government use the 'Council Manager' system of local government and not presidential. We should nail the lie on the counter and follow the path of rectitude and honour to change from the presidential system of running our local governments. The constitution allows this and we should comply with it to cross the Rubicon if only to get the best performance appraisal.

FUNCTIONS OF LOCAL GOVERNMENT

Local Government would have improved but for the fact that state governments have continuously whittled down their powers and have continued to encroach upon what would normally have been the exclusive preserve of local *governments.*

For instance, many states took over without consultation with tile Local governments, many revenue yielding functions of local governments like markets, motor parks, building plan approvals, liquor licensing, tenement rating, the collection of royalty and many more.

Also, it was reported that poll-tax, community tax and cattle tax have been abolished by some state governments to make local governments ineffective, impotent and sterile.

The effect of this as reported by Dasuki Report is to make local governments unhealthy by depleting the internal sources available to tile local governments with the result that 1iost local governments lack tile financial resources required for the effective service delivery to their communities.

"With all these scenarios, how can one make local governments viable since after tile taking of all these revenues yielding resources from them by such state governments, what remains usually for local governments are only for staff salaries and nothing more.

With objective consideration, therefore, one should refrain from passing adverse comments on local governments but to blame in all sincerity their respective state governments and that was why the Dasuki report recommended that state governments which eroded the constitutional functions of local governments should hand over such functions to local governments on mutually agreed terms. Honestly, it should not be on terms but such state governments must imperatively do so. They must obey the provisions of the constitution without resistance.

However, the local government and legilative committee gave this a serious thought at the 1988/89 Constituent &sembly in Abuja, and they put a provision in the draft Constitution forbidding state governments from encroaching into the exclusive functions of local governments; but alarmingly such a prohibitive provision was left out in the final draft.

It is therefore of a national interest to think on what to do in order to allow local governments perform their duties uninhibited. One feels that statutory provisions should be made against this unwholesome practice by the state governments. The laws or statutes to be made should provide for gadgets to enforce compliance since behind any society or organization lies the force of the law. Therefore, state governments should not be allowed to continue with these types of nefarious actions if we want our local governments to satisfy the yearnings and aspirations of the people at the grass root.

PERFORMANCE AND EXPENDITURE

The Federal government with the public have accused the local government of not performing or of gross under performance; while local governments i some quarters have been branded as extravagant organizations; but since there are two sides to a coin, what has the local governments got to say by way of defence under the principles of audi alteram pane-listen to the other side the mile of natural justice?

So far, the local governments arc. grateful to the Federal Government for giving them the statutory allocation as at when due; but they are complaining that they could not effectively discharge their duties because of overheads and certain depreciating and despicable behaviours of some past governors as follows: Local governments pay *65%* of their allocation for teachers *salaries* (primary educational) while *15%* was used for the payment of pensions and *5%* was used to sustain the traditional rulers and so on mention a few.

For instance, local governments pay 1% of their allocation to the local government service commission for the training of their staff, they also contribute to the sustenance of the Nigeria Police and Voters registration exercises, they make payments of salaries to the political office holders in their establishments, while the payment of over bloated security votes for political office holders on local governments still persists. With all these and the persistent abuse of the State/Local Government Joint Accounts by the State governments, the chances of viability of local governments look deem, remote and questionable, hence something must be done to do away with all these loopholes.

They also state that since it is part of their duties to maintain law and order, they purchased 1000 jeeps and handed them to the police for the effective discharge of their duties. Lastly was pointed out the indecorous attitude of some past governors who took from the "State and Local government accounts" a sum of ten million (10 million) from each local government to fund their re-election bid. These must not be allowed to rear their ugly heads again if we want a virile and effective local government system in Nigeria.

With all these scenario, and the payment of staff salaries, local governments have found it hard to perform their duties up to the pole and ad libiturn. I am therefore of the immutable belief that local government performances will definitely reach the Olympian heights, and be as fit as a fiddle if the funding of primary education is made to be the joint responsibility of the Federal State and Local governments respectively. Anything short of that will be a fall out between founding and effectiveness of service deliveries.

INTERNALLY GENERATED REVENUE

It must be noted that although, the relief which local governments are going to have over the joint responsibility for the teachers' salaries is going to be predominant, but that will not be a complete solution for the effective performance of local governments without addressing their management ineffectiveness. That is, deducible because local governments in Nigeria lack all indices to make their performance, effective, "irile and satisfactory and that is why we are recommending the retention of the parliamentary system of local governments over the years. It is also noted that some o the functionaries of local governments are riot dedicated to their duties, some of them to not even care for the survival of this democracy which **our** heroes past have brought into being with lots of sacrifice. Their absolute dependency on statutory grants without tapping their internally generated revenues accounted a lot for operational lapses which are not the case in such countries like America, Japan and Brazil to mention a few.

For instance in America, about *57%* of the local government expenditure comes from the property tax, while the state government only gives up to *35%* and after which other internally sources make up the difference. These make local governments there to be functionally autonomous and were hence able to perform excellently their functions to the people at the grass root. in Japan. for example, local governments are expected to raise between 40% to 60% of their revenues also From internal sources and that is why they are able to perform more effectively than what we have in Nigeria.
By the 1967 reform in Brazil, attempts were made to produce virile and strong national system of local government, hence all regulations and laws binding the local governments were thus entrenched into their Constitution.

Thus the Brazilian Federal government will intervene in any situation wherein the functional integrity of local governments is impaired or appropriated by the State governments. The Nigerian Federal Government must borrow a leaf from the Brazilian system bearing in mind that in terms of history and culture, Brazil has a lot in common with Nigeria. The Nigerian government must make it an offence punishable by dissolution for any local government's inability to meet the stipulated target for its internally generated revenue within two or three months. That is, on no account should a local government fail to realize its internally generated revenue of 50% or there about, monthly. If this is put in place, everybody will work hard to make a success of the institution for fears of dissolution of the Council; which hangs over them thus like swords of Darnocle.

PROJECT FINANCES

Local governments in Nigeria should be result-oriented and therefore they should be encouraged to enter into meaningful commercial undertakings; however in order to do these, they need lots of money to prosecute many projects. In this regards, more liberal attitudes should be given by the banks towards the financial aids of the councils. At present, money is too hard to obtain in order to prosecute the needy projects of some local governments and in some occasions, stringent conditions are usually attached when some local governments do apply for loans to prosecute some projects. As a matter of fact, the Dasuki committee recommended the establishment *of* a national municipal bank from which local governments can borrow money to fund projects, but this was turned down by (lie then Federal government because it is felt that existing financial institutions could meet such needs.

The government puts it in this way:

"There are other existing financial institutions like the Nigerian Bank of commerce and Industry (NBCI), government-owned banks, federal Mortgage Bank, Agricultural and co-operative Bank and the Nigerian industrial Development bank, (NIDB,) from which local governments can borrow money with the state governments acting as guarantors".

But one could argue that if there are state governments' banks, and the Federal Mortgage Bank, there should be a National Municipal Bank for Locai Government since equality is equity and since local government is said to be a third — tier of authority. In view of the above and in few of the fact that there are lots of projects which may need bank facilities to prosecute in future by local governments, one would therefore urge the federal and state governments to be sympathetic to the cause of local governments and help positively over these issues.

THE VOICE OF WISDOM

Apart from what has been written above, many seminars, workshops and conferences have been field and recommendations were made towards the emergence of a vible and self sustained local government, but it would appear as **if** both the Federal and State governments have either turned left handed compliments to them or are still sitting on the fences to effect changes. Therefore, the underlisted recommendations call for serious consideration:

1. That the local government funding by the states should be guaranteed in the constitution and that the violation of such a provision by any state government be made an impeachable offence.

2. That there should be a constitutional provision forbidding state governments from encroaching into the exclusive functions of local governments.

3. That local governments should now redeem their lost glory e viability and effectiveness by sitting up to tap more effectively all their revenue yielding resources in order to compliment the efforts of both the Federal and State governments.

4. That the imposition of external duties and functions on loca governments apart from those recognized by the Constitution should be discouraged.

5. While it has been suggested that every state should appoint locai government inspectors to look at the books of their loca governments periodically, also must be stated that each state government should set up a State/Local Government, Joint Forum —. comprising arious stake holders in local

government Administration which should meet periodically to assess progress, plans and review performance of each local government council ir the state.

6. It has also been suggested that local government projects verifications teams should be created by state governments in order to verify claims of expenditure on projects of local governments. while all major transactions by local governments should b properly receipted. And for this purpose receipt booklets for all local governments should be printed by the security printing and minting company and distributed by the state to various local governments.

7. It is also opined many a times that while state governments should. set a ceiling limit on the amount of money a local government can spend without approval of state government, the state government should also place a ceiling on how much local governments car borrow from banks without pri r approval of a state government.

Lastly, it has been suggested that all key officers of local governments should declare their assets at the beginning and end of their tenure in accordance with the law.
Many other recommendations have been made with regards to the traditional rulers which are not within the scope of this paper.

CAREER OFFICIALS AND THE POLITICIANS

Local government officers and the politicians must see themselves as partners in progress in order to achieve a reputable standard in service delivery-unlike what happened during the. Late Adegoke Adelabu administration of the then Ibadan District Council, which recorded lots of failure and ended up with dissolution and shame. It is therefore the theme of this paper that local governments will be able to score successes where the career officers and the politicians do cooperate with each other and one another.
There should be mutual understanding and senses of public probity.

The politicians must concede the management and the administration of the local government to the officials, while the politicians should be in full control of the policy matters of the Council. The two organs in local government should jointly and severally adopt a policy of self sufficiency in resources of the local government. This implies according to Adediji exploration and exploitation of all available resources that bring tangible revenues and managing such resources wisely and in a way that the present trend of heavy dependage of local government both on the Federal and State governments could be drastically reduced, while effective mechanisms must be put in place to tap all the revenue yielding resources of the local; government.

Above all, it must be noted that the effective mobilization of the people is a sine qua none for the effectiveness and viability of any local government. Thus, unhealthy relationships, political intolerance and lack of cooperative federalism *from* both sides must be avoided and made a thing of the past.

REFERENCES

1. William. F. Coventry — Management made easy page 2. W. H. Allen, London.
2. These are the directives of Marke Kean in Brian W. Rapp.
3. OYEWO A. T. — The administration and management of 1badan Municipal Government *1954* — 1979. M. Phil theses submitted to the University of Ife, Department of Public Administration 1983.
4. (See Rehald Wraith, L. Gray Cowan in Local government in West Africa, as reported by Alex Gboyega — unpublished Ph.D thesis, 1975 — University of Ibadan, Nigeria.
5. Wraith, Renald — The quality of Councillors in West Africa (Land 24t /9/1 *955* page 901.
6. Orewa. G. U. — Report on the problems of Local Government Finance in Western Nigeria.
7. Humes, S. Local Government Quarterly journal of Administration (Ife)5(1)atpp9l —110(1970)
8. Oyediran O. — Town Councilors Quarterly Journal of Administration (Ife) 7(4) PP *453-402* July, 1973.

CHAPTER TEN

AN EXAMINATION OF PRESIDENTIAL PRIMARIES ELECTION IN NIGERIA: A COMPARATIVE ANALYSIS OF PEOPLES DEMOCRATIC PARTY (PDP) AND ACTION CONGRESS OF NIGERIA (ACN)

OLAJIRE A. BAMISAYE PH.D AND
AYODELE M. BELLO M.SC

INTRODUCTION

Electoral contests in Nigeria are wars. They are not shooting wars, but, they are not just continuation of war by other means, as defined by clausewitz. They are real wars. The contestants are combatants who aim at winning by all means. Those who lose understand the language, they do not concede defeat; but live to fight on. This "fight to finish" saga characterized the 2011 presidential primaries of two contending political parities in Nigeria PDP and ACN. However, the scenario witnessed from PDP's primary was quite different from that of ACN's primary. This and other related issues or features shall be succinctly examined and analyzed in this paper.

A war is usually not fought, won and lost in a day. Victory comes after series of campaigns and losses and victories on the battle field. The side that starts strong may not in the final analysis be the ultimate leader if it makes costly mistakes along the line or gets battle weary. This is also captures most of the circumnavigating activities that usually accomplish electoral contests among the competing candidates for elective posts e.g the President of a country. All the major political parties in Nigeria were gripped by internal convulsion as January 15, 2011 deadline set by Independent National Electoral Commission

(INEC) for them to conduct their primaries for all elective offices (Presidential) inclusive. Many events occurred before and during the proper presidential election in the presidential primaries conducted by both PDP and ACN. These events shall be the examination of this paper'

Background to PDP Presidential Primary

Before a meaningful analysis could be made, it would be necessary to discuss what could be termed as "battles before presidential convention" of PDP and in turn, for ACN. The Nation Newspaper, of Thursday, January 13, 2010 gave a comprehensive record of what considered as battles before presidential convention and mostly related to various political parties in general and PDP in particular.

Zoning

This is one of the issues that have dominated discourse for more than six months. It has refused to go away. Northern Political Leaders Conference, met between June and November 2010 attempted to mobilize Northerners to reject the idea of President Goodluck Jonathan running on the party's platform. Four aspirants, former President Ibrahim Babangida, former Vice-President Atiku Abubakar, former National Security adviser Ibrahim Gusau and Kwara State Governor Bukola Saraki, submitted themselves to the process pleading to work for whomever a committee led by Mallam Adamu Ciroma picked as the North's consensus candidate to square up against the President.

At the end of the exercise, without announcing how the nine-man committee arrived at its choice, the mantle was handed to Alhaji Atiku Abubakar.

The panel simply said: "We are pleased to announce that we have concluded out assignment of arriving at a consensus candidate today and one out of the four aspirants who submitted themselves to the process has emerged. He is ATIKU ABUBAKAR.

It was further stated "we are glad and proud that we have finally arrived at this outcome after several weeks of hard work and wide consultations. We are proud because of the unusual honour and extraordinary privilege given us by the four gentlemen who placed their political destinies in our hands. We are humbled by the strength of their faith. We appreciate their humility and cooperation. We have been reassured by all of them that they will work together to enable

ATIKU ABUBAKAR clinch their party's ticket in the presidential primaries.

"We thank all Nigerians, supporters and critics alike for their views over these past several weeks. While we note these views and respect each one of them, we insist that no individual, organization or society dreaming of success and greatness can achieve these dreams without respect for others and honouring agreements voluntarily entered into. This is especially so where these agreements have been transformed into a binding document, a constitution, which governs the conduct of those who subscribe to it".

The battle over zoning has been using various forms and strategies. At the National Executive Committee meetings, the pro-zoning group argued forcefully that, with the South, through General Olusegun Obasanjo, having ruled for eight years, the baton should be handed to the North in keeping the Article 7 (2) of the PDP constitution. This was rejected by the anti-zoning group. The supporters of President Jonathan insisted that the constitution might have spoken about rotation of power, but it never specified rotation between the North and the South. For emphasis, the group has said the primaries of 2002 and 2006 were contested by aspirants from the North and the South.

Besides, the constitution of Nigeria that guarantees unfettered right to vote and be voted for that is subject to qualifications was cited. It was held that President Jonathan is thus qualified to contest and any effort to shut him out would infringe on his constitutional right.

Finally, the national leadership of the party held that the party's constitution truly specifies zoning of the offices, but the President was, due to exigencies of the moment, allowed to participate in the process. Legal attempts to erect further hurdles on the path of the president on this basis equally failed as the Chief Judge of the Federal Capital Territory, Lawan Gunmi, ruled that the cited provision of the PDP constitution is not justifiable.

That ought to have laid the matter to rest, but it did not. The controversy is endless. The debate continues in open and private places. Associates of the two major aspirants put the argument in favour of their chosen one. It may end tomorrow.

Order of Primaries

This was another matter that gave fright to the aspirants. At a point, governors elected on the platform of the PDP, constituting a very powerful bloc, got involved in the preparations for the primaries. Their leader, Governor Bukola Saraki was involved. He tried his hands at obtaining the party's ticket. He failed even before the primaries as the consensus committee shunned him. His colleagues did not think much of his bid and rather opted to protect their individual and collective interests. While the leadership of the party proposed to the NEC that the presidential primaries he held first, the governors who considered it deleterious to their interests, fought vigorously to hold the governorship before presidential primaries. The governors won. The President, who had supported, and probably sponsored the Presidential primaries first motion, lost the battle. The table one below shows voting pattern for the Presidential primary in which Umaru Yar' Adua won gallantly.

Should Lawmakers be Members of NEC?

The presidential battle did not extent to the governors only. The National Assembly members also sought to be power brokers. They attempted to use their power to make laws to whittle down the influence of the governors and many suggested that the President could be behind their bold moves. In the process of amending the constitution and the Electoral Act 2010, they made a move to make all National Assembly members automatic part of the NEC of their respective political parties. In the PDP where this could have meant so much that in any other parties, the governors who had always influenced policy matters en bloc felt threatened.

While there are 27 Governors, there are more than 300 Federal lawmakers. The governors went to work. After one of their nocturnal meetings ahead of the December 15 meeting of PDP NEC and crucial decision on the Act by the Senate, the governors threatened literally to walk out of the party if the lawmakers were allowed to introduce the toxic provision. At the precipice, the presidency, PDP leadership and National Assembly baulked. They backed down and peace returned to the party at least on a temporary basis.

Super Delegates?

It is an old argument. According to the old constitution used for the 2003 National Convention, presidential appointees were allowed at the convention. Thus, if the president chose to appoint so many advisers, special assistants, he could just sway things in his favour.

Article 13 (18) (A) (IV) provided that: "All ministers, special advisers, and special assistants to the president and the vice president and all chairmen of boards of federal parastatals who are members of the party shall be participants at the national convention and shall have voting rights".

The provision was changed just before the 2007 presidential primaries to accommodate more than 10 of such presidential aides. In 2011, the party leadership, believed to be supportive of the president, attempted to reintroduce the pre-2003 provision. It was defeated. Again, the President lost a golden opportunity to definitively tilt things in his favour.

Staggered or Central Primary

When the decision on the mode of the presidential primary election was first taken in August 2010, at a time that INEC had fixed the election for January, the presidential aspirants were told that voting for them would be held at the zonal level by delegates from the state. By that arrangement, the hands of the governor.

Battle for Delegates

Again, so far, the president has won this battle. Delegates across the zones and critical sections of the party, including the governors, have all endorsed him openly. At the meetings of the NEC, when the governors dithered, President Jonathan reportedly reminded them that he understood the language of power and would not hesitate to wield and use it in the electoral process. That was enough to get him the required unanimous endorsement. In return, he pledged to support the return of the Governors. Now that the governorship primaries have been concluded, it appears that the president has kept his words. Would the governors reciprocate?

Factors that will drive the process

The first factor is, understanding who the delegates are. Till date and before the correction, no one has the list of the delegates. However, going by the 2006 convention where 4,101 votes were cast, it is expected that there may be a little less than 4,000 delegates since some of those who were automatic delegates then have been sidelined. The statutory delegates now are the President, Vice-President, National Chairman and NEC members, all National Assembly members, all Governors and Deputy Governors, all the governorship candidates who emerged from the state congresses and House of Assembly.

Members of the Board of Trustees, Zonal Working Committee members, state party chairmen, state party secretaries, all women leaders from the states, local government party chairmen and all chairmen of local government councils are also automatic members.

Others include former Senate Presidents and their Deputies, Former Speakers and ex-deputy speakers who remain members of the party and all former National Working Committee members.

Apart form automatic delegates, one national delegate was elected from each local government area. Other factors that will decide where the pendulum will swing include the power of incumbency. This has already been seen in the protests by the Atiku Campaign Organization that has alleged that the rules remained shrouded in secrecy of 72 hours to the day of convention. The organization further alleged that the Convention Committee was packed with those who had openly professed commitment to the emergency of President Jonathan. However, the question has been asked if there are delegates who remain neutral at this point.

One critical question being asked was whether the loss suffered by the lawmakers at all levels would not affect how they vote at the day of convention. In many of the states, majority of the House of Assembly members lost. The same applied to the tussle for seats to the House of Representatives and the Senators from the PDP in which 50 had lost the tickets. This has left a window for the main challenger to President Jonathan, Atiku Abubakar. Reports indicate that he is working to explore the development.

As it is said, 24 hours is such as long time on the political playing field. The two major aspirants were still juggling the facts and reaching out to the delegates. The rules, mode and setting appear to favour the incumbent.

To round up this prelude to the PDP Presidential primary, a

typical question can be asked-Will it be Jonathan or Atiku? The answer to this costly question was answered by Lawal Ogienagbon (2011). He has this to say, since the Northern Leaders Political Forum (NLPF) chose former Vice-President Atiku Abubakar as the North's consensus candidate for the April election, it has been battle royal between the Atiku camp and the Jonathan camp. By virtue of his adoption, all other contestants of northern extraction are expected to support Atiku in his bid for the ticket of the Peoples Democratic Party (PDP) to be able to run in the election. Without the ticket, Atiku cannot run in the election. To get the ticket is not going to be easy not only for him but also the North.

President Goodluck Jonathan holds the four aces in this battle. Besides being the President, the leadership of PDP and majority of its governors are for him. Is that really so? But it is not going to be an open and shut race for the President. From all indications, he is going to fight hard for the ticket. It is not going to be like 2006 when he got to the convention ground in Abuja as a governor armed with a ticket, but left as the running mate of the late President Umaru Yar' Adua, without lifting a finger. Such a fortuitous turn of event will not rear its head this time.

It is going to be a fierce battle. So far, Jonathan and Atiku have shown that they are determined to get the ticket. In words and deeds, they have taken the fight to each other's territory. As if he has already been chosen, Atiku has been going round the country canvassing for delegates' votes in the party primary which will climax the national convention of PDP.

The week of convention is a crucial and a week for the country as more presidential candidates are expected to emerge between 10-15, January 2011. But the PDP show is generating interest because of the high wire politics over its presidential ticket. In the other parties, the acrimony over the ticket is not as pronounced as in PDP. We have all witnessed the political horse-trading that characterized the party's congresses at the ward, local government and state levels. Many who had thought that securing the ticket to run as National and Houses of Assembly and governorship candidates was a foregone conclusion are still licking their wounds over what happened to them. Their ambitions crashed before their own eyes. Those who banked on the

President helping them to get the tickets are now wondering if they were not led by the nose to the slab to be slaughtered. Will they plot against him?

These acrimonious primaries may be nothing compared to what may happen at the presidential primary which is going to be a straight race between Jonathan and Atiku. Anyone of them stands a chance of picking the ticket, but one of them has a better chance. That person enjoys the support of the party, which is ready to adopt him as its consensus candidate if not for the fear of incurring the wrath of the North. Although many from the North support the President, the party cannot afford to be seen to be overtly backing one candidate over the other. But the party leadership will no doubt be happy if Jonathan emerges its candidate.

Atiku's chances would have been brighter if not for what happened in the past that made him to severities with PDP. Although the party claims to have accepted him back like a prodigal son, but it seems it is not ready to put its money on him. Atiku, who understands the politics being played like the back of his hands, is undeterred. He is in the race to beat Jonathan, if the party provides a level playing field. Things, as Atiku knows, will no doubt be skewed in the President's favour, but like the tested warhorse he is, he is ready to live with that as long as he is allowed to test his popularity at the polls.

It is going to be an exciting battle between the duo in Abuja. No matter what happens, we already have Atiku's assurance that he will abide by the outcome of the exercise. That is how it should be; the contest should not be seen as a do or die affair. The best candidate should win. In any contest, there will always be a winner and a loser. Whoever wins should be magnanimous in victory and whoever loses should be sportsmanlike in defeat. The interest of Nigeria should be paramount in their minds as they fight for the ticket. They should not do anything to compromise the stability of the country because of the lust for power.

The delegates and supporters of the aspirants should let peace reign. They should conduct themselves in and out of the convention ground because the world is watching to see how things will go. It is understandable that the PDP presidential primary is generating tension. As the party in power, people are waiting to see if it will conduct a peaceful primary. If it does not, they will be right to ask: Can the PDP government ensure hitch free elections in April? The test is in the party's ability to conduct a transparent and credible presidential primary. May the best candidate win.

ACN: Battles before Convention

Since this is a comparative analysis research paper, it can instantly be mentioned, that the battles before the convention of ACN is not as tough like that of PDP. The road leading to the emergence of ACN Presidential candidate could not be considered as "war" in its true sense of it like that of PDP among the three contestants. This is well stated below.

It is a historic convention, the first of its kind since the party changed its name from Action Congress (AC) to Action Congress of Nigeria (ACN). The national congress billed for the Onikan Stadium, Lagos, is crucial to the future of the acclaimed progressive party. When the ACN presidential candidate emerges, he will not be perceived as the candidate of a tribal platform aggressively seeking for relevance. Already, the party is becoming a force to reckon with, following the recovery of its stolen mandates in Edo, Ekiti and Osun states. It now controls four states in the old Western Region.

The national outlook of the party will be demonstrated by the presence of party chieftains who cannot be ignored in the politics of Nigeria. New stalwarts expected at the convention cut across the six geo-political zones. They include former Governors Achike Udenwa (Imo State), George Akume (Benue), Saminu Turaki (Jigawa), Senators Ifeanyi Ararume, Senator Joseph Akaagerger and Senator Joel Dalami, Dr Abiye Sekibo, James Akpanudoedohe, Alhaji Abdullahi Gwarzo and Densil Kentebe. The three presidential aspirants-Alhaji Attahiru Bafarawa, Mallam Nuhu Ribadu and Mallam SeiduMalami-are relatively new in the party and they have track records in public life as politician, anti-corruption curator and technocrat.

The aspirants are scrambling for the presidential ticket of the leading opposition party in the country, at a time many Nigerians are looking for a credible alternative to the ruling Peoples Democratic Party (PDP). They are jostling for presidential power at a time their party, the Action Congress of Nigeria (ACN), has become the new bride in the polity. They are eager to make a difference at a time the party has made a lot of inroads into their region of birth, following the crisis rocking the ruling party at the centre.

Ahead of the convention, ward, local government and state delegates have been elected. They will in turn perform the duty of choosing a befitting flag bearer, who will immediately appear on the weighing scale before prospective voters. Before the convention, the trio appeared before the Screening Panel chaired by Ekiti State Governor Kayode Fayemi. The committee subjected them to a thorough screening. The criteria employed to assess them include educational qualifications, integrity, depth of experience, political consistency, vision for the country, international exposure, public perception, and marketability. All of them met the criteria in varying degrees.

However, and more importantly, the presence of the three aspirants underscore their willingness to abide by the progressive ideology, irrespective of their aristocratic and conservative backgrounds.

Malami: Little is known about the aspirants from Nasarawa State. A 1982 graduate of Ahmadu Bello University, (ABU), Zaria, the Nasarawa State chapter of the party has described him as a committed party man without any record of blemish in his career. For him, the contest is not a do or die affair.

Bafarawa: Bafarawa is not a baby politician. He was governor of Sokoto state for eight years on the platform of the All Nigeria Peoples Party (ANPP). To that extent, he is rated as a man of experience. In 2007, he was presidential candidate of the Democratic Peoples Party (DPP). He lost to late President Umaru Yar'Adua. In his state, he was brought before a panel of inquiry which looked at the financial books of his administration. The governor cried foul, saying that he was been politically victimized by the administration now presided over by his former deputy, Governor Wamako.

Since Bafarawa joined the race, he has been targeting delegates from the North. He is perceived as a moderately rich candidate who can run an effective campaign. But his views on contentious national issues are not known. The odd against him is that there are certain leaders of the party rooting for the idea of generational shift.

Ribadu: Ribadu is a household name. He is new in politics. That is why opponents describe him as a man of little political experience.

He was the Chairman of the Economic and Financial Crimes Commission (EFCC). He fought the anti-graft war with relentless zeal, although at a time, the agency was accused of witch-hunting perceived political enemies of former President Olusegun Obasanjo, who set it up.

Many Nigerians see him as a principled man who may not compromise his integrity. He is perceived as the face of the younger generation, which is the major victim of bad leadership in the country and, therefore, in a better position to fix the economy, restore social harmony, ensure security, fight corruption and other vices and reposition.

President Goodluck Wins

President Goodluck Jonathan on Thursday, January 13, 2011, defeated former Vice-President Atiku Abubakar and Mrs. Sarah Jibril. The build-up to the election suggested that it would be a keenly contested primary as earlier discussed but turned out to be one horse race, as he won convincingly in most of the states such as; Abia, Adamawa, Akwa Ibom, Anambra, Jigawa, Osun, Benue, Rivers, Taraba, Bauchi, Nasarawa, Lagos, Gombe, the Federal Capital Territory and others. The former Vice President led in Sokoto and Zamfara States. The build-up to the election was extremely tense, with the two major gladiators, President Goodluck Jonathan and former Vice-President Atiku Abubakar, being very combative. They heated up the polity with their accusations and counter-accusations so much that fear gripped the people. The last few days were particularly terrifying, as expletives and verbal missiles from both camps rent the air. The campaign had the appearance of a people preparing for war rather than a preparation for deciding a party's candidate. The situation before the primary could not have been worse than what Ivorians are currently going through.

The primary election campaign nearly divided the nation along ethnic line, especially with the issue of zoning being a major factor. Up till the time voting started, ethnic card was still being played up. The Abubakar camp went into the contest believing that head or tail, it would win because, as it claimed, an Abuja High Court had ruled that the zoning arrangement in the party must be respected.

Ribadu Emerges:

The direction of the battle for the presidency was on Friday narrowed down as the pioneer Chairman of the Economic and Financial Crimes Commission, Mallam Nuhu Ribadu, emerged as the candidate of the Action Congress of Nigeria. Ribadu, who became the party's presidential candidate in what was regarded as a voice vote, will ultimately join others to face the Peoples Democratic Party's candidate, President Goodluck Jonathan, in the April election.

The emergence of Ribadu followed the stepping down of the two other aspirants in the race, Alhaji Attahiru Bafarawa and Alhaji Sheidu Malami, at the special convention of the party at Onikan Stadium, Lagos. Before announcing that the other aspirants were stepping down for Ribadu, Bafarawa, a former governor of Sokoto State, said he joined the ACN, not only to become the presidential candidate, but to join hands with all other progressives to wrest power from the PDP during the April general elections. In his acceptance speech, Ribadu noted that his emergence would address the failed leadership of the ruling PDP, saying the password for that change as a generational shift in the leadership pattern of the nation.

He added that the lack of change in the leadership style of the nation in the last 50 years was responsible for the drift currently being experienced in all sectors of the nation's economy.

Ribadu said, "I humbly accept this challenge with an enormous sense of responsibility. The forthcoming elections will determine whether Nigeria is ready for a change. The PDP administration has had more money than any other administration in the country, but Nigerians should ask the moral value the PDP has brought.

PDP, ACN Primaries: Beyond the Clash of Political Titans:

One may be interested in Chux Ohai's analysis of the two primaries. The PDP primaries no doubt, appears to be more rigorous than that of ACN. The picture given was that, the PDP primary to select the presidential candidate seems to appear as if, the real presidential election for the whole country is taking place. This can be confirmed by the "Thank you" message from one group called "Nigeria Coalition". It was reported that all Nigerians were appreciated for voting Goodluck, as if all Nigerians were responsible for the voting.

Whereas, this is not true. Members of PDP are fractional part of Nigeria. The message of coalition as appeared on the Punch, Monday, January 17 of page 62 is stated below:

"Nigerians from every tribe, tongue, zone, region and religion spoke with one voice on Thursday, January 13, 2011 at the PDP Convention in Abuja: they voted massively for the transformation of Nigeria through ideas, humility, courage and national consensus. They sowed the seed for the glorious future where Nigerians will be judged by the content of their character and not their accents and tribal marks. They voted massively for Dr. Goodluck Jonathan as the flag-bearer of the PDP as we journey to a new Nigeria shaped by unity in diversity, peace and progress. Now that Nigerians form 36 states of the Federation and FCT have spoken with one voice, Nigeria's journey to greatness has just begun. You are welcome on board." The same comments came from the same group of one Nigeria coalitions, when asserted that "Nigerians, this is the time to make your vote count. Jonathan will never let you down" (Thursday, January 13, 2011 on The Punch, (Newspaper).

Before the presidential primaries of the Peoples Democratic Party and is main rival, the Action Congress of Nigeria, which took place in Abuja and Lagos respectively, both parties had probably given hints of their preferred candidates for the 2011 presidential poll. While the ruling PDP had to grapple with the contentious zoning formula that nearly tore the party into shreds, as well as sundry issues, the ACN had little problems announcing its intention to field the former Chairman of the Economic and Financial Crimes Commission, Mallam Nuhu Ribadu, as its preferred candidate.

A great deal of public attention had riveted on the ruling PDP as a result of the peculiar drama unfolding within the party in the months leading to its presidential primaries. For a while, the major gladiators, President Goodluck Jonathan and his major opponent, former Vice-President Atiku Abubakar, engaged themselves in the task of convincing their numerous supporters that they truly deserved to earn the party's ticket for the forthcoming presidential election. Eventually, on the day of the PDP presidential primaries, both men found themselves squaring up for the first time in a crucial battle for the survival of their political careers, alongside the only female contestant in the race for the party's nomination, the indefatigable Mrs. Sarah Jibril. Jonathan finally emerged the candidate of the PDP, pooling 2,736 votes to beat Atiku, who garnered 805 votes.

On January 14, 2011, the ACN held its presidential primaries in Lagos amid fanfare. Actually, it would be incorrect to describe what happened at Onikan Stadium, the venue of the event, as a contest. There was no contest. Ribadu was virtually proclaimed winner by all the delegates of the party across the country after other contestants voluntarily withdrew from the race. The outcome of the ACN presidential primaries clearly reflects the thriving spirit and culture within the party. Unprecedented as it seems, the withdrawal of Ribadu's opponents, the former governor of Sokoto State Alhaji Attahiru Bafarawa and Alhaji Sheidu Malami, from the contest to pave the way for his nomination as the party's presidential candidate, is enough proof of the maturity of the politicians themselves and their commitment to the practice of politics without bitterness.

In comparison to the ACN event, the PDP primaries would have paled into insignificance, but for the fact that the latter turned out, against all expectations, hitch-free and transparent. For once, the organizers of the PDP event did well to provide maximum security at the Eagle Square, venue of the primaries and scene of the bloody October 1, 2010 bomb blasts, and to ensure that it was not marred by any violent incident. Our final analysis reveals that what actually worked in favour of Ribadu has to do with a "concretized internal democracy" of ACN. The internal democracy of ACN gives no room for political hurly-burly or rancour among the "rank and file" of the ACN party leaders. This is contrary to what had prevailed at the PDP rank and file caucus before the presidential primary. It may interest one therefore, to end this analysis by exposing the politics of intrigues and self-preservation in the PDP presidential primaries which did not come into fore in ACN.

Meanwhile, pro-zoning elements, including Kwara State Governor, Dr. Bukola Saraki, had realized that, self-preservation was the first interest in politics. He, therefore, decided to negotiate with the President's camp. He had probably realized that the crisis currently rocking the PDP in his state, which had led to exit of his father, Dr. Olusola Saraki, from the party, was a pointer that he would need the support of the President to survive. While the senior Saraki wants the governor to hand over to his daughter, Senator Gbemi Saraki, the governor is of the opinion that it is morally wrong to do so. The governor's position infuriated his father, who defected from the PDP with his daughter to the Allied Congress Party of Nigeria, which he formed. The governor, therefore, saw the writing on the wall with the defeat the party suffered in the Offa Local Government Area by-election to the opposition party, the Action Congress of Nigeria. It was with a great relief to the troubled Governor that he was able to deliver the state to Jonathan, who scored 61 votes as against Abubakar, who managed to garner 26 votes.

Jonathan's main opponent in the primaries, Abubakar, did not go down without a fight. He also made moves to sway the delegates, especially those from the North, to his side. But the Governors thwarted the moves by warning their delegates to steer clear of him. It was learnt that the governors reasoned that by electing an incumbent as the party's presidential candidate, their interests during the governorship poll in April would be protected. Aside this, the Governors believe that the President will abide by the agreement he had with them on December 16, 2010 to spend only four years in office.

Besides, many of the Governors also felt that since Jonathan, ascendancy to the presidency was accidental, they could also have such good luck in 2015. This, was the general feeling among the North that one of them could also emerge as a presidential candidate in 2015. A member of the PDP National Working Committee, who pleaded anonymity, said, "More than anything, what worked in favour of Jonathan was the ambition of the governors". With Jonathan's agreement that he will spend four years, the presidency is open to the South-East and the North in 2005. In 2015, Sambo or any of the Governors can emerge as the presidential candidate of the party. It was based on this that the Governors ordered their delegates to vote for Jonathan, who recorded 2,736 votes as against Abubakar who scored 805 votes, while the only woman in the PDP race, Dr. Sarah Jibril, polled only one. Also, to make sure that nothing went wrong with their strategies, the Governors made sure that their representatives were on the convention planning committee. Thus, Governors like

Sule Lamido, Godswill Akpabio and Theodore Orji, among others, effectively served on the committee. The governors also personally monitored the delegates to ensure that they did not stray.

The sudden release of the Senate Leader, Teslim Folarin, from detention could have come to some people as a surprise but not to members of the Senate. Our correspondent learnt that the senators impressed it upon the President that they would not attend the primaries unless their leader was released from detention where he was being held in connection with the murder of a factional chairman of the National Union of Road Transport Workers in Oyo State, Alhaji Lateef Salako (Elewe Omo). The President was in a dilemma. Should he order the release of Folarin, would that not the governor of the state, Chief Adebayo Alao-Akala? However, at the end of the day, he was able to impress it on the police to withdraw the charges against the Senate Leader with an argument that they needed to do a further investigation. When the news filtered to the delegates from the state in Abuja, they were in anger until the Governor assured them that all was well.

Finally, the PDP presidential primaries and that of ACN were not democratic enough. For PDP, the convention was not democratic to an extent because it did not protect the delegates who voted from states. The election did not accord with genuine internal democracy. The state-by-state voting pattern exposes delegates who may have wanted to vote otherwise. The way it was done, Mr President would know the states that did not vote for him. It would have been more democratic if the party should have provided a box for the delegates to cast their votes generally.

On the other hand, the manner in which Ribadu emerged as a consensus candidate was quite undemocratic. Idea of other candidates stepping down for Ribadu to emerge as consensus candidate is democratically questionable. Is the concept of "consensus" conform with the norms and values of democratic system? What qualifies Ribadu more than the other two contestants? Perhaps, Ribadu should have been allowed to compete favourably with other contestants. In this regard, to allow Jonathan to contest with other contestants made the PDP's election even more democratic than that of ACN.

The political activities have started unfolding even as gladiators are warming up to throw their hats in the ring. The sign that the nation is itching close to a new dispensation are clear: voter registration, parties' conventions and primaries. The electorates are also not folding their arms as they await the commencement of the voter registration scheduled to hold between January 15 and 29 and the eventual general elections billed for April, 2011. It is, however, vital to note that the outcome of some of the governorship, House of Representatives and senatorial primaries of the ruling Peoples Democratic Party in particular has provoked mediation in the political state of the nation. The PDP governors for sure have cause to roll out the drums, having secured the delegates' approval to re-contest on the platform of their party in their respective states. The activities of the PDP which prides itself as the largest political party in Africa are usually appealing to Nigerians as it controls the country since the dawn of democracy in 1999.

This is even more pronounced because its members not only populate the National Assembly but it also governs more states in the nation. But to the opposition parties, especially the Action Congress of Nigeria and a good number of the citizens, the PDP has not been able to put the country on a solid socio-economic and political footing. Hence, as the party observed its primaries to select the candidates to field for the various elective positions 2011 most especially the presidential, some of the opposition parties too are strategizing under all kinds of alliances aimed at dislodging it in the forthcoming elections.

CONCLUSION

The PDP and ACN primaries had taken place and gone. However, it is not yet over until it is finally over!! The two primaries of the parties were enough to assess the Nigerian preparation for the April 2011 election. The genesis and the end products of the two primaries were quite interesting and of political relevance for a journey to a democratic general election of April 2011. The affiliated lapses in the two primaries should be noted and amelioration should be made in the nearest future of 2015.

What is a bit notable in the primaries was the tenacity of the electoral campaign strategies of both political parties before the convention which was better than that of 1999 and 2003 respectively. It was an improvement but much more would be needed to be done in the nearest future. That is to say, internal democracy should be strengthened beyond imagination. Internal rancour should be avoided. The issue of who picks the presidential ticket should not be a matter of "life and death" as noticed in the PDP primaries between Jonathan and other contestants. More importantly, the era of "ethnocentrism" should be over and must be guided against in future. To this end, the idea of "zoning" should be jettisoned at all cost. The idea of a particular person should emerge from a typical zone in the Nigerian Federation is anachronistic and contrary to the international ethics of a true democratic system and this should be avoided at all levels and cost.

Nigeria does not belong to any individual or group but to all. If this is true, then any action capable of fanning the embers of discord or mocking its heterogeneous nature which should be its strength must collapse on the altar of unity and patriotism. The country has been weakened for too long by all manners of self-seeking interests. It is time to give it the desired nerve to project from its dormant state.

REFERENCES

1. Politics @ thennationonilineng.net
2. Lawal Ogienagbo's answer could been seen at the Editorial/ Opinion of The Nation, January 13, 2011.
3. Clux Ohai analysis is contained in the Saturday Punch, January 15, 2011.
4. The Nation, Friday, January 14, 2011 pages 1 and 64.

CHAPTER ELEVEN

AGITATION FOR RESOURCE CONTROL AND THE IMPLICATIONS FOR NIGERIAN FEDERALISM

OLAJIRE A. BAMISAYE PH.D AND
AYODELE M. BELLO M.SC

INTRODUCTION

Resource control in Nigeria before and after independence has been an endless and a controversial issue between the Federal Government and its component parts. The controversy has to do with the issue of "who gets what" out of the country's wealth. It has been a persistent controversial issue in the contemporary Nigerian politics as it relates to federalism as a preferred system of government in Nigeria. Given the heterogeneity of the Nigerian state, the founding fathers of Nigeria adopted the Federal system as the most viable option of protecting the core interests of the federating units. This was demonstrated in the Federal constitution especially, the 1963 Republican Constitution that clearly defined the jurisdictions of the federating units. For instance, each federating unit had its own constitutions, which is one of the key properties of federalism.

Also, by extension, the available agricultural and mineral resources were limited to the control of the regional governments in which certain percentages (10%) were remitted to the federal purse (derivative principles). Duties, functions and powers of both the Federal Government and regional governments were clearly defined without controversy and if there is any dispute at all, the Supreme Court is on ground to administer justice to the warring parties. This had been the structural formation of the Nigeria polity vis-a-vis the resource control.

However, it is important to note that this prototype format of resource control and fiscal federalism acquired before and after independence (1960) became a shadow of itself and non-existence owing to the historical events that over took the polity. Nigeria less than a decade after independence was bedeviled with series of nationhood problems such as social and political tensions, constitutional problems, economic sabotage (e.g corruption) power tussles, ethno-religious crisis, electoral malpractices, census crisis and intra-communal clashes.

The advent of the military in power in January 15, 1966 headed by General J.T.U Aguiyi Ironsi made a negative impact on the Nigeria's federalism owing to its hierarchical command structure. The central government became so powerful, while the component units were relegated and subordinated in order to favour their administrative command. General Ironsi was honest in his articulation of a military government, unlike his successors who engaged in political deception by describing their respective regimes as the "Federal Military Government of Nigeria without respecting the sanctity of federalism". General Gowon took advantage of the emotive sentiments of the public outcry against Unitarianism but preference for federalism, despite this, his regime was in all intents and purposes, a unitary regime. It was from this historical synopsis, that the idea of regional control of resources became a thing of the past as Nigeria had suffered from militaristic federalism. Even the few civilian governments suffered greatly from the debilitating effects of militaristic Nigerian federalism.

The practice of true federalism (fiscal federalism) become complex, difficult and unachievable even in recent times because of the elitist conspiracy, regional sentiments, fear of security and domination, imbalance socio-economic and political opportunities that may accrue from the practice of true federalism. Projecting a different position is another group within the elite, who advocates the recognition of individual, family and commercial ownership of land and the resources. To this group, agitation for resource control is a call for the ownership of the natural resources by the people within the area who later pay royalties to the federal government. Looking critically on the issue of resource control vis-à-vis federalism in Nigeria-a simple question arises. What is the circular relationship between resource control and federalism? Is that relationship circularly causal? This study intends to analyze the relationship with all its attendant positive and negative consequences.

Regardless of what the concept of resource control means to different groups, this study view it as an agitation for a better deals in the allocation of resources accruing from the oil exploited areas in order that the people are adequately compensated for all their losses and deprivation arising from the exploitation and exploration activities of the various oil companies. This study therefore, sets out to look at factors that engendered the agitation for resource control; it seeks to identify various dimensions of the agitation in recent times, as well, as its implications on Nigerian federalism.

THE AGITATION FOR RESOURCE CONTROL IN NIGERIA

The agitation for Resource Control in Nigeria is partially traceable to the nature of its federal system. Coupled with this is the fear expressed by the southern states perceived marginalization in the management of the natural resources by the Federal Government especially the oil-producing states. As explained, the various components of the federation are not equal in view of their disproportionate revenue generating capacities.

Therefore, if a mineral producing state controls the resources and appropriates the revenue accruing from it by way of derivation, the result would be first an unbalanced development; second, derivation could lead to a radical shift in revenue from majority groups, which are very influential and powerful, minority groups that are politically powerless. However, the majority groups had also agitated for derivation when it was advantageous to them.

The reforms in the national sharing of resources between 1967 and 1975 effectively reflected the politics of the dominant class because oil formed substantial revenue base of the country. Therefore, it is the oil revenue that has brought about the current struggles over the control, access and distribution by various ruling classes. The principle of derivation, if allowed to be the basis for determining revenue allocation with unduly favours some parts of the federation at the expense of the others. This explains the reason why Obi (1998) posits that:

> *The Federal Government as the very vortex of power thus becomes the ultimate prize in politics and all attention shifted to the contest for access to power and the capacity to authoritatively allocate resources at the centre.*

This centralization of power and resources is antithetical to true federalism. The concentration on oil revenue also militates against the improvement of other sector of the economy. In Nigeria, revenue allocation largely implies the allocation of oil revenue. Therefore, oil is central to the politics of inter-governmental relations in Nigeria.

The possession of the nation's oil wealth by the minority groups of the Niger Delta has led to series of agitations for better compensation and that the derivation principle was stoutly defended and applied in the 1950s and the early 1960s by the dominant power blocs- Western and Northern regions that benefited from it. During that period, the bulk of the country's revenue came from cash crops such as cocoa in the West and groundnut from the north.

In order to ensure that states producing the wealth of the nation do not stand a good position of benefiting more than others in revenue sharing both Aboyade commission (1977) and Okigbo commission (1981) did not emphasize derivation principle. The principle of derivation was also attacked before these commissions but despite the attacks; it remained the dominant principle up to the Mid 1970s (Mbanefo and Egwaikhide 1998:213). The recommendation of both Aboyade and Okigbo commissions was that the principle of derivation should not feature again in the revenue allocation scheme. In view of these principles such as: equality of access to development opportunities, minimum responsibility of government and population, social development and internal revenue efforts became the relevant yardsticks for revenue sharing in the country without recourse contributive capacity of each state.

The sharing formula depicts a political power game as emphasis shifted from derivation to other principle as revealed in the committee's recommendation thus:

1. Vertical allocation

- Federal Government - 53%
- State Government - 30%

-	Local Government	-	10%
-	Special Fund	-	27%
ii.	Horizontal Allocation		
-	Minimum Responsibilities of Government	-	45%
-	Population Responsibilities of Government	-	45%
-	Special Development factors of Government	-	15%
-	Internal Revenue Efforts	-	5%

The special fund of 7% was to be shared as follows:

-	Initial Development of Federal Capital Territory (FCT)	-	2.5%
-	Special Problem of Mineral Producing Area	-	2.0%
-	Ecological Problems	-	1.0%
-	Revenue Equalization Funds	-	1.5%

The Special Development factor of 15% was to Direct Primary enrolment was to take 11.25% and inverse primary school enrolment was to take 3.75%.

It also recommended that each state should contribute 5% of its total revenue for sharing among its local government councils.

Finally, it recommended the establishment of a permanent fiscal commission. Based on Okigbo's recommendation, a permanent Revenue Mobilization Allocation and fiscal commission was established in 1989, and this permanent commission had carried out the reviews of the vertical revenue allocations as follows:

Shared by the Western states, while the southeast shared 11.7% (the Guardian, January 25, 2002: 40). Thus, the resource control issue is considered a political matter and should be given a political solution rather than a legal approach.

Furthermore, it is not all the states in the North that introduced Sharia and even series of controversies also surrounded the introduction of the Sharia legal system by the Zamfara state Governor, Alhaji Sanni Yerima (the Guardian, December 7, 1999:8). The relevance of the Sharia to the issue of resource control could be viewed from the perspective of self-determination of the constituents of a federation. Thus, if a state Governor could unilaterally declared a Sharia state, then those with resources should also control such resources.

The decisions of the Supreme Court of Nigeria on the suit also complicated the issue. The high points of the ruling class include the followings: Derivation should begin on May 29th 2000, Federal Government must comply, Gas should be part of derivation, 1% allocation to Federal Capital Territory halted: funding of the judiciary: payment of Nigerian National Petroleum Corporation (NNPC) as first line charges is unconstitutional, non-payment of derivation on capital gain tax, and stamp duties is unconstitutional federal government perpetually restrained from further violating the constitution on first line payment (This Day April 6, 2002:1).

The decisions of the Supreme Court could have been entirely in favour of the state; especially the southern state but the low water mark of the land surface and seaward limits of inland water aspect of ruling did not favour the littoral states. The controversy generated by the court's ruling led to the south-south Government protest (Newswatch, May 27, 2002:30). Consequently, President Obasanjo realized the need for a political solution and set up a committee to resolve the conflict politically (Nigerian Tribune, May 24, 2002:20).

Given the high stakes built into the state-oil linkage in Nigeria, where oil exports accounts for 95% of exports earnings and over 85% of national revenues, politics continues to be influenced by oil. For those in power, access to oil is the ultimate prize in the political contest. For which they are ready to fight at any cost and by any means. For the out-of-power elite, it gives them everything to fight for, but most importantly, it has contributed to the marginalization of most Nigerian citizens (particularly those from the Niger Delta) form power and from the benefits of the oil economy, in spite of the unprecedented earnings from oil exports since 2000. The result has been the continuation of the militarization of the conflict between the indigenous population and the Nigerian federal state which lays claim under the constitution to be the sole owner of all oil in Nigeria for control of the oil.

BASIC ISSUES IN RESOURCE CONTROL

As part of the salient issues in resource control, matters like revenue formula allocation or sharing, fiscal policies (instrument or methodology for raising and distributing revenue) cannot be ignored. Nigerian governments had engaged in several battles over the political and economic principle, of which the various natural resources of the states could be determined, owned and control by the federation. Several commissions were inaugurated to address these contentious issues ever before and after independence. In summary, the commissions have suggested various principles for allocating revenue. The following constitutes a list of the principles suggested at various times.

- **Principle of Derivation:** This suggests that a large proportion of resources should be returned to the area (state) from which they are collected.
- **Population:** This principle calls for distribution of revenue to states according to their population so that state with high population will earn more than those low population.
- **Even Development:** The guiding principle of this is that all parts of the nation should develop. Consequently, more resources should be made available to underdeveloped, areas to catch up or that poor states should get more.
- **Equality of Units:** This principle suggests granting equal amount of resources to all the states on an equal basis regardless of size and population. This is not a popular principle with large states who feel they are being treated the same with smaller units.
- **Minimum National Standards:** As in the case of even development, minimum national standards imply that in the performance of certain functions such as health and education, efforts must be made to see that all parts of the federation maintain given standards. In order to facilitate this, funds are allocated to sates so that set standards can be met. This suggests that variation in the grants will follow needs. States where the burdens of the function are greater will receive larger grants than those with lesser responsibility.

ETHNIC MINORITIES STRUGGLE FOR LOCAL AUTONOMY

The history of the struggle for self-determination and local autonomy by the ethnic minorities of the Niger Delta is well-known. What is important to note is that it had its roots in the creation of Nigeria as a colonial state in 1914, an act that relegated the people of the region to minority status in relation to the numerically superior neighbouring ethnic groups, which dominated political life in the old western and eastern regions of Nigeria. The successive institutionalization of revenue-sharing and power distribution along regional lines tended to reinforce the politicization in the struggle for power. Smaller groups defined as "ethnic minorities" tended to lose out, while the dominant ethnic groups asserted power at both regional and national levels.

The ethnic minorities did not succeed in their quest to establish separate states before Nigeria's independence in 1960, and opportunities to resolve festering disputes in the following years were squandered. Even before the 1967-1970 civil war there was an abortive attempt by a group of Ijaw ethnic minority youth- the Niger Delta Volunteer Force (NDPF), led by Isaac Boro, to secede from Nigeria, by declaring the Niger Delta Republic in February 1966 in a bid to protect "Ijaw Oil" (Obi 2004:23). Shortly before the eruption of war in 1967 between secessionist Biafra in the Eastern region, the four regions of Nigeria (North, East, West and Midwest) had been abolished and replaced with twelve states, three of which were in the ethnic minority regions of the Niger Delta. From 12 states in 1967, Nigeria currently has 36 states.

Apart from the state creation exercise, and the centralization of the control of oil, the method of oil revenue allocation also changed over time. The share of oil revenues allocated to the ethnic minority oil-producing states of the Niger Delta fell from 50% in 1966 to 1.5% in the mid 1990s. It then rose to 13% in 1999, in response to international campaigns and local protests by the minorities and the strategy of the new democratic regime to win legitimacy by attending to the grievances of the oil-producing communities.

In order to justify the need to grant resource control right to the lower constituent units mainly because of the varieties of natural resources found across the length and breadth of Nigeria and such other related factors as argued above, it is highly imperative to discuss the state of the nation through revenue allocation especially as it generally affects the practice of federalism in Nigeria vis-a-vis resource control.

FACTORS THAT SPARKED OFF RESOURCE CONTROL AGITATION

The agitation for resource control by the Niger Delta people is borne out of perceived cheating marginalization and deprivation they had suffered in the hands of the majority ethnic groups who have dominated the corridors of power since Nigeria's independence. Due to the activities of oil companies operating in the Niger-Delta area, the people had suffered untold hardship but not adequately compensated.

One of the factors that precipitated the resource control agitation by the Governors of the South-South could be seen in the abandonment or de-emphasis on derivation as a principle of revenue sharing in the Nigerian Federation. The economic objectives of the 1999 constitution are found on the control of the national economy in such a manner as to secure the maximum welfare, freedom and happiness of every citizen on the basis of societal justice, equality of status and opportunity. Towards this end, section 162 (1) of the 1999 constitution established a "federation account" to which all revenues collected by the Federal Government are paid.

Section 162(92) then enacts the principle of allocation which includes: population density, equality of states, internal revenue generation, landmass and terrain. The provision is however, subject to an overriding provision, which states in part provided that the principle of derivation shall be constantly reflected in any formula as being not less than thirteen percent (13%) of the revenue accruing to the federation account directly from any natural resources. These provisions clearly outreach the principle of derivation of not less than thirteen percent of revenue accruing to the federation account directly from any natural resources, as an overriding allocation principle of the federation account.

This is a deliberate constitutional mechanism intended to ensure a more equitable distribution of the national revenue among the federating governments in general and states in particular which bear the burden of the exploitation of their natural resources for the commonwealth of the nation.

Another factor accountable for the agitation of resource control by the Niger Delta people could be seen in the area of the untold suffering and hardship meted out on the people of the area, necessitated by the exploration and exploitation activities of oil companies operating in the area.

According to a recent report "the environment is all the forces or factors outside the individual that operates to control his behaviour and to shape his physical and mental development. These forces include geographical, climatic and organic entities and processes that influence man and his or her occupation, institution and interaction.

The organic entities and processes are of the biological, category and indicate the photogenic germinal infestations, parasitic invasions prevalent in an area affects the health of the people and animals living in that areas. It is long accepted that a people environment determine their culture and national characteristics...therefore, the environmentalist states that when people are deprived of their natural resources, they are deprived of the most essential vehicle for enhancing the quality of life through self development in all ramifications of life's endeavours. Deprivation produces stagnation and poverty stricken and downtrodden conditions. All these factors combine together to make the Niger Delta people to agitate for resource control to enable them be in a better position to control their environment.

IMPLICATION ASSOCIATED WITH THE AGITATION OF RESOURCE CONTROL

One major problem that the agitators are bound to face is the domains of power, which is out of their control and this militates against the feasibility of their objectives, this is especially the case when considering the mono cultural nature of the Nigerian economy which has made relatively bigger but poor states to be entirely dependent on the oil revenue source from the weak but rich small states of the Niger-Delta. Thus acceding to the request will bring about disintegration of the country (Sunday Punch, March 4, 2001:15).

The double standard approach of the federal government is discernible, for instance, the President Olusegun Obasanjo during his tenure purportedly assured the seven Governors of the zone: Edo, Akwa Ibom, Rivers, Bayelsa, Delta, Ondo and Cross River States that no legal action would be taken to resolve the conflict between the states agitating for resource control and the federal government.

The Governors also promised to maintain a peaceful relationship with the federal government but contrary to the promise by the federal government. A suit was instituted against the states in the Supreme Court, despite the advice of the solicitor- General to the contrary (Tell, April 9, 2001:25). This and its subsequent determination generated a lot of controversy in the polity and the fact is incontrovertible that was embarrassed by the reaction of most Nigerians.

However, the federal government in view of its advantaged position would not like to consider any issue on a shift, which empower the states more than the centre, the president during his official visit to Delta State in January 2002, stated it categorically thus: "on the issue of resource control, the state can be managing the resources". According to him, problem will only arise when the state wants to interfere with the management of the resources (The Punch, January, 2002:10). This statement is illustrative enough. Also, in his address at the international Bitumen Conference in Ondo State, the president remarked "no state can lawfully allocated to itself the control of mineral deposits in such state or anywhere else" (The Punch January 12, 2001:13).

Furthermore, a shift opposition is expected from states and Northern politicians who are adversely affected by the issue of resource control. For instance, Alhaji Wada Nas, a controversial Northern politician once stated that:

> *This oil we are talking about is a gift from God, it is not owned by anybody and does not need waters, oil to germinate or grow, nobody should therefore claim ownership, it is God's given. (The Punch, January 12, 2002:5).*

Also, Dr. Ahmed Jalugo, a lecturer at the Bayero University, Kano and a former sole administrator of the National Union of Petroleum and Natural Gas (NUPENG) during the General Abacha era argued thus:

> *When there was groundnut pyramids, we all benefits and finished them together, when there was palm oil and cocoa, we enjoyed them together. Now that we have oil, we must finish it together.*

From the above statements, it is obvious that Northern states have benefited tremendously from the oil revenue and will not support any move for resource control.

Recommendations in the vertical allocation formula from 1989 to 2002 clearly shown in the National Revenue Mobilization, Allocation Fiscal Commission (NRMAFC) that the resource control allocation was problematic. This is illustrated in table 2 below:

The introduction of the sharia legal code in some northern states made the southern governors to device a neutralizing strategy and this strategy was consolidated at the southern governor's summit in October 2000 sequel to the call by some eminent personalities of southern descendants. Subsequently, the issue of marginalization in the Niger-Delta became an instrument to pursue the goal of resource control, and this explains the struggle of oil-producing communities which became disenchanted with the pattern of distribution of the nation's resources, which essentially was derived from their land. The demands of the newly formed oil minorities, social movement included the restructuring of the federation in a manner that gives more autonomy to the central government (Obi, 1998).

Furthermore, self-determination of the minorities within the federation, the return to the allocation principle of derivation, compensation for the oil pollution of the environment and lately the demand to control the resources within their state have become the fundamental issue which groups like the Movement for the Survival of Ogoni People (MOSOP), the ethnic minority rights protection organization and the southern minorities movement are championing. Thus, the Hamman Turkur commission on Revenue Mobilization, Allocation and fiscal commission recommended 13% derivation in the new allocation formula released in 2000, and this tallies with the recommendation of the 1995 constitutional conference (Nigeria Tribune 11th September 2001:12).

The federal government has instructed that 50% of the 13% from the derivation account go to the oil producing areas and be channeled to the newly established Niger-Delta Development Commission (NDDC) (The Punch, October 11, 1993:13). This action was protested by the people who wanted the allocation paid to their various states.

The agitation for resource control by the southern governors was premised on the fact that fiscal federal structure was merely a creation of both the military and politicians, mainly from the north (Sunday Punch, March 4, 2001:14). Therefore, agitation for resource control in October 2000 was timely as it provided a pre-emptive strategy to the Sharia Governors to achieve their objectives. The south-south governors argued that the current derivation principle in revenue allocation in which 13% of natural revenue is allocated to states is insignificant and cannot redress the ecological devastation in the Niger Delta. The federal government was uncomfortable as it viewed that true federalism in Nigeria will lead to national disintegration (Sung Punch, 4, 2001:15). To avert this situation, the federal government instituted a suit against all the thirty-six states of the federalism in response to the claim of the littoral state regarding resource control. The politics in the legal approach taken by the federal government could be seen form the position of Karibi Whyte, a judge of the Supreme Court who argues thus:

> *From my own perception of how it (resource control suit) was framed, no case was brought before the court, which the court can decide because it was brought badly. If you are asking for something... and what you are bringing is just determining boundaries how does it answer resource control, which you have brought (Nigerian Tribune February 2002:28).*

The six littoral states contended that the natural resources located off shore should be treated as being located within the territorial boundaries of the respective state like Akwa-Ibom, Cross-River, Rivers, Bayelsa, Edo and Delta states. The legal approach to solving the problem has also attracted condemnation from the public, especially the southerners as people have rather suggested a political solution to the problem because the demand was essentially motivated by political solution to the problem because the demand was essentially motivated by political considerations. Prior to the application of 13% derivation principle as recommended by the 1994 constitutional conference and implemented by the present democratic government, northern states took 52.6% of the horizontal allocation, while local councils in the north equally shared 63.9% and this was against 21%.

CONCLUSION

As this work is out to address the issue of lopsidedness in the resource control in the federation most especially in the democratic dispensation we are now, this study has contributed its quota to the ever expanding frontier of human knowledge in the area of resource control and federalism in the Nigeria's context. Consequently, it stands to also enhance proper understanding of the effects of policy makers (Government) actions or in actions on the Nigeria political system. Thus, the work while adding to the body of existing literature on the even distribution of resources particularly in the context of federalism in Nigeria, it highlights the indispensable need by the policy-makers and government to properly consider the multiple interests that characterize the pluralism of Nigerian federalism.

Finally, one must state clearly that the Federal Government under Umaru Yar'Adua/Jonathan had taken frantic efforts to put an end to the crisis as a result of resource control agitation. The activities which includes: creation of Niger Delta ministry, and amnesty option. Other governments since 1958 have set up very high powered commissions to look into the problems of the Niger Delta and the committees have submitted far-reaching and comprehensive, reports, they have suffered the same fate i.e non-implementation. In cases where some of the recommendations have been considered at all, they have been taken out of context and implemented piecemeal or without the required enthusiasm, constituency and monitoring. Some of the reports were not even touched at all; no white paper was issued, and no follow-up implementation and monitoring mechanisms were set up by Government. This meant that the will and required enthusiasm to set in motion processes for a developed, peaceful and progressive Niger Delta were absent.

It will not be out of place to state that the current condition which the people of the Niger Delta Region find themselves and the country is entangled, characterized by violence, kidnappings, oil theft, illegal bunkering, political uncertainty, economic dislocation, youth restiveness, inter and intra community suspicion and conflict is the result of non implementation of the recommendations of various reports on the Niger Delta. Insensitivity, neglect and at times, marginalization of already powerless and devastated communities have made it possible for political opportunists, bad leaders, corruption, waste, institutional decay and inefficiency to thrive.

REFERENCES

1. Akindele S.T. et al, Fiscal Federalism and Local Government Finance in Nigeria *"An Examination of Revenue Right and Physical Jurisdiction"*. International Review of Administrative Science, an International Journal of Comparative Political Administration, Brussels, Belgium, Sage Publication London (Vol. 68 number iv 2002). Pp 557-558.
2. Asisi Asobie, "Centralizing trends in Nigerian Federalism" in Tunde Babawale et al, ed, Re-inventing Federalism in Nigeria (Lagos F.E.F; Malthouse Press Ltd 1998). Pp 14-52.
3. Cyril Obi I. (1998): The Impact of Oil on *Nigeria's Revenue Allocation System: Problems and Prospects for National Reconstruction:* Kunle Amuwo et al (eds) in Federalism and Political Restructuring in Niger. Ibadan, Spectrum Books Ltd.
4. Elaigwu J.I. (1983): *Sub-National States and the Future of Federation in Nigeria.* The Journal of Political Economy Vol. 1, (2) Pp. 1-26.
5. Eme Ekekwe (1986): *Class and State in Nigeria.* England, Longman Group Ltd.
6. Garuba, D.S (2003): *Oil and the Politics of National Resources Governance in Nigeria,* A Paper Presented at the XIV Biennial Congress of the African Association of Political Science (AAPS) in Durban, South Africa, June.
7. Gini A. Mbanefo and Festus O. Egwakhide (1998): *Revenue Allocation in Nigeria Derivation Principle Restructuring the Nigeria.* Kunle Amuwo et al (eds) Ibadan, Spectrum Books Ltd.
8. Gurr T.R. (1985): *Minorities at Risk: A Global View of Ethno Political Conflict:* Washington D.C.U.S, Institute of Peace Press P. 16.
9. Gurr, T.R. (1985): *Minorities at Risk: A Global View of Ethno Political Conflict:* Washington D.C. U.S, Institute of Peace Press P. 16
10. James Onanefe Ibori (2000): "South-South Zone. The Keynote Address at the Meeting of Governors and National

Assembly Members from the South-South States in Nigeria at Government House Asaba, on Friday 31st March Lagos, Jermie Publishers (Nig) Ltd.

11. John Rawls (1971): *A Theory of Justice*: USA Harvard University Press.
12. Keith Panter (1989): *Solider and Oil:* London, Frank Case.
13. Mike Kwanashie: *Revenue Allocation Formula and the Political Economy of Nigerian Federalism in Constitutional Federalism and Democracy in Nigeria*- Etambie E.O. Alemika and Festus O. Okoye (eds) Kaduna Human Rights Monitor.
14. Ogban Ogban-Iyam; "Federalism in Nigeria; Past, Present and Future" in Tunde Babawale et al, ed, Re-inventing Federalism in Nigeria (Lagos F.E.F) Malthouse Pres Ltd 1998) pp 57-71.
15. Olowonini G.D (1998) *Revenue Allocation and Economics of Federalism*, in Amuwo K. et al (eds). Federalism and Political Restructuring in Nigeria, (Ibadan: Spectrum and IFRA).
16. Olufemi Falana (1996): *Three –and-a-half Decades of Federalism in Nigeria*. Isawa Elaigwu and R.A. Akindele (eds) in Foundations of Nigerian Federalism (1960-1995). National Council of Intergovernmental Relations, Abuja.
17. Olufemi Falana (1996): *Three-and-a-half Decades of Federalism in Nigeria*. Isawa Elaigwu and R.A. Akindele (eds) in Foundations of Nigerian Federalism (1960-1995). National Council of Intergovernmental Relations, Abuja.
18. Oronto Doglas (2005): *The Question of Resource Control and Ownership* April 28 pg. 33.
19. Oyeleye O. and Olatunji O; "The Military and the Politics of Revenue Allocation" in Oyeleye Oyediran, Ed Nigerian Government and Politics under Military Rule 1966-1979. (Lagos: Friends foundation Publishing Ltd, 1988). Pp 73-86.
20. Sagay I. (2000): *Federalism Constitution and Resource Control,* Pointer Newspaper Thursday 15, October pg. 18.
21. Wagbefo, M. (1996): *On the Rawlisan Theory of Justice* in Benin Journal of Science, Vol. 5 No. 1 and 2 November.

ABSTRACT

The paper examined the agitation for resource control and its implication on Nigerian Federalism. In achieving this, the study traced the evolution of Nigerian federalism as the trigger for the agitation for resource control in Nigeria, political antecedents of resource control right from the inception of military rule in Nigeria in (1966), examined the agitation for resource control in Nigeria, and basic issues in resource control on Nigerian federalism.

With all these, the paper established the relationship between Nigerian federalism and the agitation for resource control. It also examined the logic of resource control in an emerging democratic rule in Nigeria. The issue of resource control should be seen as a pointer towards enjoyment of democratic rule in Nigeria. The issue of resource control should be seen as a pointer towards enjoyment of democratic dividends for the oil producing areas; however, reverse is the case for Nigeria. The results showed vices among the youths as inconsistency in government policies had led to the bunkering and kidnapping of expatriates for money.

The study concluded that the Federal Government under the current dispensation had played a crucial role towards the distribution of resources in the oil producing areas in order to reduce the persistent agitation for resource control. In the process, several measures had been taken to ensure even distribution of resources, providing the right and enabling environment for the oil producing areas, enhance proper understanding of the effects of policy maker's actions or inactions on the Nigerian federalism as it relates to resource control.

CHAPTER TWELVE

AN EX-RAY OF THE JUDICIARY AS AN ARM OF GOVERNMENT IN NIGERIA 1960 - 1999

PROF. A.T OYEWO AND M.L.A SALAWU (PH.D)

INTRODUCTION

The Judiciary all over the developed countries is being accorded greater respect and better treatment, than in Nigeria. The Judiciary is the hope of the common man, for justice is an indispensable prerequisite for the orderly existence of any society and if justice is removed, then what one gets in return is disorderliness, breach of peace, near anarchy and kingdoms of gangs of criminal at a large scale; hence the light of justice must not be quenched at any given time, in order to promote stability of happiness 'cum' orderliness for the generality of the people living in a particular society. Thus, the judiciary must be accorded a pride of place in any democratic society – if we are to build a stable and prosperous nation.

This paper scans through the ways Nigerian judiciary has been handled and being manipulated within the hierarchies of government and concludes that the Nigeria judiciary has been terribly neglected; relegated to the background; seriously undermined and slighted within the rank and file of the entire government.

The Institution has not been accorded the dignity and entailing respects which it deserves, and it is a serious conjecture, if it is being considered as a related atom in the building of the nation in Nigeria.

We should therefore not be deceived, but change our non-challant attitude to give the institution adequate recognition and respect since it is saddled with the duty of dispensing justice; for any nation that does not do justice cannot know peace and that is why in all religions, justice is basic, otherwise there will be no peace except peace of the grave yard.

The judiciary plays predominant roles any where in the world, like in Nigeria, for the organic growth of the nation, its dogged determination to give equal justice both to the rich and the poor alike, without a differential category of justice to the rich and another category to the poor is unparalleled. Its duties of impartiality, are praise-worthy and its uncompromising attitude, in giving judgments against the government, whenever a government errs, are exemplary since the body does not surrender leadership to the garment, while the shoe does not tell the foot how big to grow.

Nigerian Government must therefore have a change of mind, in order to accord our judiciary respect and a pride of place.

Areas of Disparity

Our judiciary became downgraded, turn-turtled, despised and looked low upon with jaundiced eyes, a few years after Nigeria got independence.

Many degrading changes took place, that were sufficient enough to take the wind out of judiciary's sails, but for the aptitude and stead-fastness of our judges, who refused to budge or allow the turn of events and seeming opprobrious treatments to affect their judicial oath of office.

Take for example, before independence and up to the 30th day of September 1963, a Chief Justice of Nigeria or of any Region of Nigeria could not be removed from office unless a consent was obtained from the Queen-in-Council.

Equally, as soon as a person is appointed to fill such a post, he became automatically by the Queen of England; but the turn of events became glaring and evident from the 1st day of October, 1963 when only the British subjects were entitled to be knitted automatically on getting appointed to such posts in the judiciary.

Another discouraging factor is that, while top-most civil servants and other senior administrative officers, like Secretaries to Governors get recognition by decorating them with such titles on appointment in 1976, yet Chief Judges of States, Justices of our Court of Appeals in addition to the Supreme Court Judges were not thus, decorated as of right with a CON or CFR on appointment.

This disparity can neither be justified nor equitable. One feels that, our judges should be better handled with the kid's gloves and accorded heavy recognition than administrative officers. After all, the work of judges cannot be compared favorably with those of the administrators.

Our judges, do a lot of work under unbearable conditions than the administrators. As a matter of fact, Nigerian Judges are doing their utmost best by maintaining and enhancing standard in the administration of justice despite all odds, and notwithstanding the facts that many of their Courts and Chambers lack many infrastructural facilities, which are normally pertinent and conductive to the discharge of their duties.

For instance, they have to work under stress and strain by listening to the litigants, take down their evidence personally, go to their chambers and or libraries, to refer to authorities in aid of their judgments, unlike what happens in America and England.

One will be worried to stay in any of the Courts for hours, because of the incessant shortage of electricity which more often than not, make people (including the judges) to sweat profusely, contrary to the use of nature.

Also, one notices that their Chambers and in fact the Courtrooms are not averagely equipped with books, law journals and periodicals, owing to lack of funds to purchase them. To add to the avalanche of problems facing the bench in Nigeria, is the fact that more often than not, the magistrates are not equipped with books; hence, unless a Counsel parts away with the authorities cited by him, it is an uphill task for such Magistrates to cross Check. We really pity such trial judges and magistrates, who in the circumstances are made to act like students, by their regularity of library attendance.

Something definitely ought to be done. The States and the Federal Governments must provide sufficient in their estimates, in order to obviate the obtaining malaise and improve the system of the administration of justice in Nigeria. After all, Counsel take it as their important duty in the administration of justice to cite authorities which will support their arguments, while if the judge makes a brief note of the argument and authorities, he would read those authorities cited, in order to assist him arrive at a good judgment.

Lastly, one may draw an inference from the decision of Ibrahim Vs. States that judges in this part of the world needed to be pitied for lacking infrastructural facilities to cope with their duties.

Ubeazone, JCA., said as follows in the case:-

> "It must be realized that judges in this country work under severe strain and are subject to great stress.
> Unlike some countries like the United States of America where judges have attorneys attached to them who do the research for them under computerized system, and produce a draft judgment; the Nigerian judge has to hear a case, take evidence and counsel's address in hand, take the record book home and write the judgment after doing the researches himself, including looking for law reports and other books with which to write his judgment. The Nigerian judge deserves sympathy and commendations rather than condemnation, in view of the nature of his work and the circumstances under which he operates".

Apart from the few instances given above, some states in fact, do not have adequate living accommodations for their judges, who have to travel many miles before getting to the courts, at the risk of their lives. One feels seriously that, it is high time, Nigerian Judges were handled with the kid's gloves that they deserve. A halt must therefore be made, to these acts of deficiency in order to honour our judiciary, while the Courtrooms decorum has to be maintained with all seriousness. To us, we feel the judiciary has been neglected in a number of ways, too numerous to be mentioned in this chapter.

Judges Salaries

Added to the disadvantages scored against the judges, is the fact that, they salaries *are not as high as those in the civil service* nor are they, all that enhancing, as would be found in all developed countries. For instance, a High Court Judge in England and Ireland to mention a few, earns a higher salary than the Prime Minister of the United Kingdom of Great Britain, whereas the contrary is the position in Nigeria. It must be realized that, the responsibilities of the judges are much more preponderant than, both the legislators and the executives, hence they do deserve higher pay. What one notices is, when the legislator are elected, they would be asking for quixotic amount for accommodation with other comforts, whereas nothing by way of an enhanced payment, is accorded to the offices of the judges.

Judges cannot table motion on the floor of the house, to air their grievances and thus they suffer in silence. Something figuratively has to be done so as not to relegate this arm of the government further into the background, like fags to be seen and not heard.

The Protocol:

The judiciary has suffered a lot of denegation of their rights in Nigeria, even under State/Federal Protocol – and experts on Constitutional Law, have not been happy over this unacceptable treatment, which is difficult to understand, like a Greek puzzle.

It must be remembered that, Nigeria practices a sort of government, which recognizes the system of separation of powers. Thus, their constitution favors a tripartite form of government which predominantly consists of (1) The Executive (2) The Legislature and (3) The Judiciary. These three bodies, must all join hands together, like equal partners to steer the ship of the nation. It is unequivocally laid down that none of the bodies should transact and or usurp the functions of another.

Equally recognized under that order of protocol, is that the President representing the Executive is No. 1 person, while the President of the Senate and the Chief Justice of Nigeria should be No. 2 and No. 3 citizens respectively, in the order of protocol. Students of constitutional history, will note that, before Nigeria became a Republic on the 1st of October, 1963, the Chief Justice of Nigeria was usually regarded as No. 2 citizen on the protocol list, and it was so much obviously imperative for him to act as Governor-General, whenever the then Governor –General was on leave.

Equally notable, is the fact that, the 1963 Constitution like the earlier one of 1960, recognizes the distribution of powers into what we have discussed above as (1) The Executive (2) The Legislative and (3) The Judicial bodies. One is therefore worried, to see how and why the Chief Justice of Nigeria has been conspicuously undergraded in the protocol list. Why must he not retain his constitutional position and be ranked as No,. 3, at least on the protocol list?

This agitative question, became pronounced during the military regime which made our Chief Justice of the Federation, to rank after even lieutenant colonels of both the Supreme Military Councils and then armed forces ruling Council. This is an aberration from the path of rectitude and it should be corrected now, at the nick of time, in order to achieve the dividends embedded in the spirit of co-operative federalism.

One on this score, may postulate likely problems. That is, one may imagine a situation where the executive president, the president of the Senate, the Chief Justice of Nigeria, the Vice-President and the Speaker of the House of Representative may have occasion to be together on a national function. What will then be the protocol order? Who sits before whom and what number does he take? It is the unshaken belief of these writers that, the President takes his No. 1 position, the Senate President takes his No. 2 position, and the Chief Justice of Nigeria will take his No. 3 position; while *the Vice-President and the Speaker of the House of Representative should* take the 4th and 5th seats/positions respectively.

We are fortified by this stance in that, since the only recognized substantive organs of the government are:- (1) The Executive, (2) The Legislator and (3) The Judiciary, it is then obvious that, after the substantive holders of those posts have been accorded recognition comes the Vice-President and the Speaker of the House of Representative, *for one does not consider for one does not consider an alternative claim in law after the main claim has been granted and concluded.*

It will therefore be as deceptive as the mirage of the desert and incongruous, as opposing situations to allow either the Vice President or the Speaker of the House of Representative to unsurp the place of the Chief Justice of Nigeria. For, to do so, is not only perilous and risky, if we want co-operation to exist, but also hazardous, untenable and unjustifiable.

The Recovery of public property and its effect on the exalted position of the Judiciary

As soon as Shagari Government was overthrown by a military coup detat, the Federal Military Government passed a Decree (Supremacy and Enforcement of Powers) Decree No. 13 of 1984, which effective date was from May 17, 1984 and subsequently the Recovery of Public Property (Special Military Tribunals) was enacted.[3]

Those Decrees, No. 3, 8 and 14 of 1984 were made to commence, as from the 31st day of December, 1983 retrospectively. And by the provision of the Decrees, any public officer who-

(a) has engaged in corrupt practices or has corruptly enriched himself or any person;
(b) as by virtue of abuse of his office contributed to the economic adversity of the Federal Republic of Nigeria;
(c) has in any other way been in breach of the code of conduct, or
(d) has attempted, aided, counseled, produced, or conspired with any person to commit any of the offences set out in this section will be guilty.

Panels were chosen which consisted of some judges from the court of Appeals as members only. Each of the panels was to be headed by a member of the Armed Forces (As Chairman).

This contravened the long cherished practice in the judiciary, and the judges protested; but despite their protests and unity of purpose not to serve in such tribunals, the then Chief Justice of Nigeria called the judges individually and instructed them to proceed as directed by the Military Government.

We do not feel that the then Chief Justice did that on his own free volition, but we are inclined to suggest that he has been subdued so to do by forces beyond his control. This is a glaring example of the usurpation of duties and ill – treatment of the judiciary by the Executive.

However, thanks to the courage and fortitude of the members of the bar, who stood their grounds unrelentingly, to uphold the integrity of the judiciary by boycotting appearances before such tribunals. This proves glaringly that, there is no limit to the contribution which the legal profession could not make to the improvement of the administration of justice, which should be enforced by positive action.

The lawyers have also proved that, the law all over the world, is expected to be catalyst of societal values, attitudes and development. It is the last hope of the common man to be applied by the judges. Therefore, if the judiciary is made to take a back seat, by making laymen chairmen of tribunals, where the judges are just mere members, it means then that, the judges have been made lame ducks and irrelevant in the administration of justices[4]. This has shown the disgraceful manner, under which the judiciary has been handled. The poser is, whether the executive should be allowed to do the work of the judiciary, in blatant contradiction to the rule of law and the ever cherished principle embedded in the doctrine of separation of power?

We are convinced like a multiplication table that, such an act will never happen in any civilized country, which adorns justice in all its entirely and respects its judiciary, as the last hope of the common man.

Definitely, this incident in Nigeria, where solders are made to entertain and decide cases, (and judges thus relegated to the background), will lend a lot of weight to deciding cases with manifesting prejudices, whimsy, ignorance and venality with each decision not connected, but poles apart from the theory and practices of the legal norms leading then to arbitrariness and victimization,. The practice should not be allowed to rear its head again.

Other Factors

Judges in Nigeria appear not to be adequately motivated, nor compensated in many respects for the judiciary on many occasions is usually and at random, left to the whims and caprices of the executive, like dominant masters to their servants who then could toss them up and down intolerably.

It is a known fact that, generally the judges movement are restricted, unlike that of any member of either the legislative or executive arm of the Government because of the nature of the judges' work, so as to ensure impartiality. A judge for instance must refuse to go out with, a person standing trial before him, when the proceedings are pending and up to a reasonable time after judgment must have been delivered, unlike what happens to the members of both the House of Representatives and the Senate, in the cases of Hon. Salisu Buhari and Senator Ewerem, who mixed freely undisturbed with their other members during the pendency of actions taken against them.

Added to this disparity, are the enormous incursionary devices done by the Executive to the Judiciary, by curtailing most of their beneficial needs in order to make the judiciary a lame duck or to reduce them to the position of a dog that can only bark and not bite. One considers some of the measures taken as repulsive and or contemptuous, calling therefore for an urgent re-orientation, since law is a catalyst of social value, attitudes and development.

The Judiciary is expected to be a bulwark of safety, for the people in all respects and particularly, whenever the executive goes wrong or becomes oppressive. Hence, it is the contention of this chapter that if the judiciary is driven to a corner where it takes a back seat like this in Nigeria, it will soon become a lame duck and irrelevant in the reckoning of the statutes or even the common man. Something positively should be done to arrest the ugly situation.

Comparative Studies

Judges in Nigeria are as effective as their counterparts all over the world; and since Nigerian government is a borrowed relics of both the English and American systems, it therefore calls for reason why, we should emulate those countries like the United States of America, the United Kingdom, Japan, Australia and Newzealand to mention a few, where judges are only enjoined to attend the Courts not more than between 32 and 40 weeks a year. That stance, is denied to Nigeria judges who were even expected to work from mornings till very late at nights during the 1982 election.

Moreover, a time lag stipulation imposed by section 140 (2) and 129(2) of the 1982 Act, making it mandatory for election to be concluded within 30 days appears to infringe the provisions of section 258 of the 1979 Constitution which make it mandatory for Courts to deliver their decisions in writing not later than 3 months after conclusion of evidence and final address. The limitation period of 30 days as contained in the Act, affects both the members of Courts and litigants considerably. It has been branded as an unwarranted interference in the affairs of the court of judicature. Apart from working hardship for the judges, it has proved inimical for the people, since judges will have to work throughout the nights on such election petitions. That and many others are the situation in Nigeria. And as a matter of fact, in March, 1976 leave of judges were curtailed in Nigeria to 30 days only in a year.

In the same vein, judges were banned from spending their leave abroad – (overseas) where they could rest better and gain better enlightenment, even if such judges could personally meet all necessary expenditure entailing such a leave.

As if these were not enough, Aguda[6] pointed out that attempts were even made in 1976 to equate the workload of a civil servant or a soldier, as equivalent to that of the judiciary; hence judges were made to report for duties from 7.30a.m to 3.30.p.m.

It would appear that Nigerian Government, should be made to realize the essential value of the principles engulfed in the IN-SERVICE -TRAINING. Therefore, the prohibition of judges from attending international conferences as at that time, should be made a thing of the past and terrible to relate in this exercise. International conferences for the judges, must be made compulsory; after all, both the executive and legislature, travel incessantly outside Nigeria for comparative advantages, hence judges should be made compulsorily to attend international conferences for the cross fertilization of ideas.

The Purge of 1975 – 1976

The greatest mistake made by the Military Government in Nigeria, was the purge of the entire civil service, which was undertaken during the Muhammed and Obasanjo regimes. The (the Military Government) then undertook to do this on the pretext of alleged, alarming rate of corruption, abuse of office and or inability to perform effectively, duties and functions bestowed on the civil servants.

However, General Obasanjo halted this process, because of the negative impact it has received among the members of the community, and resultantly, because the good elements in the bureaucracy were also affected, much because their heads of department do not like their faces, or because they had personal animosity between each other and or one another – i.e, factors that were irrelevant to the continued existence of their jobs.

Thus, the effects of the purge were essentially negative and those officers who survived it, began having second thoughts about the job – Security, and whether staying in the service was worthy the risk of the humiliation involved?

What surprises reasonable men and lovers of justice, is to discover that, the judiciary was also affected by this odious exercise in so much that, dedicated, hardworking, analytical and productive judges were rid of their exalted positions unfairly and unjustifiably. The judges were not alleged of any wrong doing and they were not given any opportunity, in compliance with their constitutional rights, to defend their good names and reputations. And as Aguda commented, their exercise became counter productive for it was capable of producing a weak and trembling bench.

Other facilities

The judiciary in Nigeria without fear of contradiction, appears to have suffered enormous depression and it ought to have been affected by diseases and illnesses, owing to the following list of symptoms:-

For instance, it has suffered considerably from the hands of the politicians, who make/made oscillatory and unfavorable decisions against it on many occasions. And most especially and spectacularly, the Military Governments have taken serious annihilative measures to disrupt the continued survival of the system. It has infact, been made to suffer an acute shortage of funds, since its financial base and avenues for monetary support, are too narrowly based, to be all that enhancing and effective.

What is worse is that from time to time, it receives left handed compliment and looked low upon without recognition, by both the Executive and the Legislative arms of the Government, just because the judiciary refused to dance to their music.

Lastly, many restrictive orders and legislations were made either against the proprietary, fundamental or constitutional rights of the judges, thereby subjecting both their rights of movements and health care delivery, to the whims and caprices of the other two arms of

Government. As a case study, Ogundere[8] discussed exhaustively on the Judges good health and made us to realize that, serious incursions with oscillatory and unfavorable decisions have been made against the cherished custom of taking adequate precautions for the judge's good health.

It has been pointed out that, before 1966 coup, the health of judges was accorded a priority. Many hospitals were built in some States exclusively meant to be attended by the judges. And among such hospitals could be mentioned the Jericho Nursing Home at Ibadan and the Creek Hospital in Lagos.

As at this time, a judge including any senior civil servant could call for a Senior Government Doctor to come and treat him in his house – even beside his bed.

However, all these good arrangements were changed and overturned as soon as the Military Government came to power in Nigerian scene; and it was reported that a mellowed change of mind became apparent in 1973, when immediately after the death of Alhaji Atta, the then Secretary to the Government – General Gowon ordered that, all senior civil servants as well as judges, should be allowed to have medical check up overseas periodically.

This arrangement has been accorded severe condition nowadays, for it is only when a judge is seen to be dangerously sick and/or near a point of death that he would be allowed to be flown abroad, because it is felt that, facilities ought to be available in Nigerian hospitals for all sorts of treatment, whereas our hospitals are patently seen to be without drugs and/or necessary equipment. Thus our hospitals, have been reduced to mere consulting clinics.

It is our contention in this chapter that, this accredited dogma, should change, so as to give our judges better opportunities to look after their health. After all, health is wealth and a good health scheme is the hub around which the existence of any society depends, since no society can exist for long, without good and environmental sanitation schemes. The Nigerian government should therefore take a hint from these postulates.

Evaluation of the Judiciary

Judges in Nigeria, are men of integrity who have nothing to hide and that is why, they stood their grounds under even turbulent conditions to uphold the rule of law and the integrity of their institution. They believe like Robert Ingersol[9], that domination and perdition would befall a nation which denies her people justice.

Ingersoll said as follows:

> "All the reeks on either side of the stream of time,
> and all the nations that have passed away – all her warning
> that no nations founded upon injustice can stand.
> ***From the said – enshrouded Egypt, from the marble Wilderness of Athens, and from every fallen, crumbling stone of the one Mighty Rome comes a wail as it were, the cry that no nation founded upon injustice can permanently stand".***

And that is why judges in Nigeria try their best "ad astra per aspera" – not minding the outburst of intimidation and arbitrariness of the Government, to do justice in cases meant for their determination. This was shown in many cases and particularly in Governor of Lagos State and Others Vs. Odumegu Ojukwu and Ors. [10]

Where ESO JSC said as follows:-

> ***"There essence of the rule of law is that it should never Operate under the rule of force or fear... and there must Not be ... an attempt to infuse timidity into Court and Operate a sabotage of cherished rule of might as against the rule of might as against the rule of right ... it must never be"..***

Eso further pointed out in this celebrated case that by the 1979 Constitution of Nigeria, the Executive, the Legislature and the Judiciary are equal partners in the running of a successful government. One must not exist in sabotage to the other, or else there is chaos.

In other words, Eso's views are that, an executive act of government must comply both with the principles embedded in the rule of law, and those recognized by the enabling law or else, it may be challenged in Court. Hence all exercised powers must be done in conformity with the law of the land. This was also the *ratio decidend* in the case of *Muhammed Olayori and Anor.* Vs. *The Lagos State Government11*, a Lagos suit No. M/196/69. Here the appellant and four others were arrested and detained by or under the authority of the Nigerian Army, for receiving money for services not rendered or good supplied to the Nigeria Army. But, when they promised by force to pay the money on a certain date, they were released on bail, and they were subsequently arrested, when they failed to fulfil the terms of repayment, which they promised in terorem before their conditional release.

Hence, finally they were detained under section 3 (1) of the 1967 Decree and subsequently an application for Habeas Corpus was made.

Granting the application, the judge observed that Decree No. 24 of 1967 can only be applied for the prevention of all acts tending to endanger the security of the State. It was meant to give power, to order the detention of trouble makers, and one is in doubt whether it can be applied to corrupt persons.

His Lordship, further said that although every members of our society should abhor corruption and embezzlement of public funds, but if we are to live by the rule of law, if we are to have our actions guided and restrained in certain ways for the benefit of society in general and individual members in particular, whatever post we hold, we must succumb to the rule of law. The alternative, is anarchy and chaos, and the whole purport of the Defence Regulations and emergency regulations is to prevent this state of things. Hence, an order for their immediate release was made accordingly.

The same principles was applied in the cases of Eleko Vs. Officer Administering the Governor of Nigeria and Rabbe and Ors. Vs Inspector – general of Police and anor[13] Lagos suit No. M/197/69. Also could be mentioned the case of Agbaje Vs The Commissioner of Police[14] suit No. CAW/81/69 of 27/8./60 Court of Appeal, West.

In Agbaje & Ors case, an application for a habeas corpus was filed for unlawful detention of the applicant in the Police Station, Ibadan, by the Commissioner of Police as from 31st May, 1969 to June 12, 1969, without giving him reasons why he was so detained despite repeated demands for such explanations.

In answer, the Commissioner of Police said that he Has acted under the delegated power granted him by Virtue of section 3 (1) of the Armed Forces and Police (special powers) Decree No. 24 of 1967 which provides as follows:

> ***"If the Inspector – General of Police ... is satisfied that any person is or recently has been concerned in acts prejudicial to public order in the preparation or investigation of such act, and by that reason therefore it is necessary to exercise control over him, he may be ordered in writing, directing that person incharge of any Police Station as the case may be, if an order made in respect of any person under this section is delivered to him to keep that person in custody until the order is revoked".***

In granting the application, it was held that, the orders made by the Inspector-General of Police, under which the applicant was detained in a Police Station in Ibadan, during the relevant period were not valid orders under section 3 (1) of Decree No. 24 of 1967. And the Commissioner of Police, Western State, has no authority under those orders which he relied upon, to detain the applicant in a Police Station in Ibadan, during the relevant period.

What concerns us here is the breach of the application of the rule of law. Here power has been arbitrarily exercised at the whims and caprices of the power that be, contrary to the decision of the Indian Courts in Singh Vs Delhi[15] 15 Sup. Ct. Journal 326, where it was laid down emphatically that's

"Those who feel called upon to deprive other persons of Their personal liberty in the discharge of what they Consider to be their duty, must strictly and scrupulously Observe the forms and rules of law".

In the case of Lakanmi Vs. A.G. Western State [16], the Supreme Court held that Decree o. 45 of 1968 was ultra vires since it was nothing short of a legislative judgment, an exercise of judicial power. The Court held also that, the doctrine of

separation of powers exists in Nigeria and it cannot be whittled down.

This judgment frightened the Supreme Military Council which necessitated, their passing of another decree which abrogated this judgment and its effects.

There are lots of interesting decisions, which show the forthrightness, bravery and ingenuity of the judiciary in Nigeria but space and time will not permit us to write on them.

However, it suffices to say that, the judiciary in Nigeria does not succumb to pressure from any arms of the Government. They constantly follow the rule of law and comply with the rules of natural justice, notwithstanding the ill-treatments meted to them as above written.

Judges in Nigeria do believe that, to achieve a safe society, they must follow the rule of law, without yielding to pressure, arbitrariness and victimization, no matter what the people and authority say or perceive. They believe in the following Biblical quotations[17]

> "But and if ye suffer for righteousness sake, happy are
> Ye; and be not afraid of their terror, neither be troubled.
> But sanctify the Lord God in your heats; and be ready
> always to give an answer to every man that asked you
> a reason of the hope that is in you with weakness and
> fear....
> For it is better if the will of God be so that ye suffer for
> Well doing than for evil doing".

National Judicial Council

The establishment of the National Judicial Council as enshrined and entrenched by section 20 of the 3rd schedule to the 1999 Constitution of Nigeria will go a long way in improving our judicial system.

First, the appointment of the judges will no longer depend on the swing of political pendulum, but will depend preponderantly on the integrity, ability and appropriate training or qualifications in law of each individual who aspires to go to the bench.

Second, the new appointment process devised by the constitution, will no doubt ensure that, judges shall have a guaranteed tenure until their mandatory retirement age or the expiry of their term of office where such exists.

Thus, the question of arbitrary exercise of powers in dismissing judges from their exalted positions, in addition to compounded manipulation of the entire judiciary as it was done during the Military Regime will vanish into the thin air. *Nwankwo and others.*[18] writing on the *Limits of justice in Nigeria* gave us comprehensive examples of the insecurity of Judicial tenure as follows:

There have been instances where the military removed judicial officers from office without giving them the opportunity to present their own defence. For instance, in the former Bendel State, in 1986, a Judge, Donald Ikomi, who was a murder suspect, was removed from office even before the case had been concluded. After he was acquitted, the dismissal was converted to forced retirement. In 1989, Usman Mohammed, a Katsina State High Court Judge accused the State Chief Judge of gross professional misconduct and interference. On April, 29, 1990 without giving him a hearing, the AFRC dismissed Mohammed. He subsequently alleged that he had received several death threats and spent several weeks in hiding. His wife, a magistrate, was also threatened with removal. According to Mohammed, "all apparatus of government were directed against me because I denied them the chance to tele-guide me on the performance of my duty".

In 1984, under the Military Government of General Muhammadu Buhari, a Lagos High Court Judge, Yaya Jinadu was forced to resign after he had summoned a Federal Permanent Secretary, John Oyegun (who later become Edo State Governor), to appear in an action against the Government for wrongful termination of appointment. After failing to appear on five occasions, Justice Jinadu issued a bench warrant against Oyegun, following which government officials approached him and asked him to go and apologise to the Federal Attorney-General. He chose to resign instead.

Not even the position of the highest judicial officer in the land has been spared this type of meddling. In 1972, the then military ruler, General Yakubu Gowon, had amended the procedure for removing judicial officers as contained in a previous decree making it a matter of his own discretion as head of State.

In 1975, his successor, General Muritala Mohammed used this provision to retire the Chief Justice, the Late T.O. Elias, who was appointed a few years earlier, ostensibly on healthy grounds.

Ironically, Elias was elected a judge of the International Court of Justice at the Hague, barely three months later. And he served at the Hague until his death in 1991.

For the inferior courts, there are also procedures governing the removal of their officers. In the absence of judicial service commissions under the military, the task goes to the various Advisory Judicial Committees. In fact, most disciplinary actions are decided by the State's Chief Judges when allegation of misconduct are made against them, it is for the Chief Judge of the state concerned to establish the veracity of the allegations and make up his mind, whether the judicial officer concerned should be removed or not.

The tenure of this category of judicial officers, is the most precarious, as their fate depends solely on the decision of the Chief Judge. There is no Constitutional protection against unfair dismissal, leaving them open to removal, should the Chief judge be out to settle personal scores.

Enforcement of Judgment

The Judiciary appears to have been seriously slighted and ignored during military era in Nigeria, in so much that, judgments given against the military were rendered innocuous or phyrrhic and/ nor laughing stalks.

However, as examples are better than precepts, Nwankwo[19] also gave us few instances as follows, to buttress our contention.

In 1987, at the University of Benin, the School Authorities compulsorily retired three of its teachers, Dr. Festus Iyayi, Professor Itse Sagay and Professor John Odita and ordered them to vacate their residences in the University Campus. The three went to the high court to challenge their retirement and restrain the authorities from evicting them. The Court made an order, restraining the University authorities from evicting the teachers. This order was disobeyed and the properties of the teachers were forcefully thrown out of their University residences.

In 1989, in Gongola State, two contestants for the post of local government chairman in the Numan and Mayo-Belwa Councils had gone to court to challenge the results announced by the National Electoral Commission (NEC). The high court upheld their arguments, nullified the results earlier announced by NEC and substituted their names as the duly elected chairmen for their respective councils. This decision was affirmed by the Court of Appeal. In his reaction, however the military governor of the State, Wing Commander Isa Mohammed, refused to swear in the two Council Chairmen on the ground that it is only NEC and not the courts that can declare who is dully elected.

Again in September, 1988, Chief Gani Fawehinmi had his passport seized by the State on his return from a trip to London. Chief Fawehinmi, immediately filed an action in the Lagos High Court demanding the release of his passport. On 14th February, 1990, Judge Moni Fafiade ordered the State Security Service (SSS) to return the passport to Chief Fawehinmi. The SSS's applications for a stay of execution of the order was refused by the Court, yet the SSS refused to release the passport. The passport was to be returned a year after its seizure by the then Information Minister, Alex Akinyele, supposedly "as an act of clemency", but probably in response to public and press criticisms of government's action.

Other instances of disobedience of Court orders by officials of the Military Government, include the incident in July, 1990 when Justice Fredrick Odubiyi of the Shagamu High Court in Ogun State made an order restraining the State Governor from installing his choice to the traditional Chieftaincy stool of Akarigbo of Remo. The Governor, in reaction to the order enacted an edict nullifying the Court order; according to him, "to ensure public peace and safety", and proceeded to install the Government' choice as Akarigbo.Again on 19th February, 1991, Judge Francis Owobiyi, ordered the Army authorities to release a certain Gloria Mowarin, detained on account of her boyfriend's alleged involvement in the 22nd April, 1990 coup attempt. This order was not carried out for several months.

Conclusion and Recommendation

No doubt, this chapter has pointed out many of the ills, that have confronted our judiciary and in order to save its skin, we are going to make few suggestions as palliative remedies.

First, let us hope that, the members of the National Assembly and the Presidency who in figurative terms have been alleged of spending

Nigerian's money like a demented drug baron[20] will recognize that the judiciary have been badly hit for lack of funds, infrastructural facilities, bad working conditions with paucity of emoluments; and candidly depressed by many opprobrious acts of both the Executive and the Legislature as outlined above.Therefore, the two bodies should also realize that, owing to the paucity of wages attributed to the judicial officers, independent private legal Practitioners loath to take up appointments as judges thus increasing the work loads of our judges. It is therefore suggested and hereby recommended that, judges remuneration should be made attractive enough to compensate for the volume of work allocated to the judiciary. They should not longer be treated as financial scums and economic dregs without any form of remunerative responsibility[21]. Second, one is equally worried to see that, while members of the Senate and those in the House of Representatives are being paid N16,000.0 and N15,000.00 per day with 3.6 million and 3.5 million Naira for furniture allowance respectively, the judiciary has been ignored and relegated to the background for any such facilities, emoluments and or motivations, we need a positive reaction on this perspective.

Third, we are glad to state however that, the judges can no longer be dismissed at the whims and caprices of the executive, without the recommendation of the National Judicial Council; thus, judges can only be removed in proven cases of gross misconduct or for inability to fulfill judicial functions owing to illness or otherwise.

Fourth, we have equally noticed that, it is the Constitutional right of the National Judicial Council to recommend judges for appointment, for disciplinary control and for their removal from office.

Fifth, we have noted the inept attitude of restraining judges from attending international conferences, and it is out fervent belief in this writing that Judicial officers should be allowed to attend Seminars, Workships and International Conferences in order to keep them abreast with both legal development and their judicial functions.

Sixth, in view of the ever increasing functions of the judges, it is our recommendation that, adequate fund should be earmarked and budgeted to the judiciary to enable them function effectively, with the provision of adequate infrastructures in Courts.

Furthermore, we are of the opinion that the protocol list and the health cares of the judges highlighted in this chapter should be given attention and adhered to in order to promote effectiveness and efficiency.

Also we are advocating for a system of co-operative federalism between all the levels of the government; that is the executive, the legislature and the judiciary must take each other as partners, work together unrelentingly in order to produce unity and harmony in our body polity, since unity is strength; for it will be tragic to reduce judges to a sterile role and make an automation of them.

Endnotes

1. A.T. Oyewo – The Trial judge and his Guides in Nigeria – 1999 Jator Publishing Company at Page 9.
2. Ibrahim Vs State (1993) 2 NWLR) (Pt. 278) 735.
3. Decree No. 13 of 1984 (Supremacy and Enforcement of Powers)
4. T. Fagbohungbe – The Judicial Universe of Jusitice Kayode Eso. (1995) Deovonics Communications Network.

   A.T. Oyewo – The Law, Etiquette and Practice of Advocacy in Nigeria where Elias address to the Annual Bar Conference in Nigeria was quoted at page 23.
5. T,. Aguda – The Administration of Some Key Services – Judiciary being the text of a paper delivered on the 20 years of Nigeria Public Administration the Obafemi Awolowo University on Wednesday 15/10/80.
6. T. Aguda – Ibid…
7. See (a) Aguda T. – Ibid…
   (b) Oyewo A.T. – Administrative Law in Nigeria
   (c) Dare L.O. – The Western State Public Service and the Impact of Military Rule being a text of paper delivered at the National Conference on 20 years of Nigeria Public Administration 1960- 1980 at the Obafemi Awolowo University on Tuesday 11/10/80.3.
8. Ogundere J.D. – The Nigerian Judge and his Court, University Press Plc. 1994
9. Robert Ingersol was quoted by Krishner as contained in the Judicial Universe of Justice Kayode Eso at page 34 .. Opcit..
10. Governor of Lagos State and Ord. Vs. Odumegu Ojukwu and Ors. (1986) 1 NWLR (Pt. 18) 621 at 634.
11. Muhammed Olayori & Anor. Vs the Lagos State Government suit No. L/M/196/69.
12. Eleko Vs Officer Administering the Governor of Nigeria.
13. Rabbe and Ors. Vs. Inspector- General of Police and Anor. Suit no. LD/M/197/69
14. Agbaje Vs The Commissioner of Police Suit No. CAW/81/69 OF 27/8/60

15. Singh Vs Delhi 16 Sup. Ct. Journal 326
16. Lakanmi Vs. A.G. Western State
17. 1 Peter Chapter 13 Verse 14, 15 and 17
18. Nwankwo C and two others – NIGERIA – The limits of Justices constitutional Rights Projects 1993 pages 24 – 26.
19. Nwankwo C and two others – NIGERIA – The Limits of Justice .. Ibid.. at ages 51 - 53.
20. Festus Adebayo – Nigerian Tribune Newspaper of 26/3/2000 at page 3.

CHAPTER THIRTEEN

AN OVERVIEW OF CORRUPT PRACTICES IN THE TIERS OF GOVERNMENT IN NIGERIA

PROF. A.T OYEWO & M.L.A SALAWU (PH.D)

INTRODUCTION

Corruption connotes a dishonest, illegal or immoral behaviour, especially from someone with power. It is a sword with double edges and it involves both the giver and the receiver. It is an opprobrious act, and it is often referred to as an endemic disease. A corrupt society is a gall and warm wood entity, and thus a corrupt country can never triumph beyond the level of ruin and total extinction. It is therefore to save Nigeria from collapse and attune to uprightness with dedication to duties that this topic is chosen for discussion and possible solution to nip the ugly anathema in the bud. Efforts will be made to discuss the topic on comparative level. The paper will discuss corruption within our legislators, judiciary, the executive and local government.

CORRUPTION IN THE PAST

Corruption is predominant in Nigeria, and almost everywhere, our system is corrupt. The evil of corruption, manifesting in inefficiency and wastage, is a canker worm that has eaten deep into the fabrics of the Nigerian Society. Unfortunately, the Local Government, being an integral part of the society, cannot be absolutely exonerated from this odious stigma.

Also, it should be noted that there is corruption in our political life, thus political corruption has become our bane in Nigeria and as Rimi postulated, corruption in this country is very easy to identify since many people live beyond their legitimate earnings without any body asking them about the sources of their wealth.

CORRUPTION DURING MILITARY ERA

There was magnifying corruption during Gowon's regime.' Taiwo' remarked that the cases of corruption perpetrated by the governors and cabinet members reached such a ridiculous crescendo that an average observer trembled for the nation . For instance, the soldiers then resorted to buying their needed wearing materials individually outside, when Gowon would not raise a hand against fraudulent criminals.

It must be noted that Joseph Tarka was the Federal Commissioner to be accused of diverting away a substantial amount of the state's funds for personal purpose and instead of instituting a high powered probe into such cases, Gowon, thought the best penalty was to reshuffle the cabinet which he never did. Thus when Aper Aku therefore filled an affidavit in court, exposing in detail the magnitude of corruption in Gowon's administration, Gowon summarily clamped him into jail under detention orders.

GENERAL MURTALA MOHAMMED

Murtala's regime was a clean up exercise. He set up various judiciary panels of inquiry and people found guilty of corrupt enrichment were fired out of office, and of particular mention was 10 of the state governors in Gowon's regime including the civilian administrations of the then East Central State. The 10 were found guilty of corruption and abuse of office.

Thus, all ex-military governors and former administrators of the East central state, with the exception of Johnson and Rotimi, were found to have grossly abused their offices and guilty of several irregular practices. The governors affected were dismissed outright while their earnings and assets were confististicated.

CORRUPTION IN HIGH PLACES AND DURING ABACHA REGIME

The African Concord of 21/8/1986 no 104 has details of corruption in high places of Nigerian society between 1960 and 1986. The paper pointed out that for a long time in Nigeria, those who pilfered public purses have sometimes gone free until 1984 when the Buhari Junta consigned them into detention and jailed many of them to give them a taste of the pains in order to learn lessons. Definitely, corruption has griped governmental administration of Nigeria and has become an endemic disease to be cured, and it has contributed to a slow down of the National Development.

A quick look at Abacha's administration will make the following revelations. Gen. Sani Abacha allegedly allocated to himself lots of properties amounting to billions of Naira, as reported by the Vanguard of 3/9/99. Thus, 18 choice properties of his in addition to some of his aides were offered for sale to the public for not less than 2.56 billion Naira.

The buildings are located at Lagos, Abuja, Kano and Zaria while top on the list of the probed properties auctioned is "Cowries House", a nine storey office complex on the Victoria Island. This complex which has a penthouse stands on a 2428.77 square metres land at plot 636, Adeyemo Alakija Street, Victoria Island, was acquired by Abacha in the name of Stalembo Properties Nigeria's Limited. Added to all these acts of corruption is the fact that, huge amount of Nigeria's money has been siphoned to overseas countries through socio-cultural constraints.

Abacha, as the Head of State, made administrators and government functionaries to bend and twist all available rules and regulations in favor of the members of his own family at the expense of the down trodden masses in Nigeria. Hence his regime witnessed lots of disunity, trepidation and grief, the killing of anybody whom he may think does not want him to stay any further in office, as well as incessant depravations of liberty and curtailment of the rule of law cum fundamental human rights. The treasury was absolutely looted, foreign reserve was dried up and completely mis-used, motorist became barefooted walkers and disaffection became the lot of Nigerians in its entirety.

OFFICIAL LOOTING AND CORRUPTION

The stories of corruption during the Military regime of the Late General Sani Abacha are on the pages of newspapers, periodicals, journals and books. Plethora of evidence, exist to prove that the administration was a stinking and corrupt one. Looting pervaded the entire fabric of the administration in both the States and National levels. In Ogun State for instance, (see Punch Newspaper of 28/5/2000), a probe panel asked Group Captain Sam Ewang, (a one time Military Administrator), to refund a sum of N28million which was claimed to have been used to purchase and convey protection equipment, which was alleged to have been bought and were no where to be found. There was also a panel set up in the state to unravel circumstances that led to the loss of N20million at the State Council of Arts and Culture.

Similarly, nearly all the 36 States in the country were accused of embezzling over N10 billion, earmarked for ecological projects under the Late General Abacha's administration.

Another scandalous revelation is that of Ajaokuta buy back scam, involving former Abacha ministers, Anthony Ani and Bassir Dalhatu. However, Mallam Mohammed Haruna, Chief Press Secretary to Gen, Abdul-Salami Abubakar had admitted that Ani and Dalhatu shared DM 1.9 billion (98.8billion through the scam instead of N2.5billion). Later, Ani was reported to have returned a sum of DM 30million and N2million back to the government coffers. As this was not enough, another revelation was made against Alhaji Gwarzo, the then National Security Adviser, who reportedly surrendered huge sum of money and properties to the Federal Government.

In addition to all these, billions of naira were stolen from the coffers of the government through over invoicing, like the sum of N20million for purchase of the 25 Tampico trainer aircraft by Abacha Government. However, up to N2billion looted money have been found in Switzerland and other European countries including the United Kingdom, France, Germany and Luxemburg.

There were lots of the looting of the Treasury during Abacha's regime which were sufficient enough to support the clamour and kindle for the present democracy with the hope that the country will improve and move forward.

Added to the fold of the brazen looting of the treasury and corruption was the illegally acquired properties of the former Minister of the Federal Capital Territory, Lt. Gen. Jerry Useni, which were confisticated and sold off by the Federal Government. Indeed, glaring abuse of office prevailed and misappropriation of public funds were glaring during the Abacha regime, both at the State and Federal levels.

For instance, the former Military Administrator of Adamawa State, Navy Commander Kalu Igboamah, was alleged of taking away a Toyota Pick-up after leaving the office, and when challenged or indicted for this opprobrious act, he became funny and said: I am still keeping the vehicle because no representation was made to return it. I do not see it as too much of a gift to a person who served Adamawa State to the best of his ability.

Also the pronouncement credited to Okadigbo (Vanguard 5/8/2000) may be considered perished, shameless and worthless for his defence during the probe when he said as follows:

> *"The office of the Senate President carried a lot of responsibilities and it is my responsibility to protect the members of the National Assembly. That is what I swore to defend. And that is what I have been doing, since assumption of office".*

Query: Is this pertinent as a defence for his indictment on the accusation of official corruption? Are these statements adequate to explain how and why he spent an additional sum of N37million for his official quarters on which a sum of N25million had already been spent? Or, are the statements credited to him apt and succinct, to explain why he became a contractor for street lightning which does not fall within his portfolio? Or how could one explain the initial estimate which Okadigbo was alleged to have by passed and awarded same at a ridiculously high price to his cohorts?

However, enough has been said on the Abacha administration and all, hence we will now consider the situation in the fourth Republic.

CORRUPTION IN THE LEGISLATIVE HOUSES DURING THE FOURTH REPUBLIC

The fourth Republic started with President Olusegun Obasanjo taking the mantle of leadership on May 29, 1999. During that era, the Senate was indicted with lots of financial impropriety, misappropriation of funds and acts of corruption, coupled with the incessant abuse of office, in contract awards.

Thus, Senator Idris Kuta panel was set up which found Okadigbo, Senator Rowland S. Ovie the Chief Whip, Senator Gbenga Aluko – the Deputy Chief Whip, Senator Bala Adamu Chairman Senate Committee on special duties, Senator Abubakar H. Girei Chairman Senate service committee, in addition to Senator Aruwa, guilty of various offences ranging from corruption to other financial impropriety.

The Committee also found Alhaji Umaru Sani, the director of finance and supplies guilty, as it was reported that Umaru Sani had shown financial irresponsibility and lack of professionalism in the performance of his duties.

It was equally discovered that Alhaji Kabir Suleiman, the Director of Budget, Planning, Research and statistics was guilty of mismanagement, for many contracts not executed but were fully paid for without his making serious objection to them. He never cared to verify the actual market value of contractor's quotations. With regards to Okadigbo, the panel in the report discovered that;

1. The welfare package of N22.95million received by the Senate President without questioning for Sallah/Christians could not be justified in view of the nation's economy.

2. That the Senate President, with the speaker of the House of Representatives, inflated the street lightning project from N57million to N173million and awarded the alleged contract to a member of the House, purportedly fronting for both the Speaker and the Senate President respectively.

3. That the Senate President acted unfairly by diverting N200million votes, allocated for the equipment of the press centers for both Senate and the House Press Corporation and spent/allocated a total sum of N100million for the purchase of vehicles for the office of the Senate President, bringing the number of his fleet cars to 32.

4. Okadigbo was found reprehensible, for spending a total sum of N32million for the purchase of eight additional cars, (which could not be accounted for) for the office of the Senate President, bringing the number of his fleet cars to 32.

5. While the Senate approved a sum of N25million for the furnishing of the Senate President's residence, it was found that, a sum of N37,211,570 was spent by Chuba Okadigbo.

6. Okadigbo was also found liable for spending N5million on the installation and commissioning of 100KVA Generator for the Senate President's residence.

7. It was discovered that an inflated estimated amount of N15million was expended for the installation and commissioning of 100KVA Generator for the Senate President's residence.

All these lapses were quoted by the panel report as constituting an abuse of office by the Senate President (see News-watch of August 14, 2000).

AND having found the President of the senate guilty, the panel then urged him;

(a) To resign honourably, failing which he stands removed.

(b) To refund the sum of N12,211,570, being the unauthorized excess expenditure on the furnishing of the Apo Mansion.

The committee/panel in addition recommended that henceforth, a Senate President should not have more than 12 cars in his fleet, while arrangements should be made to retrieve the excess number of cars currently under the fleet of the Senate President. The following Reports would be found also in the News watch in verbatim:

FINDINGS ON SENATOR ROWLAND S. OVIE CHIEF WHIP

There is evidence that, the Chief Whip was directly involved in contract awards to three companies and these are:

(i) Cleaning and Gardening of Apo Legislators' Quarters, awarded to Zibagbo (Nig.) Ltd for N17million. This contract, according to the sharing arrangement presented by Senator Aluko, was to have been shared between the Chief Whip N7million, Senator M. Aruwa N5million and Senator JKN Waku N5million. Instead, it was awarded for N17million to Zibagbo Nig. Ltd. The company was fully paid the contracts sum even though the gardening commenced only a few days after this inquiry was instituted.

(ii) The contracts for cleaning and gardening of Apo Legislators' Quarters should be cancelled and the contractor asked to refund the payment made, because the contract was signed for one year (12 months) but was not started until June 2000, six months later, only after the scandal had erupted.

(iii) The Chief Whip, failed to declare his interest in Zibagbo Nig. and his connection with its directors.

(iv) He facilitated the award for consultancy services for the street light project estimated for N18million to TEEJAY Associates.

(v) He awarded contract to Markin-Dover Nig. Ltd. for the supply and installation of a generator to his official residence for the sum of N6million. The actual cost of 100KVA soundproof generator, is N3,130,335 and it was finally decided that, Senator Owie should be held responsible for the refund of N2,869,645.00

(vi) The Committee concludes that, the above acts constitute an abuse of office and therefore recommends that he resigns his positions as Chief Whip. Please find below the report and finding of the panel also on the under listed personalities.

FINDINGS ON SENATOR GBENGA ALUKO
DEPUTY CHIEF WHIP

Sentor Gbenga Aluko is at the center of all the contract scam in the Senate. As sole administrator of the senate service Committee, he grossly abused his office and became a dispenser of patronage to a select few. He awarded several contracts at inflated prices, to two companies owned by himself and his wife, Mrs. Olufemi Shile Aluko. These companies are Associated Logistics Ltd and Independent Strategists Ltd. Contracts to several other companies whose owners/ sponsors he refused to disclose and which are believed to be his proxies. Particularly, he awarded the computer contract for the supply of laptop computers to Triech Computers Ltd and that for N36million office equipment to a total of eleven companies, all at inflated prices.

Evidence before the committee shows that, he withheld the sum of 35million out of the amount provided for disbursement for the repair of their quarters. The committee finds Senator Gbenga Aluko to have abused his office and therefore recommended that:

(iii) He should resign as Deputy Chief Whip for these abuses.

(iv) He should refund the sum of N35million and a further N39,257,598million by which the computers and office equipment were over-priced as detailed in table five.

SENATOR FLORENCE ITA GIWA APP DEPUTY LEADER

Her company, Laboil Ltd was involved in at least two separate contracts to supply office equipment worth N4,506million and the fencing of her own official residence at an inflated price of N1,062,593.04. This contradicts her widely published denial that she had not got any contract from the Senate. The Committee concludes that the above acts constitute an abuse of office; hence the committee recommends that she resigns her position as deputy leader.

Senator Bala Adamu-Chairman Senate Committee on Special Duties

(i) The N10 million released by the senate for relief materials to riot victims in Kaduna and other affected areas was not properly accounted for. The prices of the items bought as relief materials were found to be high and the N1.5million paid for demurrage is unexplainable.

(ii) In order to shield senators from possible abuse, it is recommended that senators should not be involved in the purchase of relief materials and instead, cash should be presented to the intended beneficiaries.

(iii) It is recommended that, Senator Bala Adamu should fully retire the N10 million advanced to him.

Senator Abubakar H. Girei Chairman Senate service committee.

Senator A.H. Girei admitted initiating the memo to collect N6.2 Million to purchase Sallah gifts for the Senators, in which most of the items were over-priced, especially the cows and rams, which were bought at a unit cost of N500,000 and N20,000 respectively. On the basis of market survey, the unit of the ram bought is not more than N10,000.

It was recommended that the excess prices of N12,180,000 of the rams should be refunded by Senator Abubakar. H. Girei. Furthermore, Senator A.H. Girei connived with his counter part in the House of Representatives to appoint consultants, for phase III project when this was unnecessary because the contract was a Turkey project. It was recommended that this project be handed over to the relevant government agencies.

Senator Mukhar Ahmed, Senator Aruwa, handled allocation of the 117 official cars to senators. He could not produce a list of how those cars were allocated albeit, he told the committee that one of the cars was missing (Peugeot 504 station wagon). In their testimonies, Senator Evan Enwerem, Senator Chuba Okadigbo and director of finance and supplies claimed that Senator Aruwa was responsible for the 66 new cars bought for the National Assembly. He claimed he didn't participate in the purchase of vehicles, but later said that ASD motors offered a unit price of 2.2 million. Again, evidence including vouchers from the directors of finance and supplies show that Senator Aruwa was responsible for the purchase of the cars in question, as follows:-

(i)	6 Nos. of 5050/Evolution at	-	N3,119,000 each
(ii)	7 Nos. 504 S/WA/Cat	-	N2,410,250 each
(iii)	1 Nos. 504 Pick up Van at	-	N2,132,000 each
	Delivery charges	-	N2,217.600

Similarly, Senator Aruwa was connected with the street light project from the National Assembly to the Eagles Square, as shown both by the Senate President, Dr. Chuba Okadigbo and Director of Finance and Supplies.

It is therefore recommended that Senator Aruwa should be made to account properly for the vehicles he purchased for the National Assembly.

CORRUPTION IN OTHER QUARTERS AND THE JUDICIARY

Allegation of corruption is rampart in the Nigerian scene and of contemporary relevance is that made against the judiciary which is supposed to be the last hope of the common man.

For instance, Mr. Justice Kayode Eso JSC (rtd) was the Chairman of a panel where 43 or 50 judges were found guilty of these heinous offences and thus some of them were sent packing by year 2004 – 2005.

Allegation of corruption against some members of the judiciary became so vibrant that one is worried about the future of this country, Nigeria. For instance, the Tribune of Wednesday the 16th day of March, 2011 at page 4, hinted that staggering sums of money were found in some judges' bank accounts, which tantamount to unlawful enrichment for taking part in both Osun and Ekiti Sates gubernatorial election appeals. The paper revealed that in an account belonging to one of the affected judges, a sum of 375,000 dollars was reportedly found, while an account belonging to another of the judges was said to contain M182 million. The investigation by the justice Umaru Abdulahi panel was instituted by the National Judiciary Council as a result of the alleged corruption in the handling of governorship election appeals in Osun and Ekiti States respectively.

Properties of the judges were also said to have been investigated, with a certain judge found to have renovated a house he built about 20 years ago with over N200 million naira.

What confidence do we expect to find in the judiciary as the last hope of the common man, when the President of the Court of Appeal refused, as of right, to go to the Supreme Court on elevation? The president alleged that his nomination for the apex Court job was not done in good faith, and he alleged that the CJ did that with a biased mind because he, the President, refused to toe the line and directive of the CJ over an election matter which took place in Katsina.

We may leave the judiciary alone as at this juncture and talk of the police and the community leaders like an Oba in Owena to mention a few.

There was also an allegation in the Tribune 3rd July 2005, stating that even an Oba in Owena town, colluded with and received gratifications or bribes from some ritualists who invaded his town at midnight, slept with women and caused the untimely death of their men. When luck ran against one of them, he was said to have confessed that they were carrying out the nefarious acts with the alleged consent of the Oba whom they promised to give one million naira and a jeep in appreciation of his support.

Allegations of corruption prevail also against the police, our law enforcement agents, and the case of the former Inspector General of Police, Mr. Tafa Balogun, could be mentioned cursorily on this.

One would in fact, agree with the Tribune of 26th June, 2005 stating that the guiding philosophy of "to serve and protect with integrity" introduced by Inspector General of Police, Mr. Ehindero has recently suffered a set back when two female inspectors fought each other openly over gratification. The two police officers were simply quarrelling over anticipated windfalls from a case file under investigation. They, the duos almost overturned the station previously as a result of bickering over the sharing of money said to have been taken from a suspect who had a brush with the law.

There is undoubtedly corruption in almost every public life in Nigeria. Take the N2.5 billion – contract fraud that rocked the prison in 2005 as a case study. Here the Nigerian prisons service crisis was over an alleged misappropriation of about N2.5billion capital vote contained in the 2004 appropriation Act and meant for the execution of capital projects across prison formations in the country. It was discovered that while the contractors handling the jobs have been paid, the contracts were never executed for most of the contractors have not even mobilized themselves to sites.

Also noted is that in more than 10 projects sites, there were no sign of activities as at March ending that year, while in other sites the jobs were done half way while the contractors had been paid the contract sum previously. Not to go into the catalogue of woes, it was learnt that some field officers of the prisons service collaborated with the contractors to issue false certificates of job completion, thereby facilitating payment of millions of naira without anything to show for them in terms of job execution.

This is not peculiar to a particular arm of government but of general application when one considers in depth local government administration in this country.

CORRUPTION IN LOCAL GOVERNMENT ADMINISTRATION OF NIGERIA

Corruption is a universal phenomenon in the whole of Nigeria and since Local Government workers are an integral part of the system, they can therefore not exonerate themselves. One discovers that in all facets of life in Nigeria, corruption is predominant, because we give much prominence to money. We honour only rich men not minding where and how they got their money, everybody wants money to be recognized.

You can not expect messengers in local government not to take money in order to carry your files from a place to the other; otherwise your file may be hidden some how without attention. Many a time, one finds the scheduled officers too demanding for gratifications as if he was not paid salaries by his local government.

Corruption in Local Governments of Nigeria is interdependent on many factors, which we may quickly enumerate as follows:

(1) **Traditional/Historical Influence:** bad method of recruitment, lack of motivation, incompetence, lack of proper human management, deficiency in leadership qualities, misappropriation of funds, indiscipline and too much dependence on monetary values.

Adedeji and Lawrence, lamenting on this incidence, stated that the incidence of corruption, misappropriation of funds have been much repeated that Local Government in Nigeria was once referred to as “Fortress of Corruption. They remark that Local Government functionaries and infact corporate bodies especially those who handle contracts for Local Government are having a "field day" due to inflation of contracts.

The Duo argued that the Audit report of 1979 – 1983 on nine local government councils of the then Bendel State as revealed by the commissioner for Local Government, showed glaringly that it is not possible to defend the leadership of these councils of the financial irresponsibility, irregularity in stores management and the accounting system which made the council concerned to be described as "Fortress of Corruption".

Lots of acts of corruption and irregularities were pointed out in the report like uncontroversial evidence of illegal award of contracts as well as payments made for abandoned or uncompleted projects and for orders which were never supplied or for supplies which were later removed and taken away by the contractors.

Equally, Ayoade castigated corruption and financial imprudence in Local Government and cited many examples, which include the examples of a chairman who died and left one hundred and twenty million naira in his bank account as revealed by Audu Ogbeh. This gives a serious concern to students of probity and accountability in office and for anybody to save that colossal amount after only three years in office proves the point that the office is rich and that the officers helped themselves corruptively.

Another real life examples was given of a State where Local Government Chairmen met monthly in rotation in their various Local Government Headquarters and contributed one million naira each to the host chairman. The State has 13 Local Governments so that the host Chairman earned 13 million naira for hosting meetings in 39 months, (3 years), each of the chairmen then received thirty nine thousand million naira.

In some Local Governments, contracts are used to siphon money from Local Government, through variations and contingency components. If one wants to eradicate corruption in Local Government therefore, it is suggested that the process of contract variation should be made more stringent, possibly by requiring the veto of the legislative councils of Local Government.

OTHER SHOCKING REVELATIONS

In one of the 4 Local Government areas in Ogoni, River State, a treasurer was said to have allegedly prepared and used spurious documents to withdraw N1.5million. He withdrew N623,000 under the pretext or organizing a reception for the new care-taker committee members.

He prepared two vouchers in another breath for staff salaries as follows:
In the first voucher, he gave a break down of N12 million, while in the second voucher he gave a figure of N11,168,000 leaving a balance of N812,000 for himself and cohorts.

When he was caught in the trap, he defended himself by challenging the chairman of the Local Government care-taker committee for collecting a sum of N160,000 from the Local Government account without accounting for same.

One could imagine than describe the various acts of corruption and impropriety that have plagued Local Government administration up till today. Collusive behaviour, coupled with acts of corruption, have polluted the air and administration of this third tier authority so much that the common man is groaning in silence for the dividends of democracy.

CONCLUSION

Corruption appears to be an endemic diseases difficult to be eradicated in Nigerian scene, but the efforts of the present administration is praiseworthy and commendable in waging a great battle against it.

People must give a supportive hand to government efforts; hence there is a need for a change if not a total re-orientation towards the intensive educational and moral re-training of our people in order to wipe out corruption in local government services.We should cultivate an attitude of putting the nation first in all we do and think less of our individual selves and money.

Nigerian image abroad has been battered so much that every Nigeria is believed to be dubious and dishonest. The degree of non-compliance by Nigerians on this issue has ignited the passion for bad Governance and it's attendant psychological violence. This is so, because people with very low morale tend to be living in affluence why those who stand by the tenet of building peace and enhancing good governance have nothing to show for their patriotism. We are convinced it is not beyond redemption. In order to reassure fellow Nigerians that corruption is an ill will that has no room in any civilized society, we should ombudsmanize so as to expunch from Nigerian body politics, those parochialists, whose souls are dead, and who motive in public life is all about primitive accumulation of wealth.
By so doing, we would have set in motion the task of coming home to decency, justices, morality and equity.

END NOTES

1. RIMI....................we have not done much these past six years in Saturday Vanguard May 28, 2005 at page 10.
2. See sections 422 and 4227 of the criminal code
3. Taiwo O.T ...... Nigeria on Gunpowder the climax of misrule Omoade Printing press 200 at 1 P 200 at 1p 220 221 I quoted Taiwo almost in verbatim see also Nigerian Tribune, 1/8/75.
4. See Sunday Tribune of 100/4/2005 at page 6 for a comprehensive discussion.
5. Adedeji and Lawrence...............in search of Grass Root Democracy.
6. Adedeji and Lawrence............in search of Grass Root Democracy Paper Presented at a seminar.
7. Ayoade T.A. .... Resources management in the reformed Local Government system paper presented at the Oyo Directorate of the National Orientation agency workshop for chairman and principal officers of local government in Oyo State December 2003.
8. Punch Newspaper of 20/3/2003 at page 14
9. Burke was quoted by W.J. Nichol son. Commission of inquiry into the affairs of Ibadan District Council 19555, printed in London.
10. Farudimu John Adebisi.........Corruption in contemporary local governments in Nigeria. Being the result of a project submitted to the Department of local government studies, at Obafemi Awolowo University 1987.
11. Farudimu J.A. .... Corruption in Contemporary Local Governments in Nigeria.

CHAPTER FOURTEEN

LEGAL AND JUDICIAL INTERVENTIONS IN CHIEFTAINCY DISPUTES AMONG THE YORUBA OF SOUTH WESTERN NIGERIA

PROF TORIOLA OYEWO AND
M.L.A. SALAWU (PH.D)

INTRODUCTION

Chieftaincy Institutions in Nigeria have been laden with predominant disputes which are not only odious but threatening, and as such they have been very much promotive of social disintegration, unrest, lack of peace and disunity among the members of such communities coupled with noticeable stagnation of developments. As a result of the foregoing therefore various state governments tried to enact their laws for the empowerment of the institution.

This paper will firstly define what the word "Chieftaincy" means and then unfold the reasons why people put much premium on it before considering the various problems associated with the institution itself. Thereafter the paper will take the readers to a conducted tour of legal provisions with decided cases on the chief's law.

CHIEFTAINCY DEFINITION

By Ordinary Dictionary meaning the word **'CHIEFTAINCY"**, means the leader of a tribe, but chieftaincy according to Kusamatu3 signifies the position of dignity and honour occupied by a traditional ruler like the Emir or an Oba. This definition to my mind is not all that embracing for it does not take into cognizance some other recognized and honorary Chiefs that do prevail among the Yoruba people.

Therefore not to be lost in the polemics of definition, this paper will use the definitions accepted both by statutes and the Court on Chiefs law. For instance in *Adanji V (Hunooo) (1908) INLR784* the court held unhesitatingly that chieftaincy is a mere dignity, a position of honour of primacy among a particular section of the native Community. This will no doubt include the Honourary Chiefs. However it must be noted that all matters concerning chieftaincy affairs fall within the jurisdiction of a state government, and that is why the 1999 constitution forbids the Federal Government from legislating on Chieftaincy matters.

Thus nearly all the states in Nigeria have passed Chiefs law regulating the appointment, selection, approval, suspension and deposition of Chiefs. And by section 2 of the Chiefs law of Oyo State which is in pari material with many others, "a Chief, means a person whose chieftaincy title is associated with a native community and thus includes both a minor Chief and a recognized Chief as well. The interpretation Act, Cap 192 laws of the Federation of Nigeria 1900, however defines a Chief to mean a person who in accordance with the law in force in any part of Nigeria is accorded the dignity of a Chief by reference to the past or to a community established in the past.
It must however be pointed out that certain classifications should be made on the word 'The ruling House', Chieftaincy" and the Traditional rulers as follows. A Ruling House Chieftaincy means a recognized Chieftaincy the holder of which, according to customary law is appointed from among the members of one or more ruling houses. By section 329 of the 1989 constitution the word Traditional council and what a Traditional ruler means are well defined.

Tradition Council, which includes Emirate council means a body constituted as such by the law of a state and presided over by a Traditional Ruler, and which consists of such members as may be prescribed by the law, while the words Traditional Ruler, means "the person who by virtue of his ancestry, occupies the throne or stool of an area or has been appointed or elected to it in accordance with the customs, traditions and usages of the area and has traditional authority over the people of that area or any other person who, prior to the commencement of this constitution has been elected or appointed by the instrument in order of the Government to exercise traditional authority over an area or community in the state recognized as such by the Government of a state.

The above definition to my mind will apply or refer to an Oba or Obi as a paramount Ruler of a particular Community. Please note that the expression "Paramount Ruler is used to indicate the prime position occupied by the incumbent of a particular Chieftaincy tool.

ISSUES ON CHIEFTAINCY DISPUTES

Chieftaincy disputes may arise to determine a number of issues such as:

1. Who should be chosen as a successor after the demise of an incumbent;
2. The validity of appointment or nomination of the King maker and the ruling house and of the chieftaincy committee of a council of a particular Chief;
3. The proper interpretation of some sections in the Chiefs law;
4. The exercise of the powers conferred on the Governor-in-Council by the Chiefs law;
5. The deposition and appointment of a chief under the Chiefs law;
6. The appointment and powers of the commissioner to appoint Kingmakers by warrant; and
7. The registered Chieftaincy declaration with many others to mention a few.

The problems emanating from these issues include problems of the prescribed and consenting authority, problems of improper grading and classification of recognized Chiefs, incessant in-roads being made to bastardize the custom and traditions of some part of the state, problems of faulty declaration, problems of conflict between the laws and customary usages, problems of the proper interpretation of the law, problems emanating from the vindictive application of the Chiefs laws and edicts by making deportation orders.

The application of these laws and edicts has been found to be repulsive, out of tune and inconsonant with the history, tradition and custom of the people of some communities. It is opprobrious, confusing and inconsistent with the yearnings and aspirations of the majority of the good people in those areas and had led in some cases to hatred, disunity, chaos, public contumely and serious breaches of peace and harmony. One in fact feels that chieftaincy institutions in these states will be crisis free and less problematic if it is taken off the tentacles of the muddy waters of politics and prejudices.

These disputes do more often than not eventually terminate in the High Courts under the prerogative orders of certiorari, prohibition and injunctions; but before dealing with the examples of such disputes let us cast our minds cursorily on some important provisions of the Chiefs law using the western Region/Oyo State laws as examples.

CASES ON SOME IMPORTANT PROVISIONS OF THE CHIEFS LAWS

The secretary of a competent council must announce the name of the ruling house entitled to provide a candidate not later than 11th days of the occurrence of a vacancy. This is contained in section 15(1) of the Chiefs law of Oyo State which must not be breached see Afolabi v Gov. of Oyo State (1985) NWLR 734 while section 15 (2) of the law makes provision for the method of the announcement of such a vacancy. However in selecting a candidate the rules of customary law as defined in the Chieftaincy Declaration of that particular house must be strictly complied with, while any failure to observe the customary rules relating to the selection of a candidate for the consideration of the kingmakers will be declared null and void if the exercise is challenged in Court., see Oduleye vs Efunuga (1990) 7NWLP (Pt 164) 518 where the nomination of 4 candidates instead of one as provided for by the chieftaincy Declaration was made.

Also in *Imoniche Vs Att Gen of Bendel state x others* (1992) *TSC NJ (part 1)* 197, a nomination which was done without complying with the Chieftaincy Declaration was held to be unconstitutional, null and void. But one wonders why in the case of Queen v Governor in council, western Nigeria ex-paste Bakare Ojelade and others (1992) WNLR. 240 the Ifa oracle was branded irrelevant to be consulted in choosing a right candidate according to the custom and tradition of the people and in line with their chieftaincy Declaration.

The facts of this case depend on who would succeed to the vacant throne f Agura of Gbagura in 1960.

The secretary of the Egba Divisional Council on 31/ 12 / 1960 called on the Egiri ruling House to submit the names of candidate to be sent to the Kingmakers within 14 days as stipulated by law. The names of 5 candidates including that of Raufu Adeosun and Shittu Okunade Shobayo were submitted. At the meeting of the Kingmakers on the 27th December, Shittu Olonde Shobayo was considered to be the only candidate and he was declared appointed.

The King makers later recalled that the two names of Shobayo and Adeosun were qualified but that Adeosun was not considered suitable because he had been rejected by the IFA oracle. The Executive Council or the Governor in Councillater explained that IFA oracle was never a condition to be taken into account under the custom of Gbagura in selecting a candidate and because of this explanation Adeosun was equally considered and his name was forwarded to the Governor-in-Council who had received the candidature letter of Shobayo before that of Adeosun. Trouble then started and surprisingly the Governor-in-Council approved the candidature of Adeosun.

An action based on Certiorari on the grounds that the Governor in Council approved the appointment without jurisdiction proved abortive under a flab by and flaccid reasoning of the law.

However, the decision called for comments. The question is why did the Governor-in-Council not consider the two names together before making a choice. Students of equity would be worried because where equities are equal) the law prevails and the usual vogue and principle to adopt in competing interest is first come) first served.

Moreover we feel the people ought to know the prevailing customary rights governing the selection of their chief in their local domain which is "acceptability to both the people and the oracle") in this perspective one then wonders why it was the sole responsibility of the Governor-in-Council to determine what was the governing customary law in this case. It is believed that this decision may lead the law into a blind alley and promote injustice.

This is our own opinion for there was never an appeal over the decision.

Another case worthy of consideration is Prince Aderibigbe V The Secretary Oranmiyan Local Government (2) The attom.ey General of Oyo State (33) The Governor of Oyo State.

This deals with cases where a litigant may loose his case, after a secretary had completed his own assignment under the Chief law because an interim injunction is never granted on a completed act.

The plaintiff in this suit asked for the following reliefs:

1. A declaration that their house is the rightful one to present a candidate or candidates for the filling of the stool of Ooni of Ife.

2. A declaration that the first defendant's letter inviting the Ogboru ruling house to submit a list of candidates is null and void.

3. An injunction to restrain the 3[ni] defendant from approving of any candidate from Ogboru ruling house.

4. A Declaration that the 1999 Oni of Ife Chieftaincy Declaration was the only valid one.

In order words the Chieftaincy Declaration of 1957 stipulates the following order of Ruling houses respectively.

1. Oshunkola;
2. Giesi;
3. Ogboru; and
4. Lafogido respectively.

The plaintiff/Applicant's submission was dismissed because he failed to establish by setting out in his affidavit how he has come to be affected and (2) That he has failed to establish the fact that his claim is not frivolous or vexatious, while he has not made any materials available to connect both the Attorney-general and the Governor of Oyo State respectively (3) Furthermore, the court held that the secretary, Oranmiyan Local Government who was the 1st defendant in this case is functus officio immediately he announced the name of Ogboru Ruling House in this case - which is entitled according to customary law to provide a candidate or candidates as the case may be to fill the vacancy.

Thus the candidate has been installed as the Oni of Ife not withstanding the provisions contained in the chieftaincy Declaration law of 1999.

STALEMATE IN APPOINTMENT

If a stalemate arises among the Kingmakers in choosing a candidate, it is apparent that the state government could not shut its eyes in a case of this nature, but to choose warrant Kingmakers in other to act accordingly.

This was the decision reached in the case of *Samuel Oyeleye Tuwagun V Jacob Oyedepo Oladipo and Governor of Oyo State.*

This arose because the former Oba Aresadu of Iresalu died and hence a vacancy had to be filled. After all the necessary steps were taken to call on the ruling house to produce a candidate or candidate, three people were presented to the Kingsmakers who were two in number. One of the Kingsmakers chose Oyedepo Oladapo while the other chose Samuel Oyeleye Tunwagun, hence a stalemate arose and the Government or its officer, the Commissioner can invoke the provisions of section 17 of the Chiefs law to choose warrant Kingmakers. *See Eyimode Ojo and others V s the Governor of Oyo State (1989) NWLR (Pt 89) 1 at page 19* where the supreme court held that the Governor is entitled to exercise powers under section 13(1) and 17 (1) of the Chiefs law in cases of default of any person or persons entitled to nominate, select, or appoint to vacancy.

SETTING ASIDE OF CHIEFTAINCY DECLARATIONS

Chieftaincy declarations are made in order to minimize or even prevent incessant endless litigations on chieftaincy matters. This was the ratio decidendi of the case of *Chief Michael Uwegba V s The Attorney General Bendel State and others (1986) INWLR (Pt.16) 303 at 206* where it is also decided that such a Declaration must be made by a committee of a competent council who will always hold consultations with the members of the interested groups before making the Declaration.

It must however be noted that by virtue of the provisions of section 9 of the Chiefs/laws of Oyo State, every declarations duly made and registered as required by Section 8 of the law are deemed to state the Customary law and they become the constitution and embodiment of the entire custom of the town with respect to Chieftaincy matters to the exclusion of any other customary rule or usage. See *Imonikhe and* others *V3 AH--General Bendel State and others* 1992 *7SCNJ (part* 1) 197.

Also such a registered declaration was held to be a subsidiary legislation for where a statute enables an authority to make regulations, a regulation, made under the Act becomes for the purposes of obedience or disobedience a provision of the Act. See *Willingale V Norris (1909)* 1KB X B. 57 a*t* 64 *and Uwegba V A.G Bendel State* (1986) *NWLR (p* + 16) *303.*

Thus as a subsidiary legislation, a chieftaincy Declaration must be published in the gazette after an approval, otherwise the non-publication of same will make it an impotent legislation see Popoola V Adeyemo (1992) 9SCNJ 79. Since any statutory order does not take effect until it becomes known see also *Johnson V Sargant* & *sons* (918) *1KB* 1 *v 1.*

However it must be noted that a duly registered chieftaincy Declaration which seems defective or faulty may be amended or replaced by a new Declaration by either the Executive Council or by the chieftaincy Committee which made such declaration when directed to do so by the Executive Council.

Thus the powers to amend, replace or otherwise can be exercised under the following grounds to wit.

If the executive council is satisfied that such a registered declaration does not contain a true sufficiently clear statement of the customary law which regulates the selection of a person to be the holder of a recognized chieftaincy or (b) does not contain a sufficient description of the method of selection of the holder of such chieftaincy or (C) contains an error whether as to its form or substance or (D) otherwise detective, or objectionable, having regards to the provisions of the Chiefs law.

In deserving cases, a chieftaincy Declaration may further be reviewed or amended on the recommendation of an inquiry set up at the instance of the Executive Council.

Please note that a non-competent local council can never make a valid Declaration. See *Esuola Akano & others Vs Governor Western State (1971) WNLR* 177 *AT PAGE 201).*

Thus a Registered Declaration can be challenged or attacked on the following grounds.

(1) That the said chieftaincy Declaration is not a correct statement or re-instatement of the customary law relating to the named chieftaincy see Minister *of Local Government V Odubote* (1962) while

(2) That at all material times the registered chieftaincy Declaration was (and still is) against the popular age-long tradition of the people of a particular community or chieftaincy.

(3) That the chieftaincy Declaration was not made by a committee of competent council.

(4) That the Declaration was not published.

(5) That the said Declaration was never registered as directed by Section 8 of the chiefs law.

In sum, it must be noted that a declaration remains in force until it is either repealed, amended, or set aside by a competent Court. See such cases like *Adigun A.G. Oyo State* (1987) *INWL:R (Pt* 53) 678. *Adigun V. A. G. Ogun State* (1995) *3NWLR (Pt* 385) 513. *Imoniche V.A.* G *Bendel State (1992) 6NWLR (Pt.248)* 396. *Oyelami V. Milad Ogun State* (1998) *4NWLR (Pt* 457) 624. *Popoola Vs. Adeyemo* (1992) 8 *NWLR (Pt.* 257). Oyebisi *V. Governor of Oyo State* (1998) *1NWLR (Pt* 574) 441. *Obala of Otan Aiyegbaju Vs. Adesina* (1999) *2NWLR (Pt 590)* 163. *Oyelakun Vs. Governor Osun State (2002) FWLR* (Pt. 135) 633

JUDICIAL INTERVENTIONS AND SOME PRINCIPLES

The intervention of the courts on chieftaincy matters stem from the provisions of the 1999 constitution of Nigeria.

Thus, and as decided by authorities, the courts are vested with jurisdiction to see whether a chieftaincy Declaration is in conformity with the prevailing customary law and if they find other wise, the courts can proceed to set them aside. See *Mafimisebi and Vs Ehuwa (2007)* 1 Se. *(Pt.*11) 73.

It must however be borne in mind that a person who brings his complaint to court for determination of any question as to his Civil right and obligation must of necessity have locus standi in law to sue. See such cases like Busari *Vs. Oseni* (1992) *4NWLR (Pt.237)* 557, *Chairman Gwaram Local Government vs. Dantine* (1993) *2NWLR (Pt* 275) *370 ratios 2 and* 4 at *page* 372 *Irene Thomas Vs.Olutosoye* (1986) 1 *A1 NWLR (Pot* 18) 669 *Orogun vs. Soremekun* (1986) 5 *NWLR (Pt* 44) 688 at *700. A.* G. *Kadena Vs. HASSAN* (1985) *2NWLR (Pt* 8) 483. *Fawehinmi Vs. Akilu* (1987) 11~ 12 *SCN J* 151. *Adesanya Vs. President of Nigeria (1981) 5SCl12,* 149 - *150 and Odeneye Vs. Efunuga (1990) 7NWLR (Pt* 164) 518 and many others to mention a few.

In short, a plaintiff will have locus standi in a matter only if he has a special legal right or if he has sufficient or special interest in the performance of the duty sought to be enforced and where this was adversely affected by the act complained of.

It is when the civil rights and obligation of the person who invites the jurisdiction of the court are in issue for determination that the judicial powers of the court may be invoked.

One may ask at as this junction when then does a cause of action arise under a chieftaincy declaration?

This question has been answered on many cases like Alao V s. Akano (1988) INS CC 321, A.G Kwara State Vs. Olawole (1993) INWLR (Pt

272 640, Oyelakun Vs Governor of Osun State (Supra) that a cause of action under a chieftaincy declaration will arise on the occurrence of an event of its implementation which affects the interest of a party, for example when an appointment is made under it.

That stance then holds to prove that a chieftaincy declaration can not affect the rights of persons subject to it unless and until it has been registered. See the case of *Military Administrator Ekiti State Vs Prince* B. *Adeniyi. (2007)* 4-5- SC *201* which dealt with the filling of the existing vacancy in the stool of Arajaka of Igbara Odo.

In this case, it was held that time for the Limitation law runs from date a declaration was registered and not when a commission or government make a decision.

There are many decisions on this point in the chiefs law but for the limited time at our disposal, let us deal with whether a party can bring a suit in a chieftaincy dispute without first exhausting the remedies provided by law; and the procedure to be followed once there is a question which touches on chieftaincy matters in Ondo State.

These questions cropped up in the case of *Aribisala* Vs. *Ogunyemi (2005) 21 NSCQR* 113 where it was held as follows.

1. The position of the law is that in a chieftaincy disputes as this, aggrieved person who brings a suit must show that he brought his suit only after he had exhausted the remedies provided or followed the procedure prescribed under the applicable law.

2. Under section 22 (3) of Ondo Chiefs law any dispute, even if it touches only the question of eligibility as the plaintiffs/appellants contend must be submitted first to the prescribed authority for settlement and later to the commissioner for chieftaincy matter.

This leads one to the doctrine of Ripeness in law which simpliciter states that when a matter is for the domestic domain of any body, institution or authority as enshrined in the Statute, it is not permitted to come to court until all avenues have been exhausted. Such an action will be branded as unjusticiable and premature. See such cases like *Olukoyi* Vs *Foloruriso Adedeuin,* 1/425/94 an unreported Ibadan High Court case, *Sunday Eguamevense* Vs. *James Amashizemwa. Amaqhizemuien, VOL.1 (1994) IKLR* 1 Miss *O.A. Akintemi and* 2 *others* Vs *Prefessor C.A Onwumechill* (1985) *Vol.* 1 *Part* 1, *All NLR.85* Thome *Vs. University of London* (1966) *24B.* 237 *University of Lagos* & *Zors: Vs.* Dr *Dada,* 1 *Unife Law Reports part III* (1971) 344. *Obajimi Vs. A.G. Western Nigeria (1967) 1 All NLR* 31 (1968) *NWLR* 96~ *Nigeria Cement Company Limited Vs. NRC (1992) INWLR* (Pt *220)* 747. *And the case of C.C.B Vs. Anambra State* (1992) *8NWLR (Pt.* 26) 528 *at* 536 *ratio* 14 which decides that where a statute provides a particular method to perform a duty regulated by statute, that method alone must be adopted.

Thus where statutes of chiefs law provide that disputes must be resolved by the Olubadan or the prescribed authority, an aggrieved person must of necessity avail him self of such provision of the law and if he is not pleased by such a prescribed authority, he can go to court by way of

Finally note that in any matter including chieftaincy affairs, the court will not grant any declaratory judgment where the question raised there in is purely academic or that the declaration would be useless or embarrassing.

In sum, let it be re-iterated that Chieftaincy matters are within the purviews of state government prescribed authorities and unless the exercise of the powers is inconsistent with the provision of the constitution, it can not be challenged.

CONCLUSION

This topic is of tremendous importance both to the members of the peace and conflict resolution with the general public at large.

It has been noted that chieftaincy disputes and settlement occupy some predominant positions in our society based upon many factors a few of which are:

(a) The social recognition and traditional respect always accorded the chief in their local communities.

(b) The elevated symbol of God on earth usually associated with those institutions by the Yoruba race and

(c) The political and highly influential roles of these chiefs in the development of their areas accounted for the struggle and conflicts in making laws to suit the desire of a particular government on the one hand and the possibility of making one a chief on the other hand.

Really, chieftaincy disputes should be handled by experts on conflict resolution and management, this will reduce the number of cases going to the court for determination, since according to the Yoruba people and Justice O' Connor - Courts should not be the places where resolution of disputes begun. They should be the places where disputes end after alternative methods of resolving disputes have been considered and tried".

To this end I would suggest for the involvement of experts on peace and conflict management in solving likely disputes and conflicts that may arise on chieftaincy matters; hence the state laws should be amended to accommodate these experts.

Lastly, I would suggest that who ever owns the reign of powers to depose or deport a chief must comply with the principles of natural justice for nobody should be condemned unheard as it is found in Dasuki case and others. Therefore all ouster of courts jurisdiction should be vacated in the chiefs law of each state, for where a country exists in which fundamental issues of social justice could not be resolved in favor of helpless individuals, then that country has lost its bearing.

ENDNOTES

1. See the chiefs law of Bendel State, Cap 3 of 197 **Bendel State**
   (a) Chieftaincy Edict of Bendel State 1971. The traditional Rulers and Chiefs (Edict) law 1976. **Eastern Nigeria**
   (b) High court law cap 61, Laws of the Eastern Nigeria 1963 Sections 11 and 16. **Ogun State**
   (c) Chief (Amendment) Edict No 1 of 1971 of the Osun State. Chiefs law of Ogun State, 1978 Recognised chieftaincies (Revocation and miscellaneous provisions). **Kwara State and Northern Nigeria**
      (i) Chiefs (Appointment and Deposition)
      (ii) Law in Northern Nigeria cap 20 of 1963
      (iii) Constitution of Northern Nigeria 1963
      (iv) Interpretation law (North) 1963 **Lagos State**
   (e) (i) Chiefs law, cap 25,Laws of Lagos State
      (ii) Obas and Chiefs laws of Lagos State 1981 Ondo State
   (f) (i) Ondo State Approval of Appointment of an Oba and Presentation of Instrument of Appointment and Staff of Office Edict.
      (ii) Olowo of Owo (Revolution of deposition) and Restoration) 1991. **Oyo State**
   (g) Chiefs law cap 21 laws of Oyo State of Nigeria (1978) **Western**
   (h) (i) Chiefs law cap 19, laws of Western region of Nigeria 1958.
      (ii) Constitution of Western Nigeria, 1963 (Section 33 (10).
      (iii) Prescribed Authorities (Delegation) of powers no. (1) notice 1967, W.S.L.N 63 of 1967.
      (iv) The Recognised Chieftaincies (Revolution and Miscellaneous Provisions) orders 1976, W.S.L.N of 1976.
2. Niki Tobi - Sources of Nigerian Law MIS professional publishers Limited, Lagos (1996) page 103.
3. Gboyega Kusamotu - Chieftaincy and the law Sulek - TEMIK Publishing Company 2001 at page 1.

4. Adanji V. Hunvoo (1908) INLB 74
5. Afolabi V. Governor of Oyo State (1985) NMLR 734
6. Odeneye V. Efunuga (1990) NWLR (p + 164) 518
7. Imonikhe V. AH. General of bendel state (1992) 78SCNJ) (part 1) 197.
8. Queen V Governor in council, Western Nigeria, exporte Bakare Ojelade and others (1962) WNLR 240.
9. Prince A. Aderibigbe V The Secretary Oranyinmo Local Government and the Attarney General of Oyo State.
10. Chief Michael Uwegba V The Attorney General Bendel State Xaner (1986) 1 NWLR (p+ 16) 303.
11. Willingate V Norris (1909) 1 KB 57 at 64
12. Popooia V Adeyemo (1992) 9SCNJ 79
13. Johnson V Sargant and Sons (1918) 1 King 101
14. Esuoia Akano (Basorunm of Oyo) and V. The Military Governor Western State and anar - suit No. CAW /12/70
15. Babatunde Oludare of lkare V The Governor of Western State - suit No. FSC 207/1959.
16. F. A. Olalowo Y. The Governor of Ogun State, Olba Onebade Lipede Suit No. AB/68/80 of 11/2/83.
17. Akin Olugbade ofOgun State Suit No. M/2/81/ of6/5/82
18. Elo Aiyedun, Chief Aromire Y. Yesuf Oresanya (1938) 14NLR 116

CHAPTER FIFTEEN

A MASTER SERVANT RELATIONS BETWEEN STATE GOVERNMENT AND LOCAL GOVERNMENT IN NIGERIA AND THE QUESTION OF ACCOUNTABILITY

B. OYENIRAN ADEDIJI (PH.D)

INTRODUCTION

Ever since the Federal Government of Nigeria embarked on a series of Local Government Reforms, residents of a local government have nursed great expectations of attendant, benefits usually enjoyed by the governed masses in similar situation elsewhere. General Muritala Mohammed in July 1975. The nation was informed that the new regime would undertake a systematic and deliberate re-organization of the Local Government set up'.

In 1976 Guidelines for Local Government Reform, (Federal Republic of Nigeria, 1976), the intention of the federal government is stated clearly as follows: In embarking on these reforms, the Federal Military Government was essentially motivated by the necessity to stabiles and rationalizes Government at the local levels. This must, of necessity, entail the decentralization of some significant functions of State Governments to local levels in order to harness local resources for rapid development. The Federal Military Government has therefore decided to recognize Local Government has therefore decided to recognize Local Government as the third tier of governments as the third tier of governmental activity in the nation. Local Government should do precisely what the word government implies i.e., governing at the grass roots or local levels. (Federal Republic of Nigeria, 1976: Foreword)

According to the 1976 Guidelines, … these reforms are intended to entrust political¸ responsibility to where it is most crucial and most beneficial, that is, to the people. The Government hopes that these reforms would further enshrine the principle of participatory democracy and of political responsibility to every Nigerian.

The 1976 local government reform constitutes a watershed in the evolution of the institutional arrangements for local governance in this country. The fundamental innovation in the reform was the 'formal and unequivocal recognition of local governments as constituting a distinct level of government with defined boundaries, clearly stated functions and provisions for ensuring adequate human and financial resources' **(Adamolekun, 1979:3).**

The 1999 constitution guaranteed the statutory nature of the third level of government through the provisions relating to the system of local government by democratically elected local government councils', the finance of local governments and the functions of local governments. The federal government perceived reform of local government as entertaining "the decentralization of some significant functions of state governments to the local level in order to harness local resources for rapid development. The 1999 constitution of the federal republic of Nigeria provides that…

Ordinarily one would have thought that state governments would seize the opportunity of this federal government gesture as a sign of possible relief especially from the hindsight of the warning given to Moses in the Bible by Jethro his father-in-law who advised that it was not good for Moses to continue to carry all alone a task that was too heavy for him to carry unaided. In short Jethro advised Moses to decentralize the heavy burden so as to concern himself with issues relating to policy formulation and to enable trustworthy people to take decisions and execute tasks in order to make things easier for himself **(Exodus**). The 1979 constitutional provisions seek to establish strong, efficient and responsive local governments in Nigeria (**Adamolekun and Rowland, 1979 and CDC Report, Vol. II, 1976).** As a matter of fact several measures have been introduced with the intention of rendering unto local government councils the measure of autonomy necessary for achieving results.

However, judging by the hues and cries by participants at

workshops seminars, public lectures etc. Organized to examine the extent to which the current inter-government relationship facilitates the performance of the roles and functions of local government councils, the present inter-governmental relations has not improved much the master-servant relationship between the higher levels of government and our grass-roots government. Thus as of today the Federal Government and particularly the state governments are said to be constantly involved in manifestations of paternalistic tendency towards local government and in treating our grass roots government as "infants that have to be military regimented, strictly controlled, remotely tele-guided, and occasionally pushed here and there to get desired results from them".

What is a Master-Servant Relationship? Is a local Government a servant? What should be the appropriate relationship between State Government and Local Government in order to place the latter in a situation to maximize its performance? What factors have encouraged the master servant relations? Is a complete autonomy possible or desirable in Nigeria? How could the master-servant relations be modified and to what extent? These and more of such questions would find answers in this paper. Since, as well known, words have no fixed meanings, except in the context in which they are used, some classifications of important terms and expressions would be undertaken here.

The aim of this paper is to assess what has happened in practice. Have local government really become the third tier of government in the Nigerian Federal administration system?

STATUS OF LOCAL GOVERNMENT IN NIGERIA

In Nigerian, the constitution grants some measure of autonomy to Local Government as a third level of government. It also grants functions which Local Government has to perform. In civil dispensations as opposed to military system a local government is also democratically elected. What's more, by a system of performance accountability now in vogue in Nigeria, a Local Government is expected to render periodic account for its performance. By this system a Local Government deserves at least autonomy of a size that is commensurate with the functions it is expected to perform and the accounts it has to render. **Adediji, O (2003:43)**

Unfortunately "local government is still treated as a servant by the higher levels of government. It is treated and regarded, as an institution that should not be given free hand to conduct its own affairs for fear of its inability to do well. Thus, we have myriads of exaggerated incursion of the state governments into the activities of local governments.

As of today local government is more or less treated as a servant who should have no say on what functions it is legally competent to perform, as such decisions are more or less the *dictates* of the state governments. This problem is most often extended to very important areas of how much to spend, on what matters to spend grants and statutory allocations. Reports have it that sometimes this paternalistic complex of superiority is exaggerated to the extent that purchase of books, vehicles, furniture etc award of contracts are made without consultation for and behalf of local government councils, and the cost of such items, most often inflated, are deducted at source by the state government from the fund of local government. The Local Governments in Ogun State recently received 2 letters which informed them that; the state Government has just purchased for each Local Government in the state, a Toyota Camry car at a cost of N9.10 million and a Koumatsu Grader machine for N85.00 million. The fund is to be paid back by the local governments in certain installments. The above is another way by which state governments rubbish the autonomy of local governments, for instance local governments submitted that they could have been better off with a Cat Grader machine than a Koumatsu Grader, some local government could have preferred some other projects instead of buying a Toyota jeep. The present executive council members in all the local governments in Kwara state were compelled to buy monetized cars at a high cost of money which is usually deducted from the sources of every local government in the state.

The local governments are forced to sponsor some functions which have no relevance to the lives of the people of their areas. In recent times, the local governments are usually subjected to the payment of Hajj operation to Mecca and pilgrimage Jerusalem. More so, the local governments are made to buy rams during Eidil-Kabir festival for some notable royalties or some political god fathers. Even when the political god fathers have an occasion, Local Government is usually forced to sponsor it whether they like it or not.

Also some programmes of higher levels of government like the civil defence, national youth corps, government liaison office, river-rein blindness, adult education instructors, traditional institutions, village base workers, overseas scholarship holiday programmes, among others and some unbudgeted expenses such as compulsory contribution of colossal amount of money to the electoral campaign fund, are imposed on local government councils and such councils are obliged to meet the cost of such expenses from its meager resources, it was busy day in Obafemi Owode local government ably led by the executive chairman was to receive the chairperson of the gateway front who incidentally the wife of the executive Governor of Ogun-state, the executive council of the local government at its finance & general purpose committee earlier in the week has approved the sum of #2.5 million for the purpose. Various eye glasses have been purchase ready for distribution to the aged including gifts to be distributed. The gateway front is the baby of the wife of the executive governor and it's mandatory for the local governments in the state to participate. This is another load on the local government in the gateway state which inhibits the autonomy of the local government. Since most wives of the executive governors have one or two pet projects which they embark on it and inadvertently increasing the financial subordination to the higher levels of government. According to ***Wheare, K.C. (1963)*** "Fiscal subordination makes an end of Federation."

Three main sources by which a local government is supposed to derive its financial fertility are internally generated revenue, statutory allocation from state government and statutory allocation from the federation account, but the state governments has more or less become a sort of stumbling block to the sources.

Local Government *internally generated revenue* has little to write home about as the state government apparently perceives local government as too naïve to be entrusted with unchecked free hand in handling such functions which could yield such revenues. Consequently the state governments all over Nigeria have high jacked such functional as markets, control of motor parks, approved of building plans, liquor licenses, tenement rating, royalty collection and forestry e.t.c.

Part IX Clause 85 (b) of the Ogun-State law was unambiguous, it clearly gave the local government the power of refuse disposal, yet the state government established the Ogun State Environmental Protection Agency and saddled the Agency with the clearing of refuse and sanitary inspection taking the money for running the Agency from direct source of the joint account of the state/local government.

Despite the above, the Ogun State government established the rural board, the board is given the task of opening up and maintenance of rural roads this is despite the fact that the local government is saddled with the responsibilities of trunk "C" roads. The fund for running the board is taken from source i.e. the joint account of the state/local government.

With respect to statutory allocation from the state government's internally generated revenue it is an open secret that. hardly does any state in the country release the 10% Internally Generated Revenue to local government as provided by the constitution to the local government. Ogun-State is a vivid example. The state governments generally fail to remit the 10% from its own internally generated revenue to local governments as at and when due. All over Nigeria, the local governments are allegedly systematically fleeced in one way or the other by State Governments. The 20% allocation to the local government from the federation account by the federal government is paid into the state/local government joint allocation account no kobo will be released to any local government until a joint allocation account committee under the chairmanship of the commissioner for local government and chieftaincy affairs of the state meets. In most cases local government funds are tampered with impunity for instance in the month of may, 2009, the federation account gave the ijebu-ode Local Government the sum of #95.00 million as its share of the federation account, but by the time the joint allocation account committee meeting ended on the 2nd of June 2009, the local government received only #19.00 million. Which gives the state Government unhindered access to the control and management of Local Government Statutory allocation accounts There has been wide spread allegations that state governors under the guise of joint account, appropriate local government allocations to themselves. The State Government also enact laws that take away many of the functions which constitutionally belong to Local Government

As a result of Nigeria's lopsided fiscal federalism statutory allocation to local government from the federation account, as well as from state internally generated revenue, are grossly inadequate, taken into consideration the enormous (added) responsibilities they face. For instance the funding of primary education causes an average local government to be left with little or nothing for satisfying other needs.

It is another thing that most often state government highjack the statutory allocation accruable to local government from federation account through all sorts of statutory deductions sanctioned by relevant extant laws of the states. Most it not all Local Government Council irrespective of political party get only a traction of their due revenue allocation. The following cases would show the extent to which state governments exercise free hands with impurity over the fund.

In April 2004, the net statutory allocation from the federation account to local government councils in Kwara state amounted to N798, 971,556, 75 but the state government released only N659, 522,205:74 to the councils.

In May 2004, the amount of money allocated to the same local government councils from the federation account was N767, 084,509:49 but only N528, 393,373:55 was actually released to the councils by the state government

In July 2005, the statutory allocation from the federation account meant for Ekiti Local Government of Kwara State was N46, 350,676:82 but the state government released only N5, 587000 to that Local Government.

In July 2005, the sum of N5478, 297 was allocated from the federation account to Oyun Local Government council of Kwara State but the State release N23,035318 to that council.

In December 2008, it was revealed that Anambra State Government had continued to take over markets and motor parks which were constitutionally the exclusive preserve of and major source of revenue accruable to the grass root government *Compass, (2008)*.

Around that period again, out of N1, 109, 2017,296 allocated to 16 local government councils of Kwara State from the federation account only N778, 807,835 was actually released to the councils by the State Government.

In the same Kwara State and around the same period, it was alleged that Local Governments were made to contribute N20, 000,000 each to cater for travel expenses of political party members, families and friends of the state executives. At another time the same State Government was alleged to have mandated the sixteen local government councils to contribute N5, 000,000 each for the travel expenses of political party members to private occasions. The Gateway Television Abeokuta in her breaking news in Tuesday 1st of April 2008 announced that the Ijebu-North Local Government has been dissolved by the State Governor; in its place a caretaker committee, against the spirit of part II item 7 of the Nigerian constitution. The federal radion corporation on Wednesday 11th , November, 2009 in her 7.00am news announced that Ikot Abati Local Government of River State has been dissolved by the state House of Assembly, the offence of the local government is bordered on corruption of funds of the council, the news read. The above are the pawn which local government had become in the hands of the local governments. Local Government Administration in Nigeria has been starved, emasculated and crippled to such an extent that they exist more as more inconsequential shadows of what they ought to be with little or nothing left to take care of the community as mere sharing centre of whatever amount remains with little or nothing left to take of the community.

In virtually all the states of the federation, the local government executives daily lament a development in which they are forced to sign for money not received at the end of the month and any local government executive who manifests reluctance, not to talk of who refused to cooperate stand removed and his Local Government automatically dissolved, and a caretaker committee is appointed to run the affairs of the councils, or the chairman is suspended and a sole administrator appointed to run the council. In almost all states of Nigeria, Council Chairmen are suspended or removed from office and a sole administrator appointed to run the council. Chairmen of local governments are removed with the filmiest of excuses thereby eroding the autonomy of local governments. And till date some local governments in the country are still being run by caretaker committee which is against the law of the country.

Some elected local government chairmen who found themselves removed by the governor of Kwara state includes the following. Chairman Oyun Local Government, Chairman Irepodun Local Government, Ekiti Local Government Chairman.

In Ondo State, Governor Mimiko unilaterally sacked the 18 elected local government chairmen of that state on ground that their election was illegal. The matter was dragged to court where the court held that the governor had no right to sack the elected local government chairmen. *Nigerian Compass, (2009) p. 23, Daily independent Monday, (2007).*

The National Union of Local Government Employees (NULGE), Ebonyi State chapter launched a protest against indiscriminate deduction of council funds through the State Local Government Joint Accounts.

Many state houses of assembly have interpreted the constitutional provision that the state government shall make laws for Local Government to mean the day to day running of Local Government; they do not give the Local Government chairman breathing space to perform their functions, state governments are not contempt with the supervisory role assigned to them by the constitution.

In short, at present the State of Local Government has degenerated to such a ridiculous extent that it resembles "Zombie" who cannot think unless you tell him to think, who cannot talk unless you tell him to talk, who cannot move unless you tell him to move.

The state which ought to nurture, sustain, guide and encourage Local Government Councils to boost their service delivery has paradoxically become a *spoke in the wheel* of their progress – abusing the process by making them incapable of living up to expectations. As allocation to them are criminally diverted by the over-bearing state authorities, local governments become cash crunched and consequently are unable, though not unwilling, to perform their functions.

While majority of Local Government executives play safe by *suffering and smiling* over their present predicament, for lack of temerity to question their state Government deducations knowing fully well that they themselves have no clean hands as their councils have nothing to show for huge resources they have so far collected from the federation revenue allocation, a Local Government Chairman in Imo State has decided to call in the judiciary to interpret the constitution as regards the relationship between state Assemblies and Local Government Councils.

In an originating summons supported by a 21 point affidavit, the Local Government chairman averred that constant threats from Defendant and the chairman House committee Local Government and chieftaincy affairs is making the entire indigenes of the local government restive and setting back the progress of the legislative arm of the local government.

The Local Government Chairman subsequently sought for the following relieves;

(a) A declaration that the invitation of the elected councilors of the Oru West Local Government Area is illegal and unconstitutional as it contravenes S.7and S. 128 of the constitution of the Federal Republic of Nigeria 1999.

(b) A declaration that defendant is not competent to suspend or remove any of the democratically elected officers of the Oru West Local Government.

(c) An order of perpetual injunction restraining the chairmen, their agents, privies and assigns from removing or suspending any *demo*cratically elected *executive* or, interfering, in any manner whatsoever with the internal administration of the said local government. The decision of this court would certainly chart the future course of our Local Government councils in Nigeria\er

In short the Local Government is constitutionally not a servant. It is a Government like others with functions constitutionally set aside for it to perform, and provisions for fund or source of fund with which to carry out the functions. It has however been turned into the status of a servant of the state Government. The Appropriate

Relationship should therefore not be that of Master-Servant but rather partners-in- progress in an effort to develop Nigeria. It is only this kind of inter governmental relations that can place the Local Government in position of being able to maximize its performance, and that can justify performance accountability on the part of Local Government Councils. Adediji, B.O (2003:44) there is also … copy from p4 master-servant Relation

The question may be asked why the state governments apparently manifest a oil of disregard for Nigeria's so called decentralization

Root Causes of Master-Servant Relationship

Several factors are behind the present Master-servant relationships between State Governments and Local Governments.

Firstly is the fact that the present distribution of national resources has been such as to make the higher levels of government to have lion shares while Local Government Councils are left with little. Financial predicaments into which Local Governments find themselves make them to accept by conduct the master-servant relationship, as most often they have to go cap in hand to cadge for financial assistance from the higher levels of government and like a servant, oblige itself to dance to the tune dictated by the state. ***Adediji, (2005) p. 44***

Secondly, most Local Government councils can hardly boast of tangible revenue. For example, a comparison of the percentage of internally generated revenue over total revenue of each of the Local Government Councils in Osun State showed that none of the thirty Local Government Councils was viable based on the number of Local Government that were able to generate at least 10% of their total revenue. Adediji, O ( ) the inability of Local Government to generate revenue internally undermines the ideas of its autonomy.

Thirdly, some local government councils have been allegedly caught red-handed behaving irresponsibly in questions of financial management. The ever present cases of financial dishonesty which made Local Government Councils to get the tag of *fortress of corruption* ***Adedij, B.O (1991:72-78)*** has led to occasional dissolution of the councils and the curtailment of their financial autonomy through administrative regimentation which includes the demand for submission of their budgets to the State Governments for approval before spending. The constancy or re-occurrences of this financial dishonesty has led to a situation in which the generality of Nigerians see as sterile the call for autonomy of Local Government Councils. For example an author once said without mincing words.

"It would be more productive to minimize sterile academic debates on the utopian concept of absolute autonomy in the full recognition that there is no way that local Government functionaries could be allowed to behave in a fashion that could be inimical to national unity and/or development" Aikhomu,*(1989) cited in Adediji, B.O (2003:45)*

It is also important to note that Local Government Councils have not been awarded pass marks for the use of the autonomy so far granted them. During the six month abrogation of Local Government Service Commission the autonomy was generally misused and Council Bosses became petty tyrants *Adediji, B.O (1995)*

Additionally, political and social instability, which Nigeria has witnessed since its independence, has led to the demand for a strong center to hold units that may attempt to secede. The experience of the civil war encouraged the Federal Government to strengthen itself against the state governments and to strengthen the state government against the local government councils. For this reason, autonomy of local government is dicated by prudence to avoid its being exploited to break up the country. There exists problems of widespread dissatisfaction of the general public with the operation and management of the affairs of some of the councils. The performances of many of them are below expectations and have failed to justify the purpose and the autonomy. **Adediji, B.O (2003:45).**

More so, constitutional limitations also stand on the way of Local Government autonomy. According Nwadialo, Local Government is not a third tier of government under the constitution. Matters over which Local Governments have jurisdiction are still state matters in the scheme of division of powers between the federal and state government. The functions of Local Government Councils as set out in 1999 constitutions are all of Local concern falling within the purvieu of a state Government. Therefore through such councils, state government plays the role of maintenance of law and orders. *Popoola (2003)*

Thus constitutional limitations have ended up making a Local Government Council a mere appendage of the state government in which it is a unit and therefore it is not free to conduct its own affairs as a result of directions and counter-directions from the state government.

Another major development in the relationship between the state and local government is the autocratic way in which the state governments relate with the councils. The instrumentality of the state house of assembly which is put in place to check the excesses of the state governors as it affects local government councils has proved inactive by the impotence of most of the state houses of assembly.

Worst still, the constitution has put local governments under the state government. The constitution says that democratically-elected government at the local level is hereby guaranteed. It stopped at that level whereas like what happened at the state and the federal level, it is supposed to have entrenched the autonomy and financial independence at the local government level also. With this, there is no way local governments can operate effectively. As long as this situation continues, it means local government can only operate at best as area offices of state governments. This means that the three tiers of government are being collapsed into two because of the overbearing power of the state over local governments. Whereas in a federal structure, the three tiers are supposed to be independent, autonomous and inter-related, instead of a master-servant relationship.

There is need to look into the status of local government in our federal structure. Should local government be totally independent of the state government? or an appendage? Both options are fraught with challenges. The recognition of the local government as independent third tier government can be a recipe for chaos, if the state governments are perpetually at log a head with local government Being left as an appendage of state governments will also deny them of the needed independence. There is need to strengthen the constitutional provisions to give more autonomy to local government particularly in the areas of finance, personnel and election of its leadership. There is also need to protect funds of local government from state officials who are always too eager to convert it to slush funds, and to protest local government personnel from state officials who use them as pawns in the chess game to subjugate local government councils. Presently the servant status of Local Government implies the fact that it is not a free legal person and as such it would be unfair to insist that institution to account for teleguided actions or to account for money which it has signed for under dures exerted upon it by the state Government but which in fact it has not fully received, otherwise the objective of accountability becomes defeated.

How to Reverse the Master-Servant Relationship

The current master-servant relationship between higher levels of Government and Local Government can be reversed if the following strategies are prudently made use of.

Self sufficiency in Resources: The autonomy of Local Government can be improved and local government can get out of servant status vis a vis the state government, if each Local Government council adopts a policy of self-sufficiency in resources. This implies exploration and exploitation of all available resources that can bring tangible revenues and by managing such resources wisely and in a way that the present trend of heavy dependence of Local Government on federal and state Government could be reduced drastically or reversed. Autonomy of Local Government Councils would be much more easily demanded and would be much more easily granted when and if local governments show evidence and guarantee of self-sufficiency in indispensable resources. A Local Government that wants to ask for more autonomy needs to prove that it deserves it and not merely demand it: ability to stand on its own through self-sufficiency in resources is not only a justification for demanding more autonomy but also for deserving it.

Prudent management of revenues of Local Government Councils could encourage ratepayers to pay rates, which would swell up the revenues of Local Government Councils. Wide publicity of executed projects at the Local Government Council areas and of problems confronting Local Government Councils especially such problems, which serve as barriers to better performance, would be useful and effective strategies in projecting and portraying good image and durable reputation of Local Governments Councils. Such image and reputation would serve as factors, which could motivate the residents of Local Government Council areas to participate actively in measures capable of making such councils to have more autonomy.

Moreover, by allowing the virtues of probity, accountability, transparency and honesty to be their watchwords, (especially now that the government is determined more than ever before to decisively deal with any form of misappropriation of public fund and any proven case of abuse of office) the councils would have justification for demanding more autonomy.

Efforts of Local Government Councils along acquisition or improvement of high calibers of human resources and procurement of technical equipment would be right path towards more autonomy.

Training programs for all categories of staff and judicious management of human resources within the Local Government Councils would be a highly effective strategy.

Avoidance of Ultravires Acts : Local government councils would have to avoid ultra-vires acts and omissions such as those that are contrary to laid down rules, regulations and procedures as well as those which violate the constitution and the directive of higher levels of government.

Change of Attitude of Higher Levels of Government: There is need for higher levels of government to change or at least moderate their attitude towards the Local Government Councils. If Local Government is supposed to be government, then it should be given autonomy necessary for the accomplishment of its functions. Local Governments should be allowed to learn through trials and errors, as the best way of learning appears to be through one's mistakes.

CONCLUSION REMARKS

The relationship between the States and the Local Government Councils is at present more or less that of master and servant relationship in an apparent doubt as to the capacity of Local Government to execute its constitutional functions without endless number of control and tele-guidance, which frustrate the so called governmental status of local Government. The way state governments descend their crushing weight on daily basis does not portray local government as a real government. The constitution maintains ambiguous posture towards local government as it proclaims its recognition as a government on the one hand, and goes ahead to make other provisions which apparently regards it as subservient to the state government. The state government takes advantage of such provisions to enact all sorts of obnoxious laws, rules and regulations mainly skewed to perpetrate all sorts of absurdities against the local Government to the extent that the councils have become more or less units under the state governments, which is not the intendment of the 1999 constitution. The lopsided nature of allocation is at the disadvantage of local governments, while the channels through which the fund gets to local government facilitates its manipulation by the state government. Unfortunately, local government councils pay little or no attention to the efforts at securing adequate financial resources which could have made it financially independent.

Worse still, there are ever present occasions of financial mismanagement which provoke myriads of rules and regulations that local government must get clearance for almost everything it would do and every step it would take. Despite the fact that no law gives the governor any power to remove any government executive, dissolve the council, or appoint caretaker committee to run the affairs of Local government and the fact that section 7 of 1999 constitution and a line of decided cause cases guarantee the system of democratically elected Local Government and does not permit their appointment, selection of local government caretaker or transitional committee or sole administrator to run the affairs of local government. State governments all over Nigeria generally derive pleasure in violating the law.

It is summated that with clean hands Local Government authorities can restore their almost lost autonomy

After going through the myriads of gestures, controls, tele-guidance, supervisions, and directives exercised by the State Government it is submitted that "A situation where the State Government behaves as big boss to Local Government can hardly present an ideal relationship among the levels of Government but sub-*servience*. Any level of Government that is legally expected to render account for its stewardship deserves such measure of autonomy necessary for performance of its duties". The constitutional provisions which State Government take advantage of its ambiguity should be reviewed otherwise Local Government would hardly every get free of the claws of the State Government, and yet would sometimes bear responsibilities for acts committed when the mind is not present.

REFERENCES

1. Adediji (2003) Accountability and Challenging Issues in Nigeria Local Government, Book Press, London.
2. Adamolekun, L (1984) – The Idea of Local Government as a third tier of Government Revised. The Quarterly Journal of Administration Vol. XVIII Nos three & four P115
3. Adediji, B.O. (1990): *Fundamental Barriers and Limitations to Local Government Autonomy* ABI Print Publishing Company, Ibadan p. 101.
4. Adediji, Master-Servant Relations P.43
5. Adediji, B.O (1985): Politisation et corruption: problems Actuals de L. Administration du development au Nigeria Doctorate Degree Thesis Institute d'etudes politiques, university of Bordeaux, France.
6. Adediji, B.O. (1995): Perception and Treatment of Autonomy B L G Political functionaries During the six-month Abrogation of the Local Government Service Commission in
7. Adediji B.O. – *Challenging Issues in Nig Local Government,* Sedex Publishers Lagos pp 76-86
8. Awolowo, (1947): Path to Nigerian Freedom London: Faber and Faber Ltd p.47
9. Adediran, Olu (2003: 133-134) Federalism and Local Government Autonomy in Nigeria: An Appraisal in Yakubu, John (Ed) *Socio-Legal Essays Local Government Administration in Nigeria* Damyaxs Law Books Ibadan Nigeria.
10. Balewa, (1981:5) cited in Adediji B.O (1985)
11. Bhattacharya, State control over Municipal Bodies in Abbijit, Datta (Ed.) *Local Government*, New Delhi: The Indian Institute of Public Administration, 198 pp 58-64.
12. Bourdillon, B. Cited in Adediran, O. (2003) Federalism and Local government autonomy in Nigeria in Yakubu, A. (Ed) *Socio-legal Essay in Local Government Administration*, Demyaxs Law Books Ibadan p. 133 - 136
13. Burns, A. (1949) the colonial civil servant London, Allen and Unwin.

14. Burns, A. cited in Simpson (2004) *History of Nigeria*, P.2
15. Clifford Cited in Adediran, O. (2003). - Federalism and Local government autonomy in Nigeria in Yakubu, A. (Ed) *Socio-legal Essay in Local Government Administration.* P. 133
16. Chief of General Staff quoted in Egwurube, J.O. (1989) Growth or Statis Development in Local Government Structure and Administration in Nigeria during the Political Transition Programme 1987 – 1989 in Aborisade, O. – *Nigerian Local Government Reformed,* Local Government Publication Series Ile-Ife. p – 499.
17. *Compass, (2008),16 July*
18. Daily independent, (2007) Monday July 23
19. Daily Independent (2007), 20 December
20. Daily Sketch, (1947) Ibadan June 4
21. de Gaule, (1968) *Le Monde Diplomatique 11, September p.3*
22. Honey will Larkin Brothers (1934) 1KB.191
23. Kilson, M. Simpson, *History of Nigeria,* P.3
24. Kirk Grene (1971) *Crisis of Conflicts-* Vol 2 doc 155 p. 220
25. *Le Monde Diplomatique,* (1973) p. 23. An article Le Nigeria dans la voie de l'unite national (Nigeria on the path of national unity)
26. Lyttleton, - Cited in Adediran O. (2003) - Federalism and Local government autonomy in Nigeria in Yakubu, A. (Ed) *Socio-legal Essay in Local Government Administration,* Demyaxs Law Books Ibadan p. 133 – 136
27. Macpherson, - Cited in Adediran O. (2003) Federalism and Local government autonomy *in Nigeria in Yakubu A (Ed) Socio-legal Essay in Local Government Administration,* Demyaxs Law Books Ibadan p. 133 - 136
28. Milverton, cited in Simpson, (2004) History *of Nigeria,* P. 3
29. Nigerian Compass, (2009), p. 23 Thursday July 2,)
30. ***Nigerian Compass 2009 p. 23***
31. Newswatch (1993:23) December 20
32. Popoola, A.O (2003)- The Taxing Power of Local Governments Under the Nigeria Constitution in Adediji B.O (Ed) *Emerging Trends in Nigeria Local Government* Sedexs Publisher pp 45-57.

33. This Day Sunday Newspaper, 2004 Dec 5, page.
34. The Guardian (2010:8)' Tuesday, Jan 26 p. 80
35. Wheare K.C. (1963) Federal Government (4th Edition) Oxford, p. 33.

CHAPTER SIXTEEN

CONTRIBUTORY ROLE OF THE GOVERNED MASSES IN LACK OF ACCOUNTABILITY OF GOVERNANCES

OYENIRAN ADEDIJI (PH.D)

INTRODUCTION

From the time when Nigeria got political independence till today, corruption coupled with disregard for accountability has always been *a chronic problem bedeviling* the governmental system of the country. The First Republic was treated in a way that it became suffocated, dead and buried only a few years after its birth: the Second Republic was not even allowed to last as long as the first.

From time to time, Nigerian leaders have manifested a concern for accountability of public office holders. The first take-over of the public office holdership by the military in 1966 was said to have been warranted by the urgent need to instill financial probity* (which was then missing) in public offices[1]. ***Adamolekun, (1987)*** General Yakubu Gowon, who later became head of State, following a counter-coup, claimed also that the take-over of the Government by the Military was motivated by the need to eradicate corruption and maladministration. ***Adamolekun, (1987)***

Muritala Muhammed, who 'later seized power from General Yakubu Gowon, justified his action by the fact that the administration of Gowon was not responsive to public feeling etc, ***Adamolekun, (1987)*** and that the admin was drenched in corruption.

Obasanjo, who continued that administration after M. Muhammed, perceived lack of accountability as a major problem and also vowed to prevent abuse of office and to enforce accountability. ***Adamolekun (1987)***

Shagari, the Second Republic Civilian Government Head of State, also saw Nigeria as infested with indiscipline, lack of accountability and corruption ***Adamolekun, (1987)*** He attempted to solve the problems though his famous "Ethical Revolution" which however could not bring any solution to the problem.

When **Buhari** seized power in 1983, he told the world press that his administration was to clean the Nigerian society of corruption and enforce public accountability ***Buhari, (1983)***

In 1989, **Babangida** was quoted as saying:

> "Our present economic predicament can be attributed to the nature and practice of politics and the collapse of the economy directly attributable to the bad government, corruption, and the absence of accountability". ***Babangida, (1987).*** The announcement was made by the Head of that Administration in 1985 that he would rid the Government of abuse of office and to make the Government accountable to the Governed. ***Adediji, (1995)*** Yet he could not solve the problem.

General **Abacha** also promised to ensure respect for accountability in public service and to eradicate corruption in all its ramifications. It is however an open secret that that administration has laid unprecedented record of corruption rather than bringing solution to the problem.

General **Olusegun Obasanjo** who took over power as civilian head of state after Abacha's emphasized that corruption the greatest single bane of Nigerian society would be tackled heed- on at all levels. Obasanjo set up economic and financial crimes commission EFCC which has led to recovery and repatriation of billions of naira. However, his administration ended up featuring in Nigerian Dailies as *counterfeiter* of corrupt-free administration and is currently receiving *verbal and written bullets* from all quarters till present.

President **Yar'Adua** who later became head of state in Nigeria vowed to bring solutions to the problems of corruption and accountability for which Nigeria has bad record. It is however unfortunate that Yar' Adua could not live up to his promises before he passed to the great beyond in 2010.

In short, the Military regimes that stayed in power between 1966 and 1979, and the civilian regime, which ruled Nigeria between 1979 and 1983 and between 2003 and 2009, ostensibly intended to lay a solid foundation for public accountability. However, that accountability has virtually been non-existent in Nigerian public offices is a fact that could be backed up with many evidences. The whole of the Nigeria's history since independence could be said to be littered with cases of authoritarian attitude, arbitrariness, and corruption: lack of accountability, at Federal and State and Local Governments.

In local government councils, there are also cases of embezzlement of Government funds and deliberate delay of official matters concerning certain persons or communities within local governments who refused or were unable to pay bribe demanded as condition for prompt service. There are reports, claims and counter-claims made by Chairmen and Local Government Councils all over Nigeria of corruptly awarded contracts or contracts awarded without following laid down procedures and of payments being made for abandoned projects.

The reports of these incidents of corrupt practices, of abuse of office, and complaints against public office holders are significant in that they serve as evidence to prove that there are problems of corruption and disregard for accountability in Nigerian public services presently. They also justify the current fears and worries as to whether the same "old story" would be repeated in Nigeria. These fears and worries are the more justifiable; given the way and manners by which Government at all levels are increasingly getting involved in a variety of socio-economic activities in a bid to satisfy the yearnings and wishes of ever-growing population.

The objective of this paper is to show how the attitude of generality of the masses is that of laisser-faire as if the fight against corruption is the exclusive preserve and responsibility of governments and their officials and how laisser-faire attitudes of the governed serve as tacit approval, condonation and ratification of corruption of political office holders' in Nigeria. It is our belief that a careful analysis of the consequences of such attitude on the part of the governed would serve as prevention for its recurrence in future.

What is laisser-faire? What is public accountability? How has laisser-faire, laisser-aller attitude contributed to rampant public service corruption today as ever. What were the consequences of such attitude?

These and related questions would be addressed in this paper.

Conceptual Clarifications

The expression and/or concepts, which would be clarified in this paper, include the following:

Laisser-faire and Public accountability.

1. Laisser-faire:

Laisser faire, are French expressions. Laisser faire simply means let do, allow (other) to do what they do. Laisser aller simply means let go, allow (other) to go the way they want to go. Laisser-faire, refers to attitude or policy or interfering as little as possible, or not interfering at all, with the acts and/or omissions of others. It is a policy of big tolerance, condonation and ratification of wrongful acts or culpable omissions of others. In this context, it is an attitude of big tolerance for, and/or condonation and ratification of wrongful acts or culpable omissions of the public functionaries of the Second Republic by the governed.

2. Public Accountability

The concept accountability is derived from the adjective "accountable", which simply means "liable to be called upon to account, or to answer for responsibility and conducts". ***Oxford English Dictionary (1970)*** Public accountability could from thence be defined as a system whereby public office holders are liable and are made liable morally and legally to be called upon to answer for their official responsibilities and conducts and to bear consequences for the same.

In a public organization where accountability is recognized and accepted, all wrongful acts of omissions and of commission attributable to particular officers, once suspected, investigated and detected, attract sanctions for such offices in accordance with laid down Code of Conduct, rules, regulation and procedure.

In this context, accountability implies public functionaries able and willing to answer queries, affirm or deny allegations of, or accept penalty for, wrongful acts or omissions. For accountability to be at its best, the masses must demand that the functionaries should render account while the functionaries must respond to the demand.

Examples of instances when public office holders could be held accountable include:

- Acts and omissions that breach the Code of conduct, rules, regulations and procedures concerning the use of public office;
- Other Acts and omissions which, even if they may not amount to breaches of the laid down Code of Conduct, rules and regulations, might be in form of arbitrariness, bias, unjustifiable delays or failure to take proper consideration into accounts.

Importance of Public Accountability

Public accountability is important in Nigeria. It is one of the means by which the exercise of legal or discretionary powers of public office holders could be restrained to be in conformity with the aims and objectives for which the institution is created. It is a means of ensuring that public office holders would be sensitive to the feelings of the governed.

Adamolekun, (1987) like ***Babangida, (1985)*** viewed accountability in terms of responsiveness of the Government officers to the will of the governed and in terms of preventing abuse of office.

Various forms of accountability exist for public office holders: including

- Accountability of the political offices to the electorates and to the Government;
- Accountability of career civil servants to the public they serve;
- Accountability of career civil servants to political executives.

The paper would focus its attention mainly on the first of the three directions of accountability.

Having clarified the basic concept and the direction of the paper, we could now go on to analyse the root causes of lack of accountability of political office holders in Nigeria.

LAISSER-FAIRE ATTITUDE OF THE GOVERNED-ANALYSIS

The basic reason, which can explain the problem of low degree of demand for accountability from public leaders by the masses during the Second Republic, is inaction on the part of the masses. Inaction is inability or unwillingness to act when necessary. Reasons behind this inaction are derived from many factors.

1 CULTURE OF SILENCE ON THE PART OF THE MASSES:

From the time of independence till the present time of Nigeria's history, the Nigeria masses have manifested a state of powerlessness and helplessness even at moments when their public office holders take them for *unpleasant rides*. When the public office holders of the first republic looted the treasury and treated the state as their personal empire, the masses kept silent. The earlier promise that the State would no longer be treated as personal patrimony was not fulfilled. Not only were they unable to realize this objective (which could be taken as the *raison d'etre* for their acceptance and legitimacy), later revelations about most of their fellow participants did not prove that one regime was better accountability-wise, than those of the earlier regimes they professed to correct. When public office holders trample upon their fundamental rights they keep and remain silent.

During the Second Republic, political office holders again came to power with promises to improve the state economy and the lots of individual members of the society. It turned out that the civilian regime was made up of the most corrupt men and women then ever found in public office holdership of that country. Those who contributed to the fall of the First Republic joined forces with new breed "*clever rogues*" and the Second Republic ended up being the saddest movement in the history of Nigeria's politics. The masses, as usual kept silent as if unconcerned or at least as if they had no power over their fate. **The Nigerian masses manifest a state of powerlessness and helplessness even at moments when their public office holders take them for unpleasant rides.**

Any public office holder conscious of this culture of silence on the part of the masses naturally feels tempted to take advantage of it. And so Nigerian Local Government functionaries of today take advantage of the culture of silence of the Nigerian masses, and *throw to the wind* all idea of probity and accountability. This culture of silence had been created by several factors.

Firstly is the fact that the masses have no clean hands themselves as many of them ask for and receive bribes before voting for the public office holders and consequently do not feel morally justified to demand for accountability from the public office holders. It is important to remember that every 'successful' Nigerian, including every public office holder, has a host of *hangers on* whom he has to cater for in questions of feeding, lodging and clothing. The residence of an average 'big boss' of Local Government Council is at all time packed full of those who call to demand for one favour or another. The survival of Local Government functionary is synonymous with the survival of the *hangers-on*. If a public office holder is known to be corrupt, all efforts are made to conceal his corrupt acts and omissions in an effort to guarantee self-survival by the needy who trooped into the house of such a public office holder for help in all forms.

According to ***Peil, Margaret, (1977)*** public office holders who distribute ill-gotten wealth among the less fortunate people often have considerable prestige. Those who enjoy crunches that drop down the table of such towering figures not only refuse to expose the known wrongful acts or omissions of their benefactors and bread-winners, but also do everything within their powers and possibility to cover up such acts in order to save the benefactor(s) from being subjected to account and sanctions.

In other words, the masses who have at one time or the other enjoyed one kind of benefit or the other from local ***Ikime, (1985)*** "the demands on the rulers far exceed their earnings" [15]. Having spent huge amounts while in office or before coming to office, the tendency is naturally there for a public office holder to seek to regain what he has spent and, as a result, those who benefited from his "*father Christmas idiosyncrasy*" find it difficult to ask such public functionary for accountability: they simply do not expect such local government functionary to live within his official income. This culture of silence has its roots in (i) Illiteracy, Ignorance and Lack of awareness; (ii) Belief that writing petitions is risky and fruitless; (iii) The Masses' lack of clean hands

(i) Illiteracy, Ignorance, and Lack of Awareness:

Illiteracy is one of the most important of such factor, which militated against demand for accountability in Nigeria. Majority of the masses in Nigeria are pure illiterates who either do not know that they have the right to hold public office holders accountable for acts or omissions that injured public interest or, if they know, they have no means – financial, material, time or sufficient information – to do so.

From the time of Nigeria's independence up till present, every Government that has ever ruled the country knows of this problem, but no government has been able to *hold the bull by the horns* by embarking on a policy of universal compulsory education for all Nigerians.

Consequently, a large percentage of the Nigerian masses have not been given opportunity of getting *out of darkness*. Majority of the governed masses hardly know their leaders whom they voted for: they only voted according to how they were told by their ethno-regional leaders. Many in fact the generality of the masses cannot really assess the quality of public offices holders because they don't have access to the tool with which public office holders work, access in form of information, situations, reasons why certain decisions are taken rather than others. As a result, the acts and omissions committed by the public office holders were not known.

Presently the masses generally do not have access to information held by the state or its agencies, as the masses have not yet started to enjoy the right of access to information in records.

It is an open secret that presently Nigeria operates a sort of *secret governance* as the following would reveal.

Firstly almost all important official documents are *classified* to prevent leakage of information about official business. The masses are prevented from having tangible information by all means including the following;

(a) Under Section 1(2) of the Officials Secret Acts (OSA) it is an offence for any public office holder to fail to safeguard any classified matter in his custody. The Act also makes it an offence for a public office holder to transmit, reproduce or retain any classified matter, which he has not been authorised on behalf of the government to divulge. To demonstrate the absurdity of this law, a civil servant transmitting a document or file in between government offices in different locations is, strictly speaking, a criminal. The penalty for this is 14 years imprisonment.

(b) Beside the OSA, the Oaths Act or, in the states, the Oaths Law, oblige(s) all civil servants or persons in the public service to subscribe to an *Oath of secrecy* prohibiting them from "directly or indirectly communicate(ing) or reveal(ing) any matter to any person which shall be brought under his consideration or shall come to his knowledge in the discharge of his official duties except as may be required for the official duties or as may be specially permitted by the President/Governor." The Civil Service Rules requires "every Permanent Secretary/Head of Extra-Ministerial department to ensure that all officers, employees and temporary staff in his ministry/extra ministerial department who have access to classified or restricted papers have signed the Oath of secrecy in the appropriate form before they are granted such access and that the declaration so signed are safely preserved." Under the Civil Service Rules, "Every officer is subject to the OSA." It is thus easy to see why we have 37 ministries of information, one federal and 36 states -with little freedom and no information.

(c) The National Population Commission Act prohibits staff of the Commission from disclosing or publishing demographic information so fundamental to our national planning.

The Agricultural (Control of Importation) Act, prohibits all veterinary and public health officials under pain of punishment (except the Minister for Agriculture under his discretion) from disclosing any information or conclusions from the investigation of plant disease even when such non-disclosure threatens severe harm to public health.

The Company Income Tax Act precludes officials of the Federal Inland Revenue Service from communicating with the public about their work.

The Fire Service Act contains the same prohibitions against Fire Service personnel.

Similar provisions are contained in the National Office of Industrial Property Act, the Petroleum Profit Act, and in the Civil Aviation Act (Investigation of Accidents) Regulations. The Evidence Act empowers a Federal Minister or, in respect of State matters, a State Governor, in judicial proceedings "object to the production of documents or oral evidence, when after consideration, he is satisfied that the production of such document or the giving of such oral evidence is against public interest and such objection shall be conclusive and the court shall not inspect such documents or be informed as to the nature of such oral evidence." In every sector, the law prohibits government functionaries / officers from telling Nigerians what government does and reinforces the hierarchy of citizenship based on information.

Consequently, it is not only difficult but also risky for the masses to criticize the government for its acts or omissions so long as procurement of document or official information could create legal problems. Therefore masses who speak would more or less be like that of *Biblical Job* who "speaks without knowledge; and his words would be "without insight".

Accountability and transparency will be impossible if the masses have no right of access to information held by the state or its agencies or if no mechanism exists for giving practical effects to the right to freedom of information.

Secondly these Nigerians simply do not know that they have the right to hold public office holders accountable for official misdeeds and omissions. Since such masses cannot demand, as of right, that there public office holders render account.

The problem facing an illiterate African citizen has been well painted by S. Ousmane in *Money Orde* Wake, (1972) where a postal officer used his official position to embezzle the *Money Order* of a postal client while the victim, being an illiterate, kept silent, unaware of the right to report the officer for sanctions. Lack of adequate education serves as a formidable barrier to participation in government as a result of inability to understand the principles of government and the nature of bureaucratic operations.

Today at Nigerian borders, the same ignorance and lack of awareness of one's rights makes it possible for such items as radio sets, wrist watches, foreign currency, etc. to be seized from the masses, who are coming into the country through the borders. Our custom officers take advantage of the ignorance of the masses up to the extent of threatening the extorted masses with "prosecution" Such masses, in addition to forfeiting and foregoing their confiscated personal effects (which they anyway have legal right to bring into the country), still have to bribe such officers in order to avoid prosecution.

Today, at Nigeria borders, the same ignorance and lack of awareness of one's rights makes it possible for such items as radio sets, wrist watches, foreign currencies, etc. to be seized from the masses who are coming into the country. Such officers take advantage of the ignorance of the masses up to the extent of threatening them with "prosecution". Such masses, in addition to forfeiting and foregoing their confiscated personal effects (which they anyway have legal right to bring into the country), still have to bribe such officers in order to avoid prosecution ***Adediji, (1985)***.

Illiteracy within Nigerian society makes it possible for many people not to know when political office holders had committed acts of illegality. An average Nigerian is concerned with how to survive. He does not read newspaper, does not listen to radio, T.V. news. As such, he does not even know what is going on in public offices and is not in a position to write petitions against public office holders. Those who know what is going on and are in position of writing petitions often consider such petition as a waste of time.

In Nigerian society ignorance and lack of awareness of one's rights against public office holders is a common thing. Illiteracy is one of the most important factors, which militate against demand for accountability. Nigeria has a male literacy rate of 54% and a female literacy rate of 31%. This means that majority of the masses in Nigeria are pure illiterates who do not know that they have the right to hold public office holders accountable for acts or omissions that injure public interest. They are mostly ignorant of the fact that those who conduct the affairs of the Council for example are servants of the public and NOT their masters, or, if they know, they have no means – financial, material, time or sufficient information or courage – to do so. As a result of ability to write and communicate in white man's language, public office holders are perceived as masters instead of as public servants. The government is perceived as a mysterious institution, too powerful to confront as a result of inferiority complex on the part of the masses. The perception of government in Nigeria is that of unpredictable nature. Thus, the unpredictable nature of an average government at any level is a sort of warning for prudent illiterate masses: it can turn round to arrest and deal with any person who challenges it.

From the time of Nigeria's independence up till present, every government that has ever ruled the country is aware of this problem created by ignorance, but no government has been able to hold the bull by the horns by embarking on a policy of universal compulsory education for all Nigerians.

Consequently, a larger percentage of the Nigerian masses have not been given opportunity of getting out of darkness. The governed masses hardly know their leaders whom they vote for in the real sense of it: It is important to note the fact that due to secrecy of government business presently Nigerian masses generally do not have access to information held by the state or its agencies, as the masses have not yet started to enjoy the right of access to information in records. The principles of government and the nature of political and bureaucratic operations is beyond their capacity. As a result, the acts and omissions committed or that could be committed by the local government functionaries are not known. Even where the masses have knowledge of these facts, they simply do not know that they have the right to hold public office holders accountable for official misdeeds and omissions. Historically, the government functionaries have assumed the status of 'superior bosses' vis-à-vis the governed masses. The Africans who came to fill the vacant posts left by European colonial masters inherited the culture of non-accountability to the masses. As said earlier, the western education and especially the ability to communicate in the White man's language has given them an image of importance and of superiority. How can such masses demand, as of right, that their public office holders render account?

Thirdly, societal economic hardship also influences the current 'I don't care' posture of masses. Today, Nigerian suffering masses are concerned principally with how to survive the countries nagging problems of no light, no water, no fuel, no security, no means to settle exorbitant and prohibitive school fees, books etc, despite the *noise* over poverty alleviation policy of government. They do not have time to bother themselves with what goes on in the government. Additionally, they do not have time or money to purchase and /or read newspapers, they do not even know what is going on in public offices and is not in a position to raise the question of accountability against local public office holders. It is another thing that those who know what is going on often consider demand for accountability as a waste of time.

(ii) Belief that writing petitions is risky and fruitless:

There are some masses who know their right against erring public office holders, but among such masses is a large part who believed that it was a risk and a waste of time to report such officers. Such people see Government as Rousseau sees it: as a necessary evil, which have to be tolerated so that man could survive in his battle with his colleagues. Government and Government functionaries are thus regarded as necessary evils created by man to moderate his excesses, but which he must be willing to tolerate if he wants peace of mind. ***Adediji, (1985)***

The Nigeria society apparently believe that whoever gets into power or position of authority would do virtually the same: enrich himself and his social circle. What then is the use of reporting those in power when those who were there before them were not better and those who might replace them might be worse?

There is also the fact that reports against erring public office holders, which were made in the past, have had no desired effects and in some cases the petitioners, rather than the culprits, had been ironical treated as if they were "Judas". The multi-lingual, multi-ethnic, multi-national nature of Nigeria makes petitions against serving political officers to be treated as mere sentiments of hatred or jealousy for public office holders in questions. Petitions are most often regarded as the handiwork of disgruntled persons and in most cases such petition ended up in the dustbins of Government officials supposed to act on them. Worse still, the person who wrote the petitions might become the object of pursuit and arrests, of attacks and victimization, and ridicule, by the sympathizers of the political officers implicated in the allegations.

The mysterious circumstances surrounding the death of the Barrister who spearheaded the trial of President Traore of Mail, and the death of Dele Giwa who spearheaded the crusade against corruption in high places in Nigeria are some of many examples of the risks and dangers involved in the business of "*belling the cat*" in African communities ***(Adediji, B. O (1985) P 61***

Therefore, petitions against wrongful acts and omissions of public office holders, especially *towering personalities*, are usually treated as very adventurous and risky. The petitioner, his close and distant relations, and even the community in which he lives or hails from might be made to pay dearly for his audacity.

Another typical case is that of University of Ilorin, when government white paper accused the authority of misappropriating a huge amount of money and the university council was dissolved. It was the lecturers that exposed the acts that were sacked by the chief executive of the university. The case was reported to The Independent Corrupt Practices Commission (ICPC) but since over 5 years ago nothing has been done on it. Public office holders do not like and do not forgive any people who criticize them. This is so because it is considered as *heresy* or abominations to question or even appear to question the integrity of big political figures. For haven risked their lives and all they had in order to make independence a reality, for have suffered all sorts of privations, including imprisonment, detention, etc. for the nation, these "great" people are regarded as "*sacred cows*" which should always be spared. Whether these public figures actually deserved the same, more or less of such respect is a question of great controversy, which would hardly be easily resolved.

When Dabo [30] (Adediji O. 1988) with evident proof, accused J.S. Tarka, a Federal Commissioner, of official corruption and abuse of office during the Gowon regime, the Government instead of thanking and compensating him for exposing corruption treated him with ignominy. If this could happen during a *corrective* military regime, one could understand what happens to such a petitioner during a civilian regime such as we have now. Sometimes ago, when Aku caused the then Governor or The Benue- Plateau State of maladministration and misappropriation of public fund, the case was still in court when the federal Government intervened, cleared the government of any wrong doing, and consequently blocked constitutional avenue for redress-shorting up the petitioner and his supporters. ***Ojo, Olatunde (1976)***

The belief that writing petitions against public office holders' questionable acts or omissions is a waste of time and of effort is the more reinforced by certain gestures often made by the Government, which tend to portray condolence rather than condemnation. Such gestures includes not only failure to apply sanctions as and when due against public office holders that had been reported, tried and found guilty, but also heroic release under the guise of *State Pardon* and welcome rallies often given to tried, discredited and convicted public office holders. Examples include the following:

The former Governor of Kano State, late Barkin Zuwo, who was convicted for corrupt enrichment up to the tune of over $3 million was one of those who received State pardon a few years later. The way he was received by the Government and by the society was nothing short of heroic. ***African Concord, (1988:16)***

Former Governor Adamu Atta of Kwara State, who was convicted by the Special Military Tribunal on charges of spending $2 million of the security vote, and thereby enriching members of the State legislature, was jailed 21 years, which was later reduced to 5 years by the Government. The Igbira communities of Okene and Okehi Local Government Areas of Kwara State gave this gentleman a heroic welcome when he was released from prison in. Chief S.O. Mbakwe was given a long jail term for similar offences but a few years later he was released from prison on state pardon. ***Adediji, O. (1988:8)*** The warm, heroic reception given to him by the Nigerian society, including top dignitaries, was aptly descried by the African Concord:

"... the news of the release of Second Republic Governor,

> Chief Sam Onuaka Nbakwe was enough to send citizens onto the streets in jubilation. Traders even closed shops. And at Aba, the State's commercial heartland where Mbakwe had his law chambers, market women abandoned their stalls while school children and teachers virtually lined the streets. "Mbakwe's home was besieged by all shades of his indigenes in solidarity". ***African Concord, (1988:23)***

A situation where those who have been detained or arraigned in courts for the shameful act of stealing public funds and have been granted bails by the courts are upon their return to their various communities received with pomps and pageantry, and chieftaincy titles are conferred on them by the traditional institutions that should know better is, to say the list, a counter-attack on the country's war against corruption.

If such releases, such warm and heroic reception for "*national culprits*" could bring satisfaction for the sympathizers of the public office holders in question who might see it as act of generosity and of magnanimity on the part of the Government, they are also capable of discouraging non-sympathisers from reporting further acts official misconducts against other public office holders: they were signs of weakness and of lack of seriousness (on the part of the government) with the question of accountability. There are cases of persons accused of corruption, convicted and sentenced to terms of imprisonment but granted state pardon as soon as sentenced and even appointed to more lucrative office, given national awards e.t.c. The impression, which state pardon for "national culprits" creates in the mind of an average Nigerian is that only public office holders involved in ridiculously small amount of public fund could be refused pardon and heroic reception. Prof. Obaro Ikime said this loud and clear:

"A financial secretary who could be lynched for stealing five Naira from his village purse could steal five million as Finance Minister and receive a heroic welcome at home". ***Ikime. O, (1985): 60*** Worst still, those former politicians were invited to Government function such as festivals and launchings. So who are members of the public to discredit them? ***African Concord, (1988:24)***

If the State pardon and heroic receptions for "certified corrupt officers" could be regarded as injury to the public feeling, the Government often adds insult to injuries when such discredited public office holders are again re-appointed into more lucrative, more dignifying public positions. ***African Concord, (1988:24)***

J.S. Tarka, a Federal Commissioner under General Gowon, who was discredited for official corruption and abuse of office, was later made the Vice-Chairman of the NPN during the Second Republic and even elected into the Senate. When he died in 1980, it was *quasi-state burial* for him, with the President, the Vice-President, the President of the Senate and top Government functionaries in attendance. Benue State alone was said to have spent $136,702 on the said burial. ***African Concord, (1988:24)***

Samuel Ogbemudia was among ten Military Governors dismissed with immediate effect by late General Murtala Mohmmed for gross abuse of office. This same man was latter conferred with an honorary Doctor of science Degree by the University of Benin In 1988, General Ibrahim Babangida later made Ogbemudia the Chairman of the National Sports Commission. ***African concord (1988:25)*** As Alex Gboyega summed it up:

> "The Government of the day is responsible. Those discredited politicians are invited to Government functions such as festivals and launchings. So who are members of the public to discredit them ***African Concord (1988:30)***

One cannot but totally agree with ***Peil, M. (1977)*** when she asserted:

> "highly publicized corruption trials after a military coup are more often a political gesture to gain popularity for the new Government than a serious attempt to root out corruption from public life as it was with the former Governor of Bendel State, formerly adjudged to have committed official misconduct, was later appointed as the Chairman of the National Sports Commission by the Federal Government" ***Adediji, O. (1988)***

A man who runs from one village to another in order to avoid payment of rates and taxes cannot have effrontery of demanding that public office holders should render account of their stewardship.

(iii) The Masses' lack of clean hands

It is universally recognized that "he who wants equity must do equity". Thus on the part of the people, they have grown up to believe that leadership is not for rendering services unto people but for betterment of one's lot and of the lots of one's group of belonging. This explains why during electioneering campaigns, electorates do not want to vote for any candidate except that such candidate must first offer "encouragement money" and /or grease the palm of the voter. Such electorates who asked for and receive brides before voting for a candidate would naturally not feel that they have moral right to insist that such public office holder should not be corrupt. Such corrupt electorates would and indeed are, unable to demand *loud and clear* for accountability from such public office holders, haven collected *shut up money.*

2 PARASITIC CULTURE AND POVERTY OF THE MASSES

It is important to note that every successful Nigerian, including every successful public office holder, has a host of *hangers on* whom he has to cater for in question of feeding, lodging and clothing. ***Adediji, B. (1990)***

The survival of the successful public office holder is synonymous with the survival of the hangers-on. If a public office holder is known to be corrupt, concealing of public office holders' corrupt acts and omission is an effective guarantee for self-survival by the needy who trooped into the house of such public office holders for help in cash and kind, including food, drinks, etc.

Haven spent huge amounts while in office or before coming to office, the tendency is naturally there for the public office holders to regain what they have spent and at this stage, those who benefits from his "Father Christmas idiosyncrasy" find it difficult to ask such public office holders for accountability. They simply do not expect such public office holder to live within his official income. Nigeria witnesses many cases of public office holder who seize the opportunity of being "trusted" to loot the public treasuries. It is now clear that the masses are not capable of demanding accountability from their public office holders. There is, no doubt, a problem: the political office holders refuse to respect the principle of accountability, yet the masses appear not to care much about this. In some cases the masses go as far as putting unbearable pressures on the government to release jailed corrupt public office holders who are ironically regarded as heroes in their communities of origin.

CONCLUSION

This paper made use of some case studies to establish that public accountability is not given a place of importance in the Nigerian governmental system. The paper analysed how "I don't care" attitude of the governed and the "Pardon them all" – policy of the government encouraged disregard of political office holders for accountability. The conclusion was reached that unless there is a change of this "laisser-faire, attitude of the masses as regularly exhibited in Nigeria. Public accountability would likely continue to be elusive in our governmental system.

FOOT NOTES

1. Adediji, B.O. Associate Professor, Department of Local Government Studies Obafemi Awolowo University, Ile-Ife.
2. Adamoleku, L. (1987:235-248) - Impact of the military on Accountability in O.Sanda (Ed) *The impact of military Rule on Nigeria's Administration. Ile-Ife, University of Ife Press*
3. Adediji ,O., (1995): *Topical essays on Nigeria Local Government*, Sedec Publishers (Lagos) p.40
4. Adediji, B.O. (1985) P- Politicization et corruption; Proble-ms Actuels de l'Administration de development au Nigeria, Doctorate *Degree Theses*, University of Bordeau I, …
5. Adediji , (1990) Topical Essays in Nigerian Local Government. p. 40 Abi Print, Ibadan.
6. Agbakoba, *(1992), pp34- Human Rights and the Culture of Silence – paper presented at conference, organized by Juris Chambers of OAU, Ile-Ife, Nigeria, June*
7. Babangida ,I.B, (1985) P. 18. – Presidential "Maiden Speech" *Newswatch* (Lagos) Vol. 2 no 11, Sept 9,
8. *Daily sketch, (Ibadan*) 1982 Thursday 12 August
9. *Daily Times, (Lagos)* 1980 14th May.
10. *Daily Times, (Lagos)* 1981 25th Feb, p. 22
11. *Daily Times*, 1988 (Lagos) 12 July
12. Gboyega, Alex (1988) African Concord Vol 2 September Page 23
13. Ikime (1985) – Ambivalent attitude of Nigeria Government to public service corruption.
14. *Nigeria's Administration* Ile-Ife, University of Ife Press, 1987 pp 235-248.
15. National Concord, (1985) - Lagos 28 Oct,
16. Ojo, Olatunde (1976) ………………..
17. Olowu D. 1983. -Some Cases of Bureaucratic Corruption in Nigeria and Implications for the Search for a Panacea – *paper presented at the 4th Annual conference on the Nigerian Association of Schools of Management Education and Training* (MASMET), Kaduna, June

18. Peil, Magret (1977) – Consensus and Conflicts in African Societies: An Introduction to Sociology, Longman p. 59
19. *Sunday Concord, (Lagos)* 1980 23 Nov. p. 12
20. Sanda O., 1980s. Privatisation of State-owned Enterprises, or insolvency: The critical Choice for Nigeria on the OAU, Press Ile-Ife.
21. *The Guardian, (Lagos)* 1st August 1984
22. *The Newswatch Magazine, (1987):* Lagos April 13,
23. *The New Nigerian,* (Kaduna (1980) 14th March
24. *The Oxford English Dictionary,* (1970) P. 63 James Murray et als (Editors) Clarendon Press.
25. *Vanguard, Lagos* (1988) 5th July p. 16.
26. *Vanguard, Lagos* (1988) 5th July p. 16.
27. *West Africa*, (1984) 6 February p 257
28. Wake, C. (1972) – *The Money Order* -Heinemann London (1972) p 6. An English Edition of le mandat by S. Ousmane